Carole lives in the North Island of New Zealand. By day she works as a school librarian and every other hour she can be found writing. Her hobbies include travelling, gardening, quilting, reading, movies and music. However, she has no time for any of them! She lives with her partner, Dennis Greenwood, an award-winning New Zealand water-colourist. This is Carole's third novel.

www.carolebrungar.com
www.facebook.com/carolebrungarauthor
@nznovelist

Carole Brungar Publishing
First published in New Zealand in 2018
Copyright © Carole Brungar 2018

The Nam Shadow is a work of fiction. In an effort to create verisimilitude, many of the geographical locations described in the story actually exist or did exist. Scenes in the novel are purely fictitious, though they are woven into actual events and roughly follow the historical calendar. The characters are inventions of the author and any resemblance to real persons, living or dead, is entirely coincidental.

A catalogue record for this book is available
from the National Library of New Zealand

ISBN: 978-0-473-45081-6

Cover design by Tui Glen Design
Printed in New Zealand by Graphic Press, Levin

Also by Carole Brungar

A tide too high

The Nam Legacy

*For those women
who have loved a Vietnam veteran,
for they are the real heroes.*

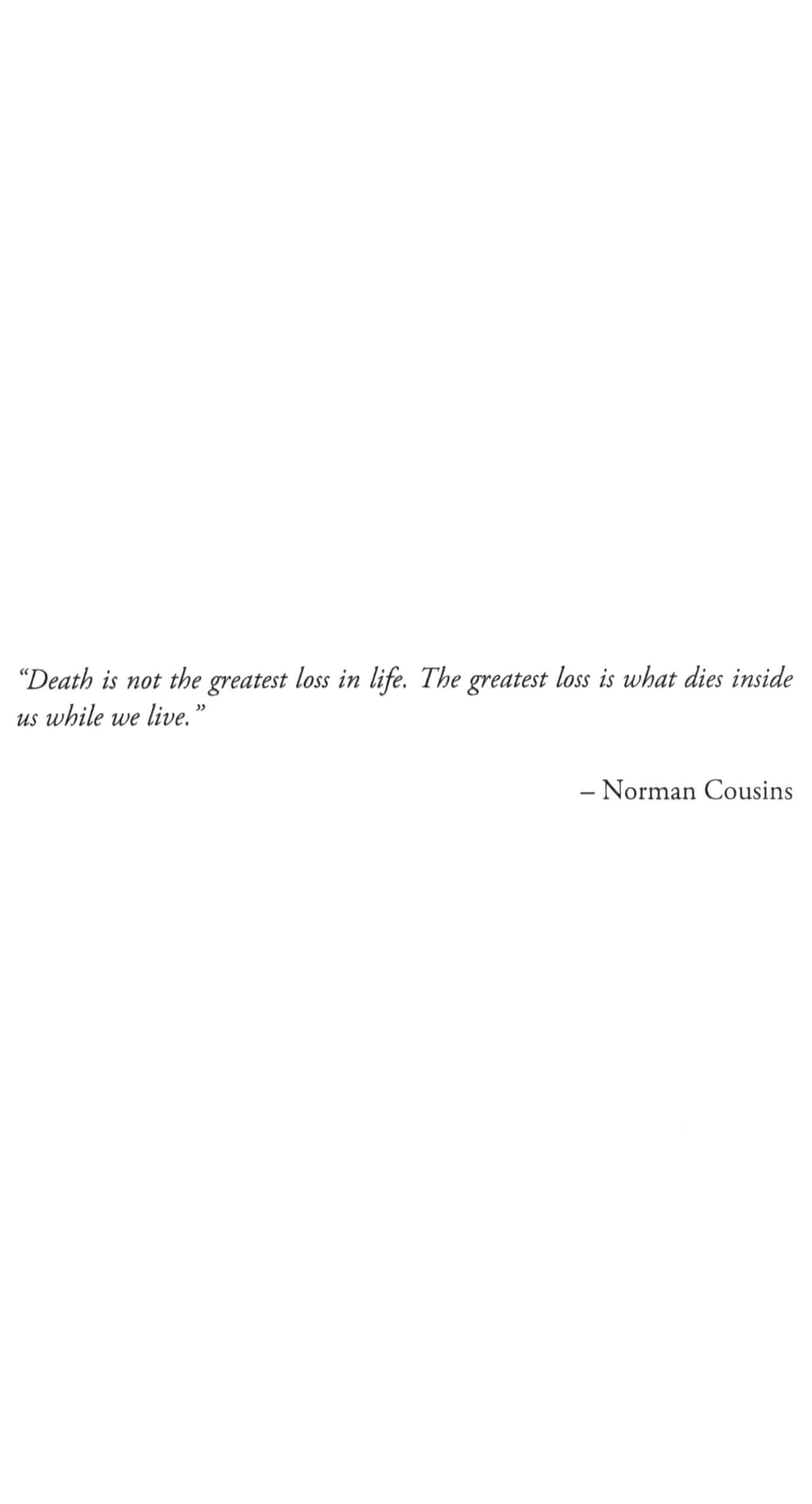

"Death is not the greatest loss in life. The greatest loss is what dies inside us while we live."

– Norman Cousins

The Nam Shadow

- a novel -

Carole Brungar

carole brungar
PUBLISHING

PART ONE

New Zealand, 1966

Chapter 1

Terry Edwards opened the door to his sleepout, felt for the thin white cord and swamped his room with light. He shrugged out of his shoes and stretched out on the comfy old mattress, glad to be away from the madness and noise of his mother's house, especially her kitchen.

Reaching underneath the bed, he groped for the stack of magazines he knew was there and retrieved the one on top. His smile widened as he flipped straight to the centrefold. There she was: Playmate of the Month. She smiled at him enticingly with her long lashes and big brown, eyes. God, he loved brunettes, especially when they wore nothing but a wet shirt. He wanted to lick every single droplet of water right off those tantalisingly full breasts.

Nice, he thought, as he took in her long bare legs. She was his idea of the perfect girl. For a moment, he imagined Evelyn in nothing but a wet shirt. He knew he couldn't have her–she was Jack's girl–but it didn't stop him dreaming about her.

He shifted his attention back to the girl draped across the centrefold. He wondered what it took to get a girl like her. There was something about brunettes that made his motor growl with longing. He hadn't got around to it yet, but this Playmate was going on the wall.

He smiled, remembering his mother's reaction when she had seen the bevy of scantily dressed women in provocative poses posted all over the walls of his sleepout. She had immediately issued a warning to the rest of the family. They were not to step foot in it, and that was just fine by Terry.

There was a knock on his door, and he looked up as his mate Jack Coles appeared.

"Jack, come on in."

"Is it safe?" Jack nodded at the *Playboy*. "Not interrupting business, am I?"

"No. I'm taking the night off."

"She's a brunette, isn't she?" Jack grinned, placing a crate of beer on the floor. "Here." He handed Terry a bottle. "Thought I'd call round for a beer or two."

"That's very considerate of you. And yes, she's a gorgeous brunette. Shift that toolbox and take a seat. I was just working out where I was going to put her. What're you doing in town?"

"Took some wild pork out to the pub for Evie's mum."

Terry levered the top off his bottle and sampled the contents. "Keeping in her good books, eh?"

Jack glanced around the room. "Doesn't hurt." He flipped the cap off his bottle and took a drink from it. "You've got this place feeling like home." He scanned the room and noticed a beer fridge neatly wedged under the bench, next to a set of drawers. "A few additions since I was here last. Nice touch. You're a natural at this interior decoration lark."

A piece of number eight wire hung across one corner of the room, supporting numerous coat hangers and several pairs of oil-stained overalls. Shelves furnished aftershave lotion, a comb, a small free-standing mirror, spark plugs, engine oil, a torch, a tin of biscuits, a stack of books and a radio. His portable record player sat on the bench together with a selection of records. A tall lamp and a pile of *Commando* comics sat on a wooden trunk beside the bed. Under the bed, an assortment of shoes and boots kept the *Playboy* and *Penthouse* magazines company. The room wasn't flash, but Terry loved it, especially the privacy it afforded him.

A map of the Tararua Ranges was pinned to the back of the door by numerous darts and surrounded by black and white photos of Terry's various hunting trophies, him with his mates, and a couple of family photos.

"Miss September's pretty bloody hot," Jack stated, fixing his eye on a girl to the left of the closed door.

"Easy on the eye," Terry agreed. "They give me something nice to dream about at night."

"You need a real girl."

"They're overrated."

"What happened to Evie's friend from the beach? The one that was hanging out with us at that party in Auckland. What was her name?"

"Joanie."

"That's the one."

"She's okay."

"What do you mean, okay? She was a knockout, *and* a brunette. You were all over her."

"Yeah, well, there's plenty of fish in the sea."

"You don't know when you're onto a good thing, mate."

Terry watched Jack empty his bottle and light up a cigarette. He couldn't very well tell his mate he had the hots for his girl.

"I've signed up," Terry blurted out.

"Signed up for what? Not the army?"

"I've been meaning to tell you. After our talk a few weeks ago, I decided to give it a go."

"I got my marching orders for Waiouru yesterday," Jack informed his mate.

Terry let out a low whistle. "That was quick. I can't wait to do basic training too and get over to Vietnam."

"I hope I get picked to go. If Evie's too busy with her singing and concerts all over the country, then I might as well be over there giving it my best shot." Jack laughed at the unintentional pun.

"I'm really hoping I'll be good enough to go to Vietnam too. Sounds like a bit of fun. Reckon they'll need me on the team."

"Is it getting a bit tough at home?"

"It's getting a bit full. Mum told us all this morning that she's up the duff again." He hadn't been over the moon about the news, but it wasn't any of his business how many kids the old lady had. She'd had Judy and him, and then his old man had buggered off. Two months later, some bloke by the name of Vernon Boyd had moved in, lock, stock and suitcase. He didn't particularly like the man, but Terry was at work, out at the beach or away on hunting trips most of the time, and they only crossed paths at the dinner table or the odd weekend when Terry was at a loose end. As long as Vernon treated his mum okay, then he guessed the relationship had nothing to do with him.

Vernon was the local bank manager; he'd needed a place to stay and had apparently decided Terry's mother could do with help to make ends meet, but it seemed he was quick to help with more than just the bills. Terry had two half-sisters and a half-brother, and now there was another on the way. They were going at it like rabbits, but he didn't want to think about that side of things.

"What's that make it?"

"His fourth," Terry answered. "Randy bastard."

"What does your old man think about you joining up?" Jack asked, getting back to the army.

"Not something we've talked about."

"Think he'll try and talk you out of it?"

"Too late. But I doubt he'd care, anyway. As long as I'm not sponging off him, he'd be happy with whatever I did."

"Be brilliant if we both went up to Waiouru and did basic training at the same time."

"You really think we might get to Vietnam?" Terry asked. "I reckon we could look after ourselves against them little fellas over there."

"Well I could, don't know about you." Jack grinned.

"They wouldn't stand a chance."

The two men talked about their last hunting trip and rugby until, eventually, Jack stood up.

"Well, better leave you to it."

Terry swung his legs over the side of the bed and joined him. "Thanks for the beer," he said, slapping his mate on the shoulder. He closed the door behind Jack and carefully slid a record from its sleeve, placing it on the turntable and lowering the needle. A minute later, John Lennon and The Beatles drowned out the sound of a wailing child coming from the house.

Terry's official letter requesting his attendance in Waiouru for basic training arrived in the mail at the end of the following week. He had three weeks to let his boss know and sort his affairs. He reread the letter and felt oddly excited. In fact, he hadn't been this excited since he'd been given that old Ford to do up two years ago. He couldn't wait to pack his bag.

His boss at the garage approved of him going into the army. He had both a brother and a father who had served, and he promised Terry his job would always be there if the army didn't work out. He claimed Terry was the best mechanic he'd employed for a long while, even if he was only nineteen, and he put on a few beers for him on his last day at work.

Rosamund Edwards made a big fuss of her eldest son joining the army. No one in her family had ever been a serviceman, and now her son was going to wear the uniform of a New Zealand soldier. The night before Terry left for Waiouru and basic training, she cooked a big roast dinner, and all the family had to be there, including his older sister, Judy, her husband, and their baby. Vernon sat at the head of the table opposite Terry like he owned the damn place. The house was bedlam and felt like it was bursting at the seams. He offered to help with the dishes, but his mother wouldn't hear of it. After a cup of coffee, it was a relief to be able to retreat to his sleepout and the company of the poster girls.

He sat on his bed, thankful for a quiet smoke, only to be interrupted by a light tapping and his sister Judy peering around the door.

"Terry?"

"Come on in, sis."

Judy sat on the bed beside her brother. "We're heading home, but I just wanted to say I'm really proud of you, and good luck."

"Thanks." He put his arm around her and gave her a squeeze.

"And if you end up going over to Vietnam, be careful."

"Don't worry about me. I'll be fine. Just keep an eye on Mum for me." He and Judy had always been close as kids, and they still were.

"I'll keep an eye on things while you're away."

Twenty minutes later, Terry had packed most of what he would need, all he had to do was throw his gear in his truck and leave. He heard the back door of the house open and close and footsteps approach.

"T-T-Terry?"

That bloody stutter drove him crazy. Terry got back up and opened the door. Vernon was standing on the other side.

"Terry, mate, can I t-ta-talk to you for a minute?"

"Help yourself." He lifted the record off the turntable and slid it back into its sleeve as Vernon stepped inside.

"Just wanted t-t-to, you know–wish you luck."

"Thanks."

Vernon shuffled his feet uncomfortably and crossed his arms. "Don't worry about p-p-paying board while you're away. Your mother and I have t-t-talked, and we decided it wouldn't be right, seeing as you wouldn't be here."

"That's very decent of you, Vernon."

"Do you think you'll be wanting to live here when you g-g-get back?"

"I'm only going to Waiouru. Why do you want to know?"

Vernon uncrossed and then re-crossed his arms, shifting his gaze to the posters on the far wall.

Mucky bastard, Terry thought as he added the record to his pile of favourites. He opened his packet of Greys and went about pulling out a measured amount of tobacco.

"Well, your mother wondered about r-r-renting out the room."

He seriously doubted his mother would have thought of the idea.

"It's little more than a shed. Not sure why anyone would want to stay in here."

"You n-n-never know."

"Perhaps I should talk to her."

"I w-w-wouldn't bother her right now."

"Right." Terry stepped towards the door. Although you could fit four or five grown men in his sleepout, it was far too small for him and Vernon. "Well, tell her I would like somewhere to sleep when I come home." He held the door open. Vernon took the hint, and with a last glance at the women decorating the walls, he retreated to the security of the house.

Terry had heard enough of his bullshit for one day. He often wondered what his mother saw in Vernon. He was overweight, with greasy, slick-backed hair and that infuriating stutter. He lived in suits and had soft white hands that indicated he hadn't done a single day's hard graft in his life. Probably wouldn't know a spark plug if he fell over one. Terry studied his own hands. The nails had oil stains around them he hadn't been able to get out, and his skin was toughened from working in the garage, the hunting trips he went on, and doing the chores around the property for his mother.

Terry lay back on his bed, hands clasped behind his head, and stared longingly at Miss September.

Chapter 2

Basic training was continuous hours of being shouted at and following orders. There were drills to learn, weapons to familiarise himself with, map reading, field work and physical fitness. Terry learned quickly and was well-liked by the other recruits.

He didn't once stop to think about how his brothers and sisters were, or his mum; whether that blue Humber that had been brought into the garage for a valve grind had been finished, or if Vernon had bothered to mow the lawn in his absence.

He caught sight of Jack during one of his drill lessons but didn't dare break formation to attract his attention. They usually caught up in the mess hall at night. He'd told Jack he was putting his name forward for Malaya, and Jack agreed and was doing the same.

Terry passed basic training with flying colours. Not only was he an excellent marksman, but he could dismantle and reassemble any of the weapons blindfolded. And it didn't stop with the small arms. Anything that could be pulled apart and put back together, Terry could do it and twice as fast as anyone else. He was simply interested in knowing how things worked, and in the army, this was an obvious advantage. He'd made friends with a number of the recruits, and they were all like him, hoping like hell they'd get called up to go to Vietnam.

But when his orders came through, he was disappointed to learn he was being sent to Burnham, down in Christchurch, and not to Terendak in Malaya. It was made worse when he ran into Jack and learned he was being sent to Terendak in seven days' time. They were sending men over to train in jungle conditions and learn about jungle warfare. There was no mention of them being sent to Vietnam, but there were plenty of rumours about how Prime Minister Holyoake would soon respond to the pressure from President Johnson. Maybe there was still hope.

One week after his arrival in Burnham, Terry was walking back to the barracks at the end of a three-day pack march and looking forward to a shower and a cold beer. His mind was on the blonde who worked in the burger bar in town; he thought he might have a chance of getting her out on a date on Saturday if she wasn't working. He heard his name being called and turned to see his commanding officer striding towards him.

"Edwards. Get cleaned up and come and see me."

"Yes, sir."

He had no idea what the boss wanted him for. When he got back to the barracks, he dropped his pack and pulled off his boots. It was good to get out of the clothes he'd worn for the last five days. Grabbing a towel, he headed for the showers. Twenty minutes later he stood in front of his commanding officer.

"Edwards, how would you feel about going over to Malaya?"

Terry couldn't believe his ears.

"I'd give my right arm to go, sir."

"That's what I thought. We've had to replace a couple of blokes. Your name came up. I'll tell them you're accepting."

"Yes, sir. When do I leave?"

His commanding officer laughed and leaned back in his seat, folding his arms across his chest. "I wish everyone was as enthusiastic as you. You're booked on a flight up to Ohakea Air Base tomorrow morning. You'll have three days to organise your personal affairs, say goodbye to your family and report to Papakura Camp, up in Auckland."

Terry couldn't believe his luck. He was going to Malaya and, hopefully, he'd go to Vietnam too. He walked back to the barracks with an extra spring in his step.

Chapter 3

Terry's mother was pleased to see him when he arrived home. She hugged him tightly and had more questions for him than he could answer. The younger children took turns to hug him too although they were now a little unsure of their big brother who looked very smart and a little scary in his army uniform. His hair had been cut short, and his mother told him he looked a handsome young man as she held him at arm's length to study him.

Vernon shook his hand and congratulated him although Terry could tell he wasn't really interested. Vernon had voiced his opinion more than once about how the government was wasting their time and money preparing men to fight in Asia. He was going through the motions to please Rosamund, and there was no doubt he believed the country would be better off investing the nation's wealth in something that gave more in return.

The younger kids wanted to know about the planes and the trucks and the strange country their big brother was going to.

"The more I hear, the less I like the idea of you going to Malaya, love," his mother stated over dinner. "I hope they don't send you to fight in Vietnam. I'll worry every minute you're over there."

"They'll train us in Malaya to look after ourselves. We'll learn about the jungle and booby traps and everything we need to survive."

"Will you get to use a machine gun?" his brother, Simon, asked, eagerly.

"I might."

"Do you get to keep it and bring it home?"

"Of course he c-c-can't bring it home," Vernon chipped in. "We don't w-w-want any machine guns here."

Terry saw the disappointment in his brother's face.

"We'll get to use hand grenades too. And set mines that will blow the legs clean off the enemy."

"Terry!" his mother admonished him.

"Ewwww!" Eileen screeched and Susan, his youngest sister,

immediately dropped the peas that had been precariously balanced on her fork.

"I want to be a soldier too," Simon declared as Susan stared transfixed at her big brother.

"We'll see," his mother said.

Simon was ten, eighteen months older than Eileen and five years older than Susan. Terry felt sorry for the kid, growing up with a bank manager for a dad. He'd probably have a healthy savings account, as Vernon had already seen to it his children were religiously saving their pocket money; but Terry doubted the kid would be going out shooting rabbits, swimming in the river or building a cart from scratch–all things he had done growing up. He made a mental note to take the kid out shooting one night when he got back.

"You'd make a good soldier," Terry said, forking up a dollop of mashed potato and pressing it into his peas.

Across the table, Simon beamed, and Vernon frowned but remained silent.

"Thought I'd hitchhike up to Auckland tomorrow," Terry said.

"Do you have to leave so soon?"

"I need to get up to the camp at Papakura. The men will be arriving already, and it would be good to sort a few things before we fly out."

"You mean g-g-get on the booze," Vernon said.

"Yeah, well, I won't say no, should the opportunity arise. Might be the last chance I get."

"Why's that?" his mother asked.

"I don't know. Plane might go down. I might get shot or blown up." He winked at Simon.

"Will people be shooting at you?" Simon asked.

"If I go to Vietnam, they will."

"Why?"

"Because they'll be trying to kill me."

"I wish you wouldn't say things like that," his mother said.

"I'll be fine, Mum."

"Make sure you write to us and let us know you're okay."

"I will." He stabbed his fork into a piece of roast pumpkin. "Susie, you be sure to draw me lots of pictures."

"I will," she said, concentrating on stacking more peas one by one on her fork.

Truth was, Terry couldn't wait to get up to Auckland. Now he knew he was going, he just wanted to get over there. He pushed his chair back, stood up and collected his plate. "I better go sort my gear." He added his plate to the collection of dirty dishes mounting up on the end of the bench. "I'll come back in and wash them for you shortly, Mum."

"Don't worry about it tonight, love, Vern and I will do them. You organise your things."

He kissed her on the top of her head as he passed her on his way to the door. "Thanks, Mum."

He packed the basics. They had been told to keep their personal belongings to a minimum; the army would provide everything they required. He just needed some gear to wear when he was on R and R. He packed a book he had been meaning to read, and the Swiss pocketknife that had saved his bacon a couple of times, which he carried as a lucky charm. He added a couple of packets of tobacco and papers, some writing paper and envelopes and gathered up the few toiletries he needed, then dropped the bag onto the floor and sat on the edge of the bed.

Miss December stared at him. She was definitely coming, and Miss September. He carefully removed the poster from the wall, along with several others, and then considered the black and white photos. In one, he and his mates had just got back from a hunting trip; Simon was wearing Terry's gun belt draped across his bony shoulder and trying to lift the head of the boar they had shot. He had it by the tusks, but it was far too heavy for an eight-year-old kid. It had been taken two years earlier and made Terry smile. He tossed it on the pile.

Another photo, from the summer before, caught his attention. Four friends sitting on the beach, Jack with a beer in one hand and his other arm slung around Evelyn. She was laughing at something Jack had said. Terry had been sitting on the other side of Evelyn, next to Joanie, who had her head on his shoulder and her hand on his thigh. Evelyn had asked a lady walking her dog to take the photo. He remembered the exact moment and the heat of Joanie's hand on his skin. He unpinned the photo, stared at it a little longer, and then repinned it to the wall.

Next, he took down a photo of his mother, father, Judy and himself taken at Judy's eighteenth birthday. His parents stood either side of their two children. His father, hands in his trouser pockets, was dressed in his best jacket and tie, and the hat he always wore when he went out; his mother in her best dress, coat with the fur collar and her cream handbag. Bill Edwards, his father, had cleared off a week after that party. He still lived in Foxton and had since bought a house. Terry went around most weekends to help him with whatever project he was working on and to escape from Vernon.

When Terry told his father he'd joined the army, he wasn't particularly surprised, and when Terry mentioned he might get called up to go to Vietnam, his father's only advice had been to 'keep your head down' and 'run like hell,' and he'd told his son he'd have a cold beer waiting for him when he got back.

Terry fingered the corner of the photo. Why he wanted to take that photo, he didn't know. Jesus, he must be getting old and sentimental.

As he lay on his bed later that night, he wondered what it would be like for them in Malaya, away from their families and friends. Jack and Evelyn had just got engaged; he was happy for his mate, he had someone special to come home to. Terry didn't.

His thoughts shifted to Evelyn's friend Joanie. He'd only met her twice; once when she was down in Foxton with Evelyn, and once at a party in Auckland. She was nice and seemed happy to accommodate his appetite for a pretty girl and a warm, soft body, but he wasn't interested in anything but having fun. Not like Jack, who wanted nothing more than to settle down. Terry didn't want anything permanent. He was far too young for all that serious shit.

Chapter 4

Frankie Proctor put down the latest issue of *Time* magazine. There were two articles in this issue about the Vietnam War. American soldiers were arriving in the country a thousand at a time every day, and yet they didn't seem to be making any headway. She drained the last of her coffee and studied the people sitting around her. People intent on finishing their meals; an elderly gentleman in a plaid jacket smoking a cigar, pen hovering momentarily in the air as he worked on a crossword; a couple holding hands, gazing into each other's eyes as they shared a milkshake. Frankie groaned.

Did any of them know what was going on in Vietnam? Did any of them even care?

She collected her shoulder bag and magazine and walked the short distance back to the offices of *The Wellington Daily*. They had given her the break into photojournalism she had so desperately wanted, but now she'd outgrown them. Or, more to the point, she had outgrown the type of work they assigned her.

Looking at the photos coming out of Vietnam made her itch to take on more challenging jobs. She'd even thought about going over to Saigon. Taking photos of community events no longer held any interest. They regularly sent her to cover educational stories, the courts or fashion. She was promised the big stories, but these promised assignments never eventuated, and she was left covering the prize for the largest pumpkin, or a pet day at school. Somehow, the editor always managed to send a man to cover the important jobs. They didn't even send her to cover the peace marches that were happening more often now.

She couldn't even begin to imagine what it would be like to get her photos on the cover of magazines like *Time* or even a spread inside one of them.

"Frankie!" Nell, the receptionist, waved at Frankie as she walked through the door. "The boss is looking for y– Good Lord, what are you wearing?" She looked Frankie up and down.

"What's wrong with what I'm wearing?" Frankie adjusted the green kerchief tied around her neck and looked down at the overalls she'd bought from the farm supply store the day before. They had a bib front, were comfortable and, most importantly, practical; with large pockets that held everything from cigarettes to her notepad, a pen, a small purse and extra rolls of film. They did nothing to flatter her figure, unlike the tight, pink twinset and pencil skirt the immaculately dressed receptionist wore. The last thing Frankie was interested in was showing off her figure in order to catch a boy. All she wanted to do was take great photos and prove herself in the industry.

"Nothing, I guess," Nell replied. "If you worked in a garage fixing old cars for a living. Anyway, the boss is waiting to see the photos you took at parliament this morning."

"Right. He'll have the contact in ten minutes." Frankie had processed the small strip of negatives and hung them to dry an hour earlier and then gone out for lunch. They looked good, as far as portrait shots went, and they made the new member of parliament look smart and sure of himself, but they were hardly going to make the country sit up and take notice.

A few minutes later, Frankie tapped on the editor's door and pushed it open.

"Ah, Frankie, come in."

Frankie handed him the black and white contact sheet, sat down in a chair the other side of his desk, and watched as William Booth, the editor of *The Wellington Daily* for the last twelve years, ran his loupe across the images, studying them in detail.

"Good work." He circled one with blue ink and handed the contact sheet back.

"It's hardly inspiring. Any photographer could take a good head and shoulders shot."

Booth ignored the comment.

"At four o'clock, it's the official opening of the new terminal at the airport. They're waiting for a flight from Sydney to land, and apparently, Holyoake will be there with some of his cabinet ministers. Catch a ride with Jim. He's assigned to the story."

Frankie didn't move. They only had two photographers on the staff, and she always got the safe jobs. Booth had refused to send her up to Auckland two years ago to cover the story about Kelly Tarlton and Wade

Doak when they recovered gold and silver coins from the wreck of the *Elingamite* which had sunk near the Three Kings Islands in 1902. In January, she had asked to fly down to cover the Strongman Mine disaster and the loss of nineteen good men, but Booth had again said no.

Booth looked up from the sheet of paper he was typing on.

"I'd like to go to Vietnam to cover the war," Frankie blurted out.

"No."

"What? Just like that?" His abrupt response took her by surprise. He hadn't even stopped to consider her idea.

"Yes, just like that."

"The New Zealand Press Association needs a photographer over there, and I know I can get good images."

"They also want experienced photographers who know what they're doing and have a proven track record."

"But how do I get that track record if I don't get the chance to show people what I can do?"

"Keep doing what you're doing, and someday you'll be good enough to cover the big stories."

Frankie was sick of hearing about 'someday.' "I don't care who grows the biggest pumpkin, or who broke into the supermarket, or who wears the most glamorous dresses." She had desperately hoped Booth would agree to send her over on a trial period. Maybe for a month. Long enough for her to prove she could handle the work.

"That may be the case, but others *do* care about new terminals," Booth replied, hitting the return lever, sending the sheet of paper and carriage careening across the typewriter. "And hospital wings and people they happen to have voted into parliament. And they want to know what's going on in their communities."

"Just for a month. I want the chance to make a difference. Help change the way people see things."

"I won't be responsible for sending you over to a war zone and then have to face your parents when you come home in a body bag. You need to think seriously about what you're asking for, Frankie." Booth picked up his cigarette from the ashtray, put it to his lips and inhaled deeply. "I am not sending a woman into a war zone. End of story."

Frankie had never felt so frustrated. It wasn't as though she would be the only woman to go to war. There had been quite a few go over already.

Booth balanced the cigarette on the lip of the ashtray and continued typing.

"What about Dickey Chapelle and Catherine Leroy?"

"Exactly! I don't want what happened to Dickey Chapelle happening to you."

Chapelle had been killed two years earlier by a booby trap while she'd been out on patrol with a Marine unit. She had been the first female reporter to be killed in Vietnam. Frankie had seen her work in *Time* magazine and even *Rolling Stone*. She'd also seen Catherine Leroy's work and admired both women.

"But she was a woman and doing a great job. Sometimes you have to do what's required to get the photo."

"That may well be, but I didn't have to face her parents," Booth replied.

Frustrated, Frankie stood. It was the last time Booth would give her the safe job.

"Then I'm really sorry, but you don't leave me much option. I'd like to hand in my resignation. I'll stay until the end of the month."

He looked up and pushed the typewriter away from him. "You're resigning because I won't send you to Vietnam?"

"Yes."

"Well, you've got guts. I'll give you that." He stood and walked to the nearest window and stared at something in the distance. "Have you found another paper to work for?"

"No."

"So what do you intend to do?"

"I'm going to Saigon."

"To work?"

"Yes." She'd worked at the paper for three years; it had been her first 'real' job after finishing university. But for the past six months, she had been thinking seriously about going to Vietnam. She had hoped she would get sent with a news agency. If she didn't, it would make things harder but not impossible, and it looked like she would be going over without the support of an agency.

"Well, I wish you luck. I think you're completely mad. War isn't pretty, in fact, it's downright ugly, and it can do terrible things to a person." He sat back down. "Mad, but gutsy," he mumbled. "Maybe you have what it takes, but I only hope it doesn't get you into trouble."

Frankie went home to her bedsit after work, feeling anxious, but excited. What if she was making a huge mistake? She needed someone to tell her she was doing the right thing. She showered and dressed and after shrugging into her winter jacket, walked the two blocks to the row of tiny two-storied houses that ran up towards the reserve. After crossing the street, she knocked on the door at number fourteen and tried the handle. It gave way, and she pushed it open then stepped inside.

"Hey. Frankie. Thought I heard a knock."

"You busy, Scotty?"

"Nah. I should be writing though, assignment due tomorrow." He put his arm around Frankie and pulled her into him, kissing her on the lips.

"Shit. I should go then," she replied, teasing him.

"Stay. I'll pull an all-nighter."

"I'd be surprised if you didn't, Scotty. What's the assignment on?"

"Unilateralism."

He was studying political science at Victoria University which seemed to be the latest trend, and his grades constantly impressed Frankie given that he was almost always stoned or drunk. At nineteen, he was also three years younger than Frankie, but she didn't care. They'd met at a local pub and got drunk together; he'd walked her home and ended up staying the night. They had fun, they laughed a lot, and they had great sex, and that was all that mattered. She was too young to settle down with anyone. She wanted to make a name for herself first.

"How you–" she started but was silenced by his lips on hers again.

"You are under my spell." He made a serious face. "Now, tell Scotty the real reason why you're here."

"I need your body."

"Yeah, they all say that."

She punched him lightly on the arm, and he grinned at her. "I need you to reassure me I've done the right thing."

He led her through the hall and into the lounge. A small, glowing heater did little to warm the high-ceilinged room. She could tell he'd been sitting on the floor reading: books and cushions were scattered in a semicircle. She peeled off her jacket and tossed it and her bag onto one of the two chairs in the room.

"I've chucked in my job."

He lowered himself to the floor and sat cross-legged, taking her hand and pulling her down to him. "That's a bit rash for you, isn't it?"

"Oh God, I think I'm an idiot. Maybe I've made the wrong decision."

"Now, you're a few things, but you're not an idiot."

"Oh really?"

"Yes." He leaned into her, lingering over the kiss.

"I'm going to Vietnam," she finally said.

There was a moment's silence.

"You're going to cover the war?"

"I'm going to try."

"Shit, you're one gutsy chick. Now, I've got just the thing for an anxiety attack." He rummaged through the papers and books on the floor and uncovered an old tobacco tin, opened it, and busied himself rolling a joint.

"Thought you might."

Drinking from a bottle of cheap red wine, they spent the night on the floor, laughing, debating and finally, making love. Frankie knew as soon as she left for Vietnam he would find someone else to share his floor, but it was fine with her. They were friends, and it'd been fun while it lasted. Now she was moving on.

She would have eventually, anyway.

Chapter 5

Now she had made up her mind she was going to Vietnam, Frankie wanted nothing more than to get over there. Holyoake was under pressure from Johnson to send more support, and with 161 Battery still entrenched in South Vietnam, rumours were rife that he would send an infantry company over. For New Zealand, the war was about to get a whole lot more real, and Frankie wanted to make sure she was a part of it.

The following day, she called into a travel agency to price tickets and hurried back to the office to do some calculations. She had enough for a one-way ticket, a spare second-hand camera, and a week in a cheap hotel before she would run out of money. She would need to find a job fast, but she was prepared do anything to start with.

Frankie rang her parents the following weekend. Now she had officially resigned from work, she wanted to plan the trip and spend a couple of days with her parents before she left for Vietnam.

As expected, her mother wasn't happy when her only daughter announced she was leaving a perfectly good job in Wellington to fly thousands of miles away to live and work in a war zone. She burst into tears, and in the end, Frankie couldn't make sense of anything her mother said and asked to speak to her father instead. She could tell he wasn't thrilled about her decision either, but at least he was coherent when she spoke to him.

He tried to make her see sense. However, nothing either of her parents could say would change her mind.

On Frankie's last day at *The Wellington Daily*, Booth put on a few drinks for her in the staffroom. By this time, most of the staff knew what her plans were and one by one they wished her good luck. Nell gave her a tube of red lipstick and a pair of pretty pearl earrings and told her she had to take them with her and wear them to remind everyone she was a woman. The other photographer gave her a pocket phrase book to read on the plane, someone else had bought her a set of luggage tags, and one of the journalists gave her a travel journal. Their support and good wishes overwhelmed her, and it was all she could do to stop herself from getting emotional.

"Can I have your attention for a moment," Booth bellowed over the din of loud talking and music. "I just want to say a few words while you're all still sober."

"It's too late," someone piped up from the back of the staffroom, adding to the laughter.

"I just want to say, on behalf of us all gathered here tonight, that we wish you well in Vietnam." He looked at Frankie. "You've been a great member of *The Daily,* and I for one am going to miss you."

Someone shouted, "*Here, here!*"

"I'm not one for long speeches, so I just want to give you two pieces of advice." The room fell silent. "The first is, keep your bloody head down and your eyes open." Booth waited until the clapping died down. "The second piece of advice is–"

"Wait for it!" Another round of laughter.

"The second piece of advice is," Booth repeated himself, "never talk to strangers, especially if they're wearing black pyjamas."

His comment fell short of being light-hearted, and the room fell silent as the seriousness of what Frankie was about to do sank in.

"Anyway," Booth continued, "we've all chipped in and got you something we think you'll find useful during your time in Asia." Booth turned, took a wrapped box off the kitchen bench and walked across to Frankie. After handing it to her, he hesitated and then wrapped his arms around her and patted her on the back.

Frankie peeled the wrapping paper off the box and discovered they had bought her a brand-new Leica camera. Her very own Leica! She had planned to buy another camera before she left, but now she wouldn't have too. It was perfect.

"Speech!"

"Speech."

Frankie blushed and then held up a hand. "Thank you all so much for your thoughtful gifts and this beautiful camera. It couldn't be more perfect. I'm going to miss you all."

Nell cried and hugged her and told her to write to let her know she was safe. Jim pumped her hand and wished her well, telling her he'd watch the wires and magazines for her images. One by one they wished her well. Finally, when they had all left and Frankie was helping Booth collect up the empty beer bottles and paper cups, Booth said he had something for her and disappeared to his office, returning with an envelope.

"What is it?"

"The names of two journalists in Saigon. One is the bureau chief for the Associated Press and the other is a freelancer. I worked with them a few years ago." He smiled as he handed the envelope to her. "Contact details are all there. I thought you might be able to look them up. If they don't have any work for you, they may know of someone or some agency that needs a stringer."

"Thank you. This means a lot."

"There's also the name of a friend of mine who works in the New Zealand Embassy in Singapore. If you're stuck over there, look him up. He'll put you up for a few nights if you tell him you know me." He hesitated. "Just keep safe over there, lass. When you get back, come and see me. I might just need a senior photographer."

Frankie hugged him, and after thanking him, she left. During the taxi ride home, she stared out into the night and thought about the brand-new Leica sitting on the seat next to her and of all the images she would take with it.

"It's not a spur-of-the-moment decision, Dad. I've been thinking about it for a while," Frankie told her father, two nights before she was due to fly out. He hadn't given up trying to change her mind. "Five thousand young American men died over there last year. Five thousand! That's a lot of men, and almost all of them were younger than me. Most hadn't even reached twenty. The more we can educate society about what this war is doing to the families of these young men, the better."

"You can't stop a war, Frances. It's bigger than you and everyone else who goes over hoping to make a difference. That's the nature of it. There are no winners."

"I know. But the New Zealand government needs to know what effect their decision to commit to Vietnam has on the young men who go over there."

"That doesn't mean you have to be the one to educate them. It's no different from World War One or Two. I dare say there are many other issues we know nothing about that come into play."

They were sitting in her parents' sitting room in Palmerston North with the fire warming the room; her mother had gone to bed earlier, complaining of a headache. Frankie loved times like this when it was just her and her father. They talked about politics, economics and social issues—subjects that didn't interest other girls Frankie's age. Most of her friends only cared about going to the movies or parties, and at twenty-two, a couple of her friends had married already and were expecting babies. Conversations with them always revolved around their homes, husbands or the babies. All topics that bored Frankie senseless.

"I think it's going to get worse. America will put more pressure on its allies. We'll be sending more men and losing more men. I want my images to help put a stop to that."

"Your images will do nothing more than stir the radicals looking for any excuse to protest. A war zone is no place for my daughter. I'd be happier if it were someone else's daughter going over there."

"There are lots of female nurses over there already, and America and France have female reporters on the ground. I've heard Saigon is safer than anywhere else in the country. I've got a couple of contacts in Saigon too. Maybe they can help me find work." They had been over it all again and again and nothing her father said made any difference.

"Well." He sighed. "All I can say is, be careful." He put his arm around her shoulder and squeezed her tight.

"I will," she promised, already thousands of miles away in Vietnam, as she imagined what it would be like on the streets of Saigon.

"Please be careful," Frankie's mother implored.

"I will. Don't worry about me." Her mother clung to her as if it was the last time she would see her daughter. "I'm twenty-two, Mum. I can look after myself."

"I know, dear, but anything could happen."

"Nothing is going to happen to me, I promise."

As she hugged her father, he whispered in her ear. "Promise me you won't take any risks." He kissed her on the forehead.

"I promise, Dad. And I'll visit the embassy in Saigon when I arrive too." He smiled at her, but Frankie could tell he was just as concerned as her mother was, only he was better at hiding it. It must have been hard for them to accept their only child wanted to go to war; that she didn't want to take photos for the soft news stories, but instead wanted to be right in the thick of history as it happened.

Finally, they called her flight. Her mother cried openly and both of her parents tried to hug her at once. As she waved to them for the last time and made her way towards the plane, she had no thoughts about when she might come home, or if she might be wounded or even killed in Vietnam. To Frankie, it felt like she was going on holiday, except she would document it with something far more significant than holiday snaps.

Her flight landed in Singapore, and five hours later she boarded her final flight to Saigon. When she eventually found her seat and stowed her bag with her brand-new Leica and her old battered Nikon in the overhead lockers, she realised many of the passengers were young men in uniform, most no older than her. As she gazed around at them, she wondered how many of these men would come home.

As the seats filled, she was sandwiched between two men. One was taking a job as a clerk in a place called Vũng Tàu, south of Saigon; the other was a civilian doctor who had been working in a hospital in Auckland and was stopping briefly in Saigon before flying further up country to join the New Zealand Civilian Surgical Team at a place called Qui Nhon. He told Frankie they helped civilian casualties of the war and also trained young Vietnamese girls to be nurses.

Frankie thought that was fascinating and made a note of his name and where he was, so she could visit his hospital and take photos. He told her most of the men on the flight were bound for Nui Dat. They were Victor Company: the first New Zealand infantry regiment to go over.

Despite the war in Vietnam, the atmosphere on the plane was light-hearted as soldiers laughed and joked with one another to pass the time. She noticed some chatted to the nurses, and others were content to read or sleep. Frankie made notes on some ideas she had for photo assignments and read her book and finally, through boredom, fell asleep.

An hour out of Saigon, she opened her eyes to find a soldier staring at her from the aisle. He seemed surprised that she had woken and caught him staring, and as he smiled at her, he tripped and landed in the lap of a matronly woman seated across from her. She bit her lip to stop herself from laughing as he apologised to the woman and beat a hasty retreat.

Frankie spent the remainder of the flight writing a letter to her parents to tell them about Singapore. She wrote about the beautiful orchids everywhere at the airport, the pretty girls who all had long straight black hair, and how the heat was barely tolerable and nothing like she had ever experienced back home. She also wrote a few lines on the back of a postcard to send to Nell at the paper. She would post both once she arrived in Saigon.

With fifteen minutes until they landed, Frankie peered past the man next to the window, looking for any sight of land, scarcely able to contain her excitement.

She would make the world sit up and take note. Her and her camera.

Chapter 6

With the training at Terendak completed, Terry and the other men had been delighted to find their names on the list that made up Victor Company, Royal New Zealand Infantry Regiment. They boarded a bus from Terendak Camp to Singapore and from there, caught a flight to Vietnam. Terry was impressed by the number of women on the flight; he had begun to wonder when he'd get the chance to enjoy female company again.

Several of the women wore the familiar uniform of the Red Cross, while some were in casual dress and others wore their nursing uniforms. Terry thought they all looked gorgeous and made an effort to spread himself around, much to the amusement of the other men on the flight. For Terry, chatting up the girls was a bit of a sport that helped to pass the time.

Some of the girls were going to the Australian Field Hospital in Vũng Tàu and others flying on to the hospital at Qui Nhon. He learned a couple of them were staying on in Saigon, too.

"For Christ's sake, sit down, Romeo," Dean Blackett said, manoeuvring past Terry on his way to the toilet.

"You've either got it, or you haven't, Blackie."

Blackie turned his attention to the girls. "Don't be fooled by his charms. He'll love you then leave you. He'll break your heart."

"Oh, but how I'll love them—that's what counts."

Giggling erupted from the row of girls.

"Yeah, right," Blackie replied, and then walked off.

The men of Victor Company made up the rest of the passengers: officers, some with their wives and children, doctors, military advisers, and several contractors.

Terry was more excited than he'd ever been in his life, and he knew he'd been lucky to be included in the ranks of those heading for a place called Nui Dat. He spent the long trip reading, playing cards, or sleeping; and to relieve the boredom, joking with the other men on board or chatting up the nurses, who were happy to indulge him.

They were a couple of hours into the flight when Terry got up to stretch his legs and noticed a woman passenger towards the front of the plane. He hadn't noticed her when he boarded, and he was sure he would have. She had the most intense dark red hair, not ginger, but the colour of polished copper. She was dressed in casual clothes and sat between two similarly dressed men. When he walked past her, she had her head in a book and didn't notice him.

Back in his seat, he could just catch a glimpse of the copper, and he noticed while the nurses chatted with others around them, she seemed to only talk to the men who sat next to her. He wondered what her reason was for flying to Saigon and decided she was probably some sort of doctor, or maybe she was meeting her husband.

Half an hour out of Saigon, he stood up to go to the toilet and decided to make his way there via the front of the plane. This time she had her head back and her eyes closed, and he was surprised to see she looked about his age and had the prettiest freckle-covered face. As he paused and nodded to one of the men beside her, she startled him by opening her eyes and staring straight at him. The intense blue mesmerised him; he grinned at her and promptly tripped, and as he stumbled and grabbed at the nearest seat, he fell into the lap of an older woman across the aisle from her. Apologising profusely, he fled to the toilet, hoping no one would notice the heat burning his face.

Why she had chosen that exact moment to open her eyes and look straight at him, he had no idea. She had startled him and made him feel like a clumsy kid. Then it occurred to him that one of her travelling companions might be her husband, and he felt embarrassment flood through him again.

When they landed in Saigon, he noticed her get off first, followed by her two male companions, and by the time Terry had disembarked and loaded his gear onto a truck, there was no sign of her. For all he knew, she had been picked up. It seemed not all the wives were happy to stay back in Terendak and wait for their husbands to return. Maybe she was one of those wives?

Chapter 7

Thick red dust swirled up behind the trucks as they drove through the main gates at Nui Dat, their base camp and home for the next six months. As the men were shown to their lines, they were told they had two days on camp duties before they would be moving out.

Kiwi lines were behind an embankment at the far end of the Luscombe Field runway, and Terry headed towards one of the larger tents between the rows of old rubber trees. At least he thought it was a tent, but as he drew closer, he realised it was actually a bunker, dug out of the earth, with a canvas tent as a roof. It had three army cots in it, and when he stood up, he could just see through the gap where the tent met the sandbags.

After claiming a bed, Terry spent the remainder of the day familiarising himself with the layout of the camp, and it wasn't until he was lying on his bed listening to the distant sound of shelling, that he remembered the girl with the copper hair and freckles. He remembered she had long eyelashes and beautiful eyes and wondered what she was doing now. Probably enjoying a grand house somewhere, or a posh hotel.

The following morning, Terry was rostered on sandbagging duty. They always needed bloody sandbags for something. By the time he had filled half a dozen, the sweat was pouring off him, and the red dust had turned him a muddy brick colour. In the afternoon, he was ordered to fill a backpack and spray the weeds around the base of each tent and the area the men would shower in. They had rigged up a platform with a forty-four-gallon drum full of water and four three-sided shower stalls.

By the time Terry finished the spraying, he had to stand-to with the rest of his section, but at stand-down, he rushed to be the first in a cold shower and, although feeling like he could sleep for a week, he took himself off to the mess for dinner and a cold beer.

"Hey, Romeo, how's it going?" Mark Murphy asked, stepping into the tent later that evening.

"I'm buggered already, and I've only been here two bloody minutes." He was lying on his cot smoking. "This heat is something, isn't it? How about a tune?"

Murphy was one of his roommates and was one of two members of their platoon who had brought guitars with them to Vietnam.

Murphy picked up his guitar and started picking notes.

"Nightcap, anyone?" Roger Harris asked, joining them. He handed a can of beer to each of them.

"Cheers, Smokey. Where did you get these from?"

"That's for me to know. Got a smoke?"

"Fair enough. Thought you'd given up the smokes?"

"I had. Got a bit of bad news, though, need a smoke to help calm the nerves."

Terry tossed his packet in Smokey's direction. "Nothing serious I hope." In the short time he'd known Roger, the man had given up smoking at least a dozen times, but no one had ever spotted him buying cigarettes.

"I just found out they've got rats here the size of cats here. Can't stand bloody rats."

"Seen any yet?" Terry asked.

"Nope. But I won't get a wink of sleep tonight."

"I reckon rats are the least of your problems, Smokey," Murphy chipped in.

"Aussie bloke down by the PX was telling me he woke up early hours of the morning, and there was this bloody big rat sitting on his pillow, eyeballing him."

"Well, you just sing out if you see any rats on your pillow, Smokey. Murph and I will save you," Terry stated, trying to keep the grin from his face.

For the following week, they were patrolling Nui Dat outside the wire; every morning, out before daybreak and then back to camp as the light faded. On the days they weren't patrolling, they were on duties around camp. There was always something that needed building, spraying or clearing.

By the end of the week, Terry was feeling frustrated and wondered if they would ever have any contact with the enemy. The only action he'd seen was in the form of an embarrassing itchy, red rash that had appeared two days after they had arrived and was becoming annoyingly sore.

During his spraying duty, he detoured past the medic's bunker to see if he could get anything for it, to save him the embarrassment of going over to the small camp hospital. He was in luck; Doc was lying on his cot reading.

"Hey, Doc. Got a minute?"

"Romeo. What can I do for you, mate?" Doc threw his legs over the side of his cot and sat up.

Terry dropped the backpack sprayer at the bunker door and stepped down into the slightly cooler air. "Well, I'm not sure. I've got this rash, and it's driving me crazy. It's itchy as all hell. Thought you might have something for it."

"I'll need to see it."

"Aw, shit."

"Drop your pants, Romeo," the medic directed.

"Steady on, Doc."

"I'm guessing it's in the groin region, and I gotta take a look."

"What if the other guys see me in your hootch, strides down around my ankles and you checking out my gear?"

"Well, you have two options. I can take a look, or you can head on over to the hospital."

Terry peeled off his shorts and underwear then stood staring anxiously at the tent ceiling.

"As I thought. Nothing more than common old crotch rot."

"Got anything for it?" Terry dragged his pants back up in quick time.

The medic retrieved a small tube of something from a trunk and handed it to Terry. "Get rid of the underwear. Your gear needs some fresh air. Underwear makes you sweat more in this heat." He nodded in the direction of Terry's manhood. "Put this on twice a day."

"Thanks, Doc."

"One of the perks of Vietnam," the medic commented. "Just be thankful you got a mild dose, and we didn't have to amputate anything."

Terry didn't see the joke, and he left the Doc laughing as he grabbed the backpack and hurried back to his bunker to relieve himself of his underwear and discreetly apply some cream. Walking back to finish the spraying a few minutes later, he decided going commando already felt better and wondered why he hadn't thought of it before.

"Edwards!" his section commander called. "Briefing, seventeen hundred hours."

"Right-o, Boss. Are we moving out again?"

"We're moving to higher ground. Carry on. You're doing a great job."

He had the officers' mess and the cookhouse to do, and then he could get rid of the bloody leaky backpack.

Orders had come through they were to move out to the Horseshoe, an extinct volcanic crater named after its shape. They were to replace an Australian infantry company: protecting an artillery battery and carrying out search and destroy missions in the area. This news seemed to please most of the men including Terry, who seemed to spend all his free time cleaning his rifle and losing money in card games; they were eager to get out in the jungle and make contact with the enemy.

At the Horseshoe, Terry shared a bunker with Blackie. He was the section's machine gunner, and as Terry had been designated his number two, they bunked together. The arrangement worked well.

Most days, One Section patrolled a designated area away from the Horseshoe, but they also helped set mines in the cleared section that spread around the base of the hill. Terry's skills were often required, even though there were a number of men capable of setting Claymore mines, no one could work as fast or efficiently as Terry. If there were any problems, Terry was always able to come up with a way to improvise.

A routine was quickly established: each night after stand-down, the men would eat and write letters or read in the last of the fading light. Terry played poker with whoever he could find to join him. Then, as the last of the light disappeared, they would try to grab some sleep, only to be woken a couple of hours later by the cry, *"Incoming!"* as the enemy let them know they were out behind the wire. The guns retaliated, and the darkness erupted in brilliant flashes of colour as tracers criss-crossed the sky and mortars and rockets exploded short of their targets.

On the fifth night, Blackie and Terry had just stood down from the nightly attacks and were making themselves comfortable in their bunker when an almighty scream pierced the air.

"Shit! That was Smokey, wasn't it?" Terry asked Blackie as they clambered back out of their cots, trying to get feet into boots and grab weapons at the same time. Smokey and Murph were in a bunker to their left, and Terry was suddenly worried that a Victor Charlie had penetrated the wire and got both men.

As Terry got to the bunker, an M16 opened fire, and Smokey dived through the opening, and rolled across the ground in front of them then sprung to his feet.

"Smokey, you all right?" Terry rasped. "What the hell's happening? Where's Murph?" Four SLRs were now fixed on the bunker, and men were running from other bunkers with their rifles. Terry could almost hear Smokey shaking and could smell the fear.

There was a brief flicker of light from within the bunker.

"Got him!" Murph called from the depths of the bunker.

"VC?" Blackie asked, holding his M60 firmly to his hip.

"Nope." Murph appeared, swinging the arse end of one of the largest rats Terry had ever seen.

"You gotta be kidding me."

"A rat?" someone asked.

"Yeah, Smokey's got a bit of a thing about them," Terry answered.

"Not much left of that one," Murph stated, hurling the remains of the rat into the darkness.

"The bloody thing was on me," Smokey said, his voice higher pitched than normal.

"You screamed like a bloody sheila, Smokey," JJ Johnson said from behind them. "Thought you had a girl holed up in there with you."

"Piss off," Murph said. "Do I look like a bloody sheila to you?"

"After I've been here a bit longer, you might start to look tempting." He roared with laughter.

"Fuck off, JJ."

"Murph saved my life," Smokey stated. "Jesus, the man deserves a bloody medal. Anyone got a smoke?" A hand reached out of the darkness with a cigarette.

"Well, let's hope he doesn't have any mates who come looking for him, that's all I've got to say," Blackie said to Terry as they headed back to their bunker.

"You and me both." Terry wasn't afraid of rats. He didn't like them, but once they discovered there wasn't anything worth eating in the bunker, he figured they'd bugger off somewhere else. Well, he hoped they would.

He stretched out on his cot, pulled his shirt collar up around his neck and draped his towel over his head. Just to be on the safe side.

Chapter 8

From the air, the shimmering blue of the sea had turned into a patchwork of lush, vivid greens, and Frankie wondered if they were market gardens, or perhaps paddy fields. Slowly, they were replaced by buildings–a river winding through them–and eventually, the runway. From the air, the country looked beautiful. It was hard to believe there was a war happening.

Frankie's flight from Singapore touched down on the tarmac at Tan Son Nhut Airport in Saigon at two minutes after one. As she stepped down off the plane, the afternoon heat hit her like a blast from a furnace, and she gasped, filling her lungs with aviation fumes. Perspiration immediately beaded along her hairline, and by the time she got to the terminal, she could feel it trickling down her back and soaking into her shirt.

In every direction, planes taxied, jets screamed, and choppers hovered above the ground as men climbed aboard or jumped out. Frankie had never seen so many different types of planes before. Soldiers in jeeps zipped between planes like snaking lifelines, and military police stood sentry at gates and buildings everywhere.

Inside the terminal, where it was barely cooler, she collected her bag then followed the stream of travellers out to where taxi drivers hawked their services. People slept wherever they could find room. Some in awkward positions in airport chairs and others lay on mats on the floor. It seemed everyone had a sleep in the middle of the day.

Three men rushed at her, all haggling to take her bag. After what seemed an eternity of arguments between the men, Frankie walked towards a car. There was a sudden burst of chatter, and one of the drivers ran to catch up with her, leaving the other two to walk back to their vehicles.

"Caravelle Hotel, please." The driver nodded and smiled, happy to pick up a fare. He opened the back door for Frankie then put her bag in the boot of the car. Booth had told her both the New Zealand and Australian Embassies were located in the Caravelle. She would start there.

The streets were beautiful, with huge trees that stretched their branches out over the road, and now and again camouflaged wrought-iron gates. Frankie caught glimpses of grand old buildings that looked like they were influenced by the French, and of courtyards littered with pots of varying sizes containing all types of plants. Motorbikes lined the footpaths and filled the streets, whizzing past the car on both sides. Women wearing traditional Vietnamese hats were everywhere, and as the car made its way through the outer districts of the city, an occasional flash of brightly coloured silk caught her eye.

The hotel was refreshingly cool inside. What an amazing place. It felt exciting, enticing. Apart from the activity at the airport, there didn't seem to be any evidence at all that there was a war taking place. To her, it looked like it was life as usual in Saigon.

An elegant sign with gold lettering indicated the occupants of each floor; Frankie noted which one she needed.

At the embassy counter, a pretty Vietnamese woman greeted her with a smile.

"Good afternoon, ma'am."

Frankie was surprised to hear her speak perfect English.

"I've just got off a flight and was wondering if you could recommend somewhere to stay."

"Are you here long?"

"I don't know. It will depend if I can find work."

"What type of work are you looking for?"

"Photographer with one of the agencies."

"Many of the journalists and photographers stay here at the Caravelle, but the Continental Palace and Majestic are favourites too." She leaned across the counter and lowered her voice. "You might find the Continental is a little cheaper than here at the Caravelle."

Frankie nodded her thanks.

The Continental was only a few metres away, on the other side of the square, and the woman told her to contact the embassy if there was anything else they could help with. Frankie thanked her and made her way back downstairs.

When she arrived at the Continental Palace hotel, they had three rooms left, and she opted for the cheapest even though it was a little more expensive than she had budgeted for. If she was careful with her money, she could stay there for a week while she looked for a job.

When she opened the door to her room, the first thing she noticed was the quaint window at the opposite end of the room. Drawn to it, she dropped her bags on the over-sized bed en route, and discovered it was actually a narrow door. Opening it revealed an intricate, whitewashed ironwork balcony much too small to stand on, but it held captive three pots of flowering geraniums that were growing through the ironwork. Frankie thought it added an element of romance to the room.

Peering down, she discovered the room overlooked a central garden scattered with small round tables and chairs. Brightly flowering bougainvillea climbed over railings and up French-looking lamp posts. In one corner of the courtyard, a solitary man sat reading a paper, and she could hear running water. Across the courtyard was a wall of small balconies similar to hers. Some had open doors, some closed. She hooked the door open, allowing the sounds from the surrounding streets to find their way inside.

A television sat on a shelf on the wall, a small fridge offered bottles of water, and an electric jug meant she could make tea or coffee. The bathroom was clean, and she was thankful to find there was good water pressure when she turned on the shower.

She couldn't wait to get out and explore the city. Hurriedly, she slipped out of her clothes and stepped under the jets of water. It was cool and refreshing and gave her a much-needed boost of energy. The heat was exhausting and inescapable.

In a thin cotton dress and sandals, with her camera over her shoulder, Frankie ventured back downstairs. It was now almost four in the afternoon, and street vendors were setting up food stalls in preparation for serving food to late-afternoon commuters. The city was alive and noisy, and still hot!

Strolling around with her camera, Frankie took photos of Vietnamese women as they squatted on the footpaths; some called out to her, happy to smile when they saw the camera; others ignored her, busy in their preparations. She didn't know what they were cooking, but the smells were heavenly.

"Xin chào," she attempted. She had no idea if the few basic words she had taught herself from the phrase book were pronounced right, but it was fun trying.

"Chào," the woman responded. "You eat?" She handed a parcel of food wrapped in a green leaf to a waiting customer and took notes in return.

"What is it?"

The woman rattled off something in Vietnamese that Frankie couldn't understand and held up one finger.

Frankie nodded. She was suddenly ravenous, and if others were eating it, it must be okay. She took the offered parcel and paid the woman, standing back out the way of pedestrians as she ate the parcel of sticky rice with, what appeared to be, beef. Whatever it was, it was well cooked and delicious. Thanking the woman, she was rewarded with a toothy smile and more chatter, and the woman was happy to continue smiling as Frankie took several photos of her.

She also took photos of the men sitting atop their motorbikes waiting to pick up rides, and young girls who walked in groups of three or four, dressed in brightly coloured silks. An old woman hidden under her conical hat carried empty baskets on a pole across her shoulder as she looked to be heading home.

Frankie walked the streets for almost two hours, fascinated by the beauty of the French architecture, the lush trees that lined the streets, and the people. Apart from the American military jeeps that threaded their way in and out of traffic and the odd small groups of soldiers in uniform, she still hadn't seen evidence of the war. It seemed another world away.

Finally, with almost a whole roll of film finished, she made her way back down Dong Khoi Street towards her hotel. It was time to sit somewhere cool in the remains of the daylight and enjoy a cold beer. She had seen the Independence Palace where the president of South Vietnam lived; sat on the steps of the cathedral and had a cold drink; and sent her parents and Nell a post card from the beautiful Post Office with its telephone booths and world clocks. There were pretty splashes of colour and parklike grounds everywhere, and she thought it was all exotic and wonderful.

By the time she got back to her room, she was exhausted. She had allowed herself to be a tourist for a few hours, but tomorrow she would need to start looking for work. Leaning out the still-open window, she could see the courtyard below was filling with diners. She hurriedly took a cold shower and changed for dinner.

Down in the restaurant, Frankie ordered something to eat. Seated at a table at one end of the garden, she was able to watch the comings and goings as she enjoyed a cold beer while she waited.

"May I join you?" A tall, tanned man stood to one side of her table.

The question took Frankie by surprise; she had been studying the little balconies and had not seen him approach. His accent was French, but his English was clear.

"Yes. Please do."

He held a hand out. "Louis Laurent. Journalist for the AP. And you?"

Frankie smiled. "Frances Proctor. But everyone calls me Frankie." She shook his hand and gestured towards the opposite chair.

He placed his glass on the table and pulled out the chair.

"And are you on holiday in Saigon, Miss–Frankie?"

"No. I am currently an unemployed photographer."

"Welcome to Saigon. I am guessing you have not been here long, no?"

"I arrived today. How did you know?" She was fascinated with him and charmed by his accent.

"You have a certain, shall we say, look of innocence about you."

Frankie laughed. "Is that good or bad?"

"Innocence is a quality we all arrive with. But unfortunately, a quality that will not last long." He paused and studied her further. "There is a lot to photograph in the South. You are looking for work with an agency?" He drained the last of his beer and signalled the waiter for another.

"I'll take whatever I can get," she replied, hoping he might have contacts. "I've got a week to find something or I'm heading back home."

"You are from Australia, I think, no?"

"New Zealand."

"You are young, very beautiful, and a brave woman coming to a war zone. But you are not the only woman to do this. It is becoming more common to see females with notepads and cameras." He nodded at the waiter as he placed the refill on the table. "Do you have accreditation?"

"No. Will it be a problem?"

"It will if you want to work as a photographer."

"How do I get accredited?" It was something she hadn't even thought about.

"If you can get work with one of the agencies, they will write you a letter of reference. You must take it to the office of the Military Assistance Command, Vietnam, or what we call the MACV."

Frankie loved the way he pronounced Mac-Vee.

"The letter explains that you are being considered for employment. If you are lucky, they will give you temporary accreditation while you impress the agency with your images."

It was a lot to take in, and Frankie was relieved when her meal arrived, as it gave her time to think about all he had said.

"Do you mind if I eat?"

"Not at all. You have the Banh Canh Ghe, a good choice. The crab is excellent here. In fact, all the food from the kitchen is of high quality, but a little on the expensive side. If you have to watch what you spend, you would be wise to eat from the street vendors."

Louis talked while Frankie devoured her meal. She found him fascinating to listen to. He told her where he had been on an assignment that day and how she would need to get some green skins if she was thinking of going out into the field. She realised there was a lot she didn't know. All she did know was that she would do whatever it took to get great photos.

"What are green skins?"

"Jungle greens. They'll help keep you safe. Plus, you will need boots. Maybe a hat to keep that beautiful hair hidden."

More things she hadn't considered. What had she thought she'd wear all day, every day? Her sundresses?

Frankie acknowledged that the meal was indeed delicious but, as much as Louis laughed at her hearty appetite, she declined his offer to buy her another course, so they settled for coffee instead.

Frankie told him she'd been given the names of two journalists who might be able to help her find work.

"You might know Robert Miller. I think he's the bureau chief at Associated Press. The other is a journalist by the name of Larry Powell."

Louis looked surprised. "Ah, Bobby. Yes, I know him well. I shall take you to meet him in the morning. I have heard of Mr Powell, but not yet had the pleasure of meeting him." Louis looked well pleased with himself as he pushed his chair back and stood up. "Thank you for the pleasure of your company tonight. I think we shall get to know each other well. I must leave you now, as I can tell you are exhausted, no? I also had an unnecessarily early morning, and I am afraid I am no longer any fun at all."

"Thank you for your company." Frankie stood too. "I am pretty bushed. It's been a long day."

They shared the elevator to the second floor where Louis got off. With a slight lift of the wrist he turned and disappeared down the corridor. Frankie remained in the elevator and got off on the next floor. Everything about Saigon filled her with excitement.

Chapter 9

In the morning, Frankie couldn't bear lying in bed listening to the city stir; she was up early and sitting at a table under the hotel's veranda drinking coffee when Louis arrived.

"Good morning, Frankie. I trust you slept well?"

"I went out like a light. Can I get you coffee?"

He grinned at her comment and shook his head, and Frankie thought how handsome he was. If she had been ten years older, they might have made a good couple. He had the rugged good looks of a young Clark Gable with flecks of grey peppering his dark hair. She guessed he couldn't be any more than thirty-two or thirty-three.

"I'm on my way to the bureau. You want to come, no?"

"Yes, please." She was thrilled he hadn't forgotten the offer he had made the night before. She swallowed the rest of her coffee and followed him out onto the street.

At the Associated Press bureau, Robert Miller sat hunched over an old Olivetti typewriter, two fingers stabbing the keys in a staccato rhythm. A cigarette hung from the corner of his mouth, and Frankie noticed half a coconut shell on his desk acted as an ashtray, threatening to overflow. One wall had various maps on it, and although Frankie couldn't be sure, it looked like they were all detailed maps of the South.

"Do you never sleep, Bobby?" Louis greeted the bureau chief.

"Morning, Louis," he replied, not looking up from the keys. "I've got a job for you."

He didn't even notice Frankie.

"Bobby, I have brought you a gift."

Robert Miller stopped stabbing at the keys and looked up.

"Frankie Procter. A photographer from New Zealand looking for work."

The bureau chief studied her over his glasses.

"How long have you been in Saigon, Frankie?"

"I arrived yesterday."

"Can you speak the language?"

"No. I'm sure I can learn though."

"What about accreditation?"

"Not yet. I worked for William Booth at *The Wellington Daily* in New Zealand. He told me he knew you and to look you up. Said you might be able to help me find work."

"Booth? Well, well, well. How is the old bugger? Still the same obviously." He chuckled at the private joke. "Accreditation is through MACV. You'll need it to work in country. It's your pass to go most places you want to go, and some you don't."

She wondered how hard it would be to get a pass but didn't want to think about the possibility of not getting one.

"Do you think you can handle being out in the field?"

"Yes."

He studied her over his glasses again.

"How old are you, Frankie?"

"Twenty-two."

"Mmm. Have you got any images I can look at?"

"Yes, back in my room. I can get them for you."

"Come back"–he looked at his watch–"about three-thirty. Louis, pay a visit to our friend Dinh. See if you can get her kitted out. Meanwhile, I'll see if I can get her a temporary accreditation from MACV. Tomorrow, the First Infantry Division is going on a witch-hunt near Chu Lai. They had a rough night last night, lost twenty-nine men with fifty-three wounded. They're waiting for reinforcements. Apparently, they're walking in, so the VC don't pick up the chopper movement and get suspicious. Then tomorrow night they're going on a hunting trip." He looked from Louis to Frankie. "Interested?"

"You know me better than that," Louis replied. "You want to come with me, Frankie?"

"Yes!" There was no hesitation, that's what she was here for. This was her big chance to see what these young men were experiencing, what it was like out there in places she had only ever read about.

"Good. Let's see what you bring me this afternoon," Booth said. He opened a drawer, shuffled through the contents and handed Frankie a sheet of paper. "Fill this in. I'll make some calls and see if I can get that pass for you."

With arrangements to use the darkroom, Frankie followed Louis down to the street where he flagged a little blue and yellow Renault taxi and held the door open for her. He gave the driver an address and sat back in his seat.

"Where are we going?"

"To get you some gear. We can't have you out in the field in your beautiful dress, as much as the soldiers would appreciate it." He grinned at Frankie.

The car pulled up in an area of Saigon known as Cholon. It was the Chinese part of the city, and Louis claimed it was full of wonderful restaurants, but no place for a woman to wander around on her own, and it should be avoided after dark at all cost. He took her hand and led her down a narrow side street to a small inconspicuous house. The door opened, and Louis shook hands with a man before they were led into a room and asked to sit. Frankie wondered what was happening. But she felt safe with Louis there. He lit up a cigarette while they waited and offered her one.

Within five minutes, all the shutters and doors were closed as a young Chinese man arrived with clothes for Frankie to try on, and she looked at Louis for guidance as to what she should do. He sat, legs crossed, smoking; obviously at ease with the process.

"Go ahead." He nodded. "Go behind the screen over there if you want."

The man disappeared and reappeared several times, and almost an hour later, Frankie was kitted out with jungle greens and boots, a hat, web belt, two canteens, a poncho and a blanket roll. All American and all sourced on the black market, or so Louis informed her. After some negotiation, Louis gave the man a handful of notes, and they left.

"How much do I owe you?" Frankie asked once they were back in the taxi. She hadn't budgeted for all these extras.

"Nothing for now. Wait until you sell your first photograph, then you can pay me back."

"I may not sell any photos."

"Or I might die before you make your first sale."

"Don't say stuff like that. You're not going to die."

"Any of us could die at any time." He was suddenly serious. "Never forget that, Frankie."

"You make it sound like we're living in a war zone. I thought Saigon was safe."

"You never know who the enemy is. There are supporters of the

North everywhere, so it is not wise to take anyone for granted."

They sat in silence during the drive back to the Continental, and once there Louis asked her to join him for lunch. She declined his offer, telling him she wanted to use the darkroom to process the roll of film she had used since she arrived. She hadn't thought to bring a portfolio of work with her, so she hoped she'd got some decent shots.

She was also worried MACV wouldn't grant her temporary accreditation, but Louis had told her that if anyone could get one, it was Bobby Miller. He was well known and respected in Saigon.

Frankie spent the rest of the afternoon working in the darkroom at the AP office, developing her film and printing a contact sheet. She picked the best two images and made larger black and white prints of each. When she finally got to show them to the bureau chief, he looked at the two images, studied the contact sheet, and then tossed them all onto the desk.

"There's no doubt you have an eye for a nice photo. Good exposure too." He paused and looked down at the contact sheet. "But I don't want nice photos, Frankie. I want great photos. I want raw emotion."

Disappointment washed over her. She could do better; she knew she could.

"So, do you think you can handle this assignment up at Chu Lai?" he asked.

"I can. I'll prove I can get you great images."

He nodded and told her what to expect and that it was a great opportunity. She was being thrown in at the deep end. Most photographers covered the daytime assignments, and although there would be no opportunity for shooting photographs at night, she would have plenty of time in the hours of daylight. He told her if she could see out a night op, she could handle anything they threw at her, and she was determined not to disappoint.

Bobby Miller handed her a temporary pass and told her they would need to be out at Tan Son Nhut by two the following afternoon. As she turned to leave, he called her back and handed her three rolls of film.

"Use as much as you need, just bring me back something I can use."

That evening, she walked down towards the river and stopped to buy food from a street vendor, unsure if it was safe to walk back on her own, she caught a cyclo on the way back. In Lam Son Square, she bought a coffee from a café and took it upstairs with her.

When she opened her door, there was a piece of paper on the floor. She picked it up and closed the door. It was from Louis. He would meet her downstairs in the lobby tomorrow at one o'clock. He suggested they share a taxi to the airport.

As she lay in bed listening to the night noises, she found it hard to believe the people bustling back and forth on the streets of Saigon were anything but friendly. Everyone smiled at her, and they loved it when she tried to speak their language. She must have fallen asleep at some stage because the next thing she knew the alarm was going off, and the sun was spilling into one corner of her room.

Today was the day. Excitement mixed with nerves and anxiety. She worried whether she'd be able to keep up with men she would be walking with. Would they even accept her? As there was no rush, she lay in bed and watched the sun creep across the wall until it hit the bed. To fill the morning, she took a walk around the streets near the hotel and found a market. She also wanted to see if she could find somewhere central to live, but she had no idea where to start looking. Perhaps she would ask Louis later.

She bought a baguette stuffed with salad from a street food seller and sat on the doorstep of a shop to eat it. The locals were getting used to seeing her, and some waved out or called to her when they saw her.

At one o'clock, she met Louis in the lobby, and they caught a taxi to the airport. Forty-five minutes later they were in a helicopter; a door gunner hung from the open door, hands gripping a machine gun, attention focused on the ground below.

Wedged between boxes of ammunition, food, and water, Frankie looked down at her green trousers and heavy black boots as she tried to control her nerves. It couldn't get any more real than this as the helicopter banked to the left and came in low over the treetops. The gunner fired in a sweeping motion into the scrub and undergrowth as the Huey turned and the pilot lowered the chopper into a small clearing.

Plumes of orange smoke swirled amongst the downdraft from the rotor blades. Men rushed to unload the cartons, and she could hear shouting over the roar of the chopper.

"Keep low and keep your eyes open," Louis ordered as he jumped clear and ran hunched over towards a small group of soldiers. Frankie followed and crouched next to Louis, who was shaking hands with a soldier and scribbling notes on a pad. She remembered she had her camera around her neck and pulled the lens cap off and shoved it in a pocket.

"This is Lieutenant Garcia. He's running this outfit," Louis said. "Lieutenant, this is Frankie Proctor. Photographer with AP."

Frankie held out her hand.

The lieutenant eyed Frankie and shook her hand then turned his attention back to Louis.

"We've got a bunch of Marines in there now giving them gooks hell," he drawled. "They had us pinned down most of the day yesterday. Reports are coming in there's a battalion of them in this area, and we wanna shut them down. Our guys are gonna retreat any time now and, hopefully, draw them out. They'll think we've retreated because we're outnumbered. Once we've squared away these supplies, we're gonna send platoons out to sweep and funnel them into our guys. I sure as hell don't like losing men."

That's all Frankie heard. She was watching four soldiers unloading cartons from the chopper. She lifted her camera and started taking photos. As quickly as they unloaded, body bags were loaded onto the chopper along with the wounded. Frankie ran back towards the chopper to take some shots of the men. Loss etched on their faces. One looked like he had been crying and she felt sorry for him. She took the photo then put her camera down; she felt like she was intruding. Two more choppers swooped down and were filled with wounded men before leaving.

The newly acquired cartons were opened and their contents distributed. One by one, others joined in until most of the boxes were empty. She took a few photos of the soldiers drinking from the bottles of water, refilling canteens, handing out mail and refilling their packs.

She was surprised at how young they looked. There were not many who appeared older than her, except for the lieutenant.

It got dark quickly, and by eighteen hundred hours they were walking. They all carried packs, including Louis and Frankie. Frankie wondered how hard it was to walk into the darkness, not knowing what lay ahead. If they couldn't see the enemy during the day, how would they find them at night?

It was hard walking. Her eyes took forever to adjust to the dark. She could barely make out Louis's outline a few steps in front of her. The platoon walked on in silence. Unfamiliar noises filled the night air. Branches scraped at her arms and legs. Before they had moved out, Louis had told her to roll down her sleeves and apply insect repellent to every inch of uncovered skin. She was thankful for the advice; she could hear mosquitoes buzzing around her face.

Twice, she was so preoccupied with the noises, she didn't realise the men in front of her had stopped, and she walked into Louis. He was quick to grab her, and together they crouched, waiting in silence for a signal to proceed.

By the time the signal they were stopping had passed back down the line, Frankie was wide awake and running on adrenaline. They had only been walking for two hours, but it felt like eight. It was hard to believe that in the surrounding darkness there were almost two companies of men waiting to kill the enemy. It felt like it was just her and Louis; she would never have known if they had all got up and left.

Then the message came back they were going to set up an ambush. There would be no digging in, boiling water or lighting cigarettes. There was to be absolutely no noise.

Frankie sat huddled in her bedroll, silently petrified. She would try to sleep, but she doubted she could; her nerves were stretched tight as she tried to work out the noises, and if they belonged to the men around her. Curled up on the ground, listening to the mosquitoes and the creatures that came alive during nighttime, she had to give these men credit. As much as she strained to hear at least one of the men, there was nothing. What were they doing? Were they out there setting mines? Trip wires? Were they all sitting with guns poised, waiting to attack or be attacked?

A hand reached out, and Louis lay down behind her. She shivered and felt him move closer, the heat from his body slowly warming hers.

He reached over her arm and pulled her tightly into him. Together they lay in silence. Listening.

Frankie wondered about Louis. She hadn't known him for more than two days, yet she felt drawn to him, and she wondered if extreme circumstances like this made people need each other more. Need moments of comfort. Solace. If it weren't for Louis, she would be tucked up in her comfortable bed at the Continental back on Lam Son Square right now. But then, if it weren't for him, she would still be wandering around looking for work. She probably owed Louis a great deal.

She heard an unfamiliar droning noise, and before she registered what it was, the earth was exploding beneath them. In a split second, the undergrowth was illuminated like a Rolling Stones concert. As the boom shattered her eardrums, all hell broke loose. Terrified, she tucked her head down and covered it with her arms. A flare went off followed by another explosion. She felt Louis pull her closer, and she curled her legs up into a foetal position.

Men yelled at each other, and guns fired all around them as she kept her head down. She had no idea what the hell was happening, but in that moment, she prayed like hell the men who had stopped to say hello in the makeshift camp before they'd started walking would be okay.

Frankie could hear bullets tearing the foliage above her head, and another explosion shook the earth; she had never been more terrified in her life. Two sets of boots ran past them, and she heard someone dive to the ground not far from where they lay.

"Ma'am? Are you okay?" someone yelled at her.

"Yes!"

"Louis?"

"We're fine."

She realised it was the lieutenant.

"Stay here and stay down. We'll let you know if you need to move."

The noise was horrendous. Another ear-splitting explosion to their far right made her jump; Louis yelled in her ear it was a mortar round, and the proper show would start soon.

Around them, grenades exploded, and the fire from machine guns was continuous. Every few seconds, the surrounding jungle flashed light then sank back into darkness. On the few inches of earth that was a safe haven, Louis was suddenly kissing her. Slowly at first then harder, as though trying to get her complete attention. Frankie found herself kissing him back, and for the longest moment, the battle around them ceased to exist, and even her shaking subsided. There was just the two of them. A scream filled the air, but Frankie tried not to hear it, to concentrate only on Louis.

He pulled free and lifted his head, craning to hear.

"Can you hear that?" he yelled at her. "That rumble?"

"Yes," she yelled, struggling to understand what had just happened.

"It's Puff. Puff the Magic Dragon. Now the fun starts!"

The rumble grew louder until Frankie could tell it was a large plane, and when it sounded like it was on top of them, the earth shook again. This time, shaking them both violently before the jungle exploded in flames.

Frankie was scared shitless. How did these young men cope with this all the time? By the light of the flames, she saw huge branches fly through the air, flames trailing from them. Louis covered her with his body. She heard men yelling, and screams, and a machine gun still working somewhere amongst it all. Debris pelted them. How could anyone survive this?

Then Frankie realised the gunfire had stopped, and for a moment, all that could be heard was the crackling of flames. Then the moaning started. All around them, men lay injured. The sound was horrific. How many had just been killed?

Louis rolled off her and sat up, and she dragged her body up too, hoping it was safe.

"My apologies for taking such liberties," he shouted at her. "Sometimes it takes your mind off the madness, no?"

"*We need help over here!*" someone yelled.

"Come on," Louis said to her. "This is where we earn our stripes."

With wobbly legs, she stood up, embarrassed when she realised she had wet herself. Thank God it was still dark. In front of her, a soldier cried out in pain, and she forgot about her embarrassment and fumbled her way towards him.

Some of the men had small torches, and Frankie could see someone working on a groaning soldier. She crouched down beside him and took his hand and squeezed it.

"You're going to be all right." She tried to comfort him, not knowing if his injuries were life-threatening or not. She could hardly see him in the darkness; he was just a shape. "I'm Frankie. What's your name?"

"Rico," he groaned. "Just took some shrapnel. I'll be right as rain after a few days. Them nurses back at the Seventy-First Evac will take good care of me. You okay, Frankie?"

He sounded too young to be lying wounded in the jungle thousands of miles from home. And she was touched he had thought to ask how she was doing.

"I've never been so bloody terrified in my whole life. I can't stop shaking. I'm not even sure I could hold my camera steady enough to use it! How the hell do you do this day after day?"

"I don't know how. We just do." He squeezed her hand. "Go help some of the others. The doc has patched me up good. I'll be right."

"Okay. I'll come back and see how you're doing soon." She gave his hand another squeeze and stumbled in the direction of another voice.

She knelt next to a soldier who had taken shrapnel to his arm and had a heavily bandaged leg. As she helped the medic to apply dressings to his chest, the medic told her he didn't know how bad the soldier was.

She found out the soldier's name was Chad, and he was nineteen; she spent an hour with him as he swam in and out of consciousness. Each time she felt him stir, she talked to him in a calm voice, reassuring him he would be fine, telling him about Wellington and where she grew up as a child, all while trying not to cry.

Before Chad, she had stopped to help another boy who was lying on the ground crying. She had groped for his hand, and when she'd discovered it was missing, had screamed for the medic, and then sat there, trying to control her breathing, trying to make sense of it all. Forcing herself to move on, she had stumbled on Chad. They were all boys. Boys sent to do a man's job; paying with their lives for the privilege.

She was holding Chad's hand, telling him about the Southern Cross, when Louis found her.

"Frankie!"

"Louis?"

"Are you okay?"

"I think so. A bit stiff."

"I couldn't find you. I was getting worried."

It was still dark, and she hadn't slept for twenty-four hours, too scared to fall asleep in case she lost Chad. She didn't want to leave any of these boys; it was like they were in her care and she needed to know they were all okay. But there were so many injured, and she couldn't help them all.

"It will be daybreak in about fifteen minutes. The medevac choppers will arrive soon. They've sent out a large party to secure the area."

"How's Rico? I need to go check on him. Hey, Chad, I'll be back in a few minutes to say goodbye before you get on that chopper." She squeezed the soldier's hand and felt Chad softly squeeze back before she let Louis help her up. The pre-dawn light made it a little easier to pick her way around the bodies. Some resting, some crying in pain and some lost to the firefight. She worked her way back towards where she'd left the young Puerto Rican boy earlier. When she finally found him, he was sitting up, leaning against a tree stump and smoking a cigarette.

"Hey," he said, recognising her in the dawn light. "Frankie isn't it?"

"Yeah, you remembered. How are you doing?"

"I've had better days." He attempted to laugh, but then clutched his stomach and grimaced in pain. "Thanks for remembering me. There aren't many soldiers lucky enough to have their own guardian angels watching over them in the field."

"I was so bloody terrified. You probably helped me more than I helped you."

"Well, I hope you got some good pictures, Frankie."

"I just wanted to check on you before they ship you out. Good luck."

He nodded. "Thanks."

Frankie walked back to where she'd left Chad. He hadn't moved, and she could see he was sleeping or unconscious; she hoped they shipped him out first. His hand felt a little cool when she touched it. She sat down beside him again and started talking to him.

"Ma'am?"

Light was finally defining the area they had spent the night in. She looked around, starting to see things for the first time.

"Ma'am?"

"Sorry?"

"Can you help me with this?"

"What is it?"

"This soldier's dead, and we need to get him bagged so we can fly him out."

"This soldier? Chad?"

"Yes, ma'am."

"How do you know?"

"Medic just checked him, ma'am."

"No, I just left him. He was alive five minutes ago. Are you sure?"

"Yes, ma'am."

She stumbled up, losing the battle to hide her tears. Dealing with the bodies was just a job. Someone had to do it. She helped the private lift Chad's body onto a plastic bag and watched as he disappeared behind the zip: a boy out here who had ended up a number, a boy just the same as everyone else who had died from shrapnel wounds.

Wiping her face on her sleeve, she went to find her camera. She was there to do a job, and she would do it for Chad and all the Chads that would follow.

Chapter 10

"Edwards!"

Terry heard his name called. He was riding the crest of a wave towards a strip of white sand, trying to impress the girl in the bikini waving at him.

"Edwards! Get your arse out of that bed!"

He opened his eyes, blinked and sat bolt upright. It was still dark. Images of the sandy beach and the bikini-clad girl disintegrated.

Craig Williams, their section commander, was losing his patience. "We're moving out. Briefing in thirty. Five nights. Get your gear ready."

Terry reached over and shook his boots, plunged his feet into them and tried to make out if Blackie was in his cot.

Terry was packed, fed and ready before many of the men in their platoon, and discovered he'd be carrying a fully loaded pack plus the ammo for his SLR and several belts of ammo for Blackie's baby, the M60 machine gun. He hoped they didn't have too many hills to climb.

Leaning against his pack, Terry dozed until someone kicked the underside of his boot. He looked up to find Jack standing over him. "Bloody Coles."

Jack offered him a hand and helped him to his feet. "Looks like we're in this one together," Jack remarked as they wandered toward the men gathering to hear what their assignment was.

They were to make their way towards the Long Hải Hills, looking for any sign of enemy movement or bunkers, and checking villages as they went. It was their job to slow down or stop the stream of VC infiltrating Saigon.

After three days march, they had found nothing more than the charred remains of trees and a small village, both possibly hit by napalm.

Each night, Terry laid Claymore mines and set trip wires while Smokey Harris accompanied him. Terry reckoned he could work quicker getting a safe harbour set up for the night on his own, but Smokey, who was walking second scout, was good at spotting trouble before it appeared. To their right, Two Section had also set up a harbour, and beyond them, Jack and Three Section also hunkered down for the night.

"What are you reading, Murph?" Terry drained the last of his coffee. The safe harbour was set, and the men were taking the opportunity to enjoy a last hot drink before they were required to stand-to.

"Letter from the missus."

"I haven't heard from my girl in a while," Smokey chipped in.

"Have you written to her?"

"You think that's the problem?"

"Yeah, she's probably forgotten about you." Murph refolded his letter.

"Tomorrow, I'll write tomorrow."

"I didn't know you were married, Murph. Got any kids?" Terry asked.

"Yeah. Boys. Two and five."

Terry could just make out the smile on his mate's face and wondered how his wife coped with being on her own for so long with two young kiddies. Murph was the oldest member of One Section and had already served in Korea. He was walking tail-end Charlie, and Terry was pleased he was in the same section as Murph.

"You got a girlfriend back home, Romeo?" Smokey asked.

"Nope."

"What? Not even one?" Murph chuckled. "That surprises me."

"Well, I guess there's one girl I went out with twice, but we weren't actually a couple."

"Twice? Wasn't she the lucky one!"

"Yeah, well, I'm not ready to settle down with one girl yet." Or rather, he hadn't met a girl who came close to Evelyn, but he wasn't about to tell anyone about his infatuation with his best mate's girl.

"I pity the girl who nails you down." Murph emptied his cup and stowed it along with his wife's letter.

"I'd like to meet her," Smokey stated.

"Yeah, me too," Terry added, grinning to himself in the fading light.

Terry was on the early morning shift. He didn't mind getting up at four and doing a couple of hours watch before stand-to if he could arrange it, as it that meant he could bunk down for a good night's shut-eye. The worst shift was the one during the middle of the night, it gave him the shits, and he was always too terrified to sleep when he got back to his foxhole after imagining every sound was the enemy creeping up on them in the darkness.

He sank into his makeshift bed and secured his bandanna carefully over the exposed skin on his neck. As he closed his eyes and lay still, he remembered the woman with the copper hair and the face full of freckles and wondered where she was and what she was doing.

Terry had just taken over the dawn shift from Elvis Waata, and as he made himself comfortable, he hoped his shift would be as uneventful as the night had been so far. It always took a few long moments to adjust to the surroundings and to work out if the shapes were in fact anything other than trees or jungle undergrowth.

BOOM!

Terry jumped and then dived for cover. He could feel his heart pounding. *Shit!* Someone, or something, had triggered a Claymore in their safe harbour. He peered into the darkness, straining to see any movement. If the enemy had triggered it, those who survived might be heading this way.

Again, the sound of another mine deafened Terry. He strained to see into the darkness; nothing caught his attention.

"What's going on?" Craig Williams landed on the ground beside Terry.

"No movement, Boss. No gunfire."

"Has to be VC though, if it had been an animal, there wouldn't be anything left to trigger the second mine. So keep alert."

"Right-o, Boss," Terry whispered, but Williams had disappeared.

Five minutes later, the boss was back. "Get ready to move out in ten. Two Section want support in a sweep. There was no exchange in fire, so it looks like they're dead or they scarpered. Either way, they know we're here."

As soon as it was light enough, One Section swept the area. Then the message came through that Coles had spotted a woman on a track and followed her to a village. They were going to check it out, and One Section would be required to form the tail-end Charlie, sweeping in from the left side of the village.

When One Section arrived at the village, it appeared empty, but they would still need to check it for tunnels and stores of rice or weapons. They were told to be careful as the whole place could be littered with booby traps. The other men made their way around a large bomb crater, and Terry thought there was a distinct stench of death and trouble, and not necessarily in that order. Jesus. He took his bandanna from around his neck and tied it loosely over his nose and mouth, hoping it would filter the stench and stop him from swallowing a mouthful of flies. The air was thick with them, and he swatted them away with one hand as he veered away from the crater.

He noticed Jack and made a beeline for him. His friend wasn't looking too hot.

"Don't go near that bloody crater," Jack said, his voice wavering.

"I don't intend to. I can smell it from here."

"It's full of bodies. The whole village by the look of it."

"Thanks for that picture."

"I've got to check out that hut." Jack pointed to one they were approaching. "Back me up. I saw a woman go into it."

"Right behind you, mate."

They approached the hut with caution as other members of the Platoon swept through the remains of the village.

Jack edged in first, followed closely by Terry. The hut was empty. Jack nodded towards the bed and gently tapped the base with his boot. Hollow. Terry would bet money that if they lifted it, they would find a tunnel entrance and who knew what else waiting for them.

Jack signalled he was going to lift the bed, and Terry moved position to cover both the tunnel and Jack. Three, two, one. Jack flung the mattress across the hut then, in one swift movement, lifted the wooden base, and both men trained their weapons on the tunnel opening. Except it wasn't a tunnel, it was a shallow dugout, and inside was the little old woman Jack had previously seen on the track and a girl who looked like she was dead.

Jack bent down and scooped the old woman up, but she wasn't going easy. She screeched at them in Vietnamese, clearly not wanting to be separated from the girl.

"Hey, mama san!" Terry yelled at her. "We help you." The screeching grew louder.

"What the hell's going on in here?" Scott Taylor, Jack's section commander, asked as he joined them.

Jack filled him in while the medic took a look at the girl and told them she was still alive, but barely.

"I'll get them choppered out. Coles, make sure the girl isn't booby-trapped, and get her onto that dustoff when it arrives."

Jack nodded.

The girl was in bad condition, and Terry seriously doubted she'd survive the trip back to the Thirty-Sixth Evac in Vũng Tàu.

Chapter 11

"Here comes trouble," Terry said, glancing up as he threw down his hand and claimed his prize of a can of beer. The company had arrived back in camp after a week out in the sticks, just in time to clean themselves up and have a late lunch. The three sections that made up their platoon were on stand-down until dusk, when they had perimeter duty.

"Boys."

Terry ripped the tab on the beer and took a swallow. It was obvious Jack's section commander was there to see Jack, not him, so he put the beer down and gathered the cards up to shuffle. It was the first beer Terry had won off Jack in a long time. He should have known better than to play him; Jack always won unless you could get away with cheating.

"Just wanted to let you boys know we're going out tomorrow. For three weeks."

"The whole company, sir?" Terry asked.

"The whole company, but I've got something for you to do first, Coles."

Terry shuffled the deck, and keeping his eyes on Jack, dealt a hand to both of them. While Jack was talking to his section commander, Terry slipped an extra two cards into his pile then deposited the deck on the table; he picked up his hand and sorted through his cards. He had to get rid of two.

Jack reached out and picked up his cards, still talking to Taylor. Terry put his hands in his lap, slipped two cards out and hid them up the leg of his shorts, then crossed his arms over his chest. Apparently, headquarters wanted Jack to fly down to Vũng Tàu to visit the girl he had saved, to see if he could get any information out of her. She was refusing to speak to anyone.

"What makes them think she'll want to speak to you?" Terry asked as Taylor walked off.

"How the hell would I know?" Jack splayed out his dealt hand and dropped it on the deck of cards without looking at it. "You need more practice at cheating if you want to beat me."

"Aw shit. I was just trying to win back a few more beers," Terry said, retrieving the missing cards and slapping his hand down in disgust.

The whole company was choppered out into the field the next morning. Once again, there had been reports of heavy NVA movement in the area south of the Long Hải Hills, and Victor Company was to slow them down, if not stop them altogether. They were being dropped into a landing zone on the far side of the Long Green, a strip of lush jungle that hadn't yet been stripped by the defoliants. The land opened out into gardens, a rice paddy, and clumps of banana and coconut palms before it gave way to more trees and scrub around the base of the hills. On the far side of the hills, huge sand dunes rolled down to the South China Sea.

The company was spread over five kilometres, moving gradually towards the hills. Terry's platoon was moving in formation at the northern-most point of the sweep and further from the sea than any of the other sections in the company. The Long Hải Hills were a known Viet Cong stronghold, the villages harboured NVA sympathisers, and the whole area was fortified with bunkers and mines.

Of all the patrols they had been on so far, Terry's nerves were wound the tightest with this one, and he wasn't looking forward to the nights, especially as the VC moved during the hours of darkness. It was going to be the longest three weeks of his life.

The order soon came through for their platoon to find a place to set up camp and lay ambushes. They were to lie low for the remainder of the day, so they were well entrenched by nightfall. Terry took Donny Tamihana and JJ Johnson with him, and while he and JJ set up mines and trip wires, Donny covered them. Terry had just fixed the wire on the last Claymore, and as he reached out to pick up his rifle, he felt something sting the side of his finger. The pain was excruciating. He dropped the gun with a clatter that attracted JJ's attention.

"What's up?" JJ hissed.

"Shit." Terry screwed his eyes closed and then opened them. "Something just got me." He gripped his hand, trying to stop the pain.

"What was it?" JJ asked. "Wasn't a snake, was it?" He took a step back, scouring the ground for movement.

"I didn't see. I just reached out for my rifle. It's not a bite. It's definitely a sting," he replied, inspecting his finger.

JJ scuffed the ground with his boot, and a large black scorpion scuttled from its hiding place, making a run for it. JJ thumped his boot down on it and twisted.

"Scorpion. Big mother too."

"Jesus, I think I'm going to die." Right now, even coming face to face with a Victor Charlie would be a more enjoyable experience.

"What are you playing at?" Donny dropped in beside Terry. "The pair of you are making enough noise to wake the dead. You're making me nervous."

"It's Romeo. He's been stung by a bloody scorpion."

"If the net's set, let's go."

"Yeah, it's all done," Terry answered through gritted teeth. He picked up his rifle with caution. Three fingers now throbbed with pain.

"Right, well, let's get you back behind the lines. You can die there," JJ said.

Terry stood up and brushed himself down. He tried to concentrate on what he was doing, where he was, and what was happening around him, but the pain was so intense nothing else mattered. He felt someone take his arm and he let them shepherd him back to the rest of the men.

"What's wrong with Edwards?" the section commander mouthed. They were on orders to keep quiet and sit tight.

"Scorpion sting, Boss. It got his trigger finger," JJ replied in a whisper. There was a snigger.

The boss leaned into Terry. "You all right, Edwards?"

"It's bloody painful. I've never felt anything like it before."

The section commander turned and signalled to his 2IC. "Get the medic over here. Keep him alive. We need him."

More sniggering.

Right at that moment, Terry prayed the earth would open up and swallow him. It wasn't like he'd been shot or wounded, it was just an insect sting. He looked down at his hand, it looked normal, but the finger in question was starting to swell.

He took his rifle and tried to curl his finger around the trigger. Pain splintered through his hand and he winced, he would be the laughing stock of the company once this got out.

The finger was getting harder to bend. Bugger it. He tried the next finger. There was still movement in it. If he had to, he could still fire his rifle. He was no good to anyone out here if he couldn't. He put the rifle down and sat with his hand to his chest.

"Edwards. How you doing?"

Terry held his hand out, and the medic studied it.

"Here's some paracetamol, get a couple in you now and then as you need them."

Terry looked at the tablets; there were twenty-four. "Thanks, Doc. The pain's killing me."

"Yeah, scorpions are good at that."

"How bad is it going to get?"

"There might be more swelling yet, and it will probably hurt a lot more before it gets better. It'll go down eventually. Maybe after a day or two you'll be good as new. Just take the paracetamol. It'll help take the edge off."

Terry nodded his thanks and ripped open the painkillers.

Suddenly, an AK-47 opened up; he could hear the bullets whizzing through the air, some sending clouds of dust as they burrowed into the dirt a few feet from him. Terry hit the ground and looked around for Blackie. He could hear him fire the M60 to his right and crawled towards the sound. A round came in, and Terry could hear the thunk as it lodged in a tree trunk to his left. He crawled faster.

"Romeo!" Blackie shouted. He was spraying the far side of a small clearing about a hundred yards to his right, and the VC were quick to target him in return.

"Two o'clock!"

Terry quickly dragged a belt of ammo off and prepared to feed it into the M60, then lined up his rifle on a spot in the scrub. A Claymore went off, showering the men in plant debris and dirt. Bullets criss-crossed the small clearing.

"You guys okay?" Murph yelled at them as he slid in beside the two men.

Terry could hear the rest of the section opening fire.

"Stoke that baby up!" Murph yelled before crawling back the way he had come as the AK's kept them pinned down.

Someone yelled, "grenade!" Terry had no idea where it was, but he put his head down and covered it with an arm. It exploded short of their lines, choking them with red dust and showering them with leaves and sticks but failing to do any damage.

Blackie had now become the target for the VC. No one liked a machine gunner who could use the gun like an extension of his hand, and the ground around Blackie was being peppered with bullets, sending clouds of dust into the air.

The exchange continued for another thirty minutes before their section commander called a ceasefire.

Everything fell silent.

"Romeo, Smokey, Elvis, JJ, go see what you can find."

The four men returned twenty minutes later, with reports of a tunnel entrance and a small bunker just outside their harbour. Everything had been set up, no doubt under the watchful eye of the VC. There were no bodies, but plenty of signs of injury. They had obviously escaped into the tunnels and taken their dead and wounded with them, along with several Claymores they had managed to disarm. The boss sent two of them back to drop a calling card down the opening and destroy the bunker.

If nothing else, the diversion had distracted Terry from the pain of the sting. He hurriedly took a couple more tablets.

Their company was ordered to pack up and join an Australian company and two platoons of Americans. After two hours' march, they reached their camp for the night and set about establishing a perimeter defence and roster.

Terry dug his foxhole and carefully checked it. *"Fucking scorpions,"* he muttered to himself. God knows what might crawl over him, with his luck it would probably be one of the venomous centipedes or a bloody tarantula. He heated some food and made a hot drink and read the book he'd picked up from the mess back in camp. After five minutes, he put the book away; the throbbing in his hand was so bad he almost felt like throwing up.

Then word came back that a forward party had stumbled on a small village in the middle of the jungle. Apparently there were more men disappearing into the hut than it could reasonably fit. Jack had found what looked to be an entrance to a tunnel system.

The ensuing attack on the village lasted two hours. The village had turned out to be more important than HQ had thought, and it was heavily protected. Fire was returned from the undergrowth surrounding the village as the VC counter-attacked, trading bullets, rocket-propelled grenades, and mortars.

However, the attacking forces were too strong and had the element of surprise on their side. No mercy was shown to anything or anyone, and when the arrival of a company of NVA surprised the attackers, air support was called in to the north of them, driving the NVA into the village and certain death for those who couldn't make it into a tunnel.

They found and destroyed a large cache of weapons, along with a hut packed with rice. Tunnel rats were brought in to go underground. Those who had been using the tunnels had left in a hurry. News filtered in that units covering areas to the south and beyond the front lines had captured VC emerging from tunnels, all armed and prepared to fight. Overall, the operation had been a huge success, with a high enemy body count and only eight wounded between the Australians, New Zealanders, and Americans.

Terry was still running on adrenaline when his platoon leader checked on him after the jungle had returned to normal and they had been told to stand-down. He was feeling seedy, and his whole hand had swollen, the skin stretched tight. He was not required on watch during the night; they would cover for him. Although Terry was thankful, he might as well have been sitting watch, because sleep didn't come easily. As he lay in his foxhole, listening to the night noises, he replayed the firefight over and over, remembering how the ground shook when the fire support arrived: anything to keep his mind from dwelling on the constant throbbing. Although he'd been popping paracetamol every three hours; it dulled the pain, but never completely removed it.

Terry woke just as darkness gave way to dawn and the shadows began to fade. He couldn't remember when he'd dropped off, but the first thing he noticed was that the swelling wasn't any worse. Making himself a hot drink, he realised he still felt seedy and couldn't eat anything. At least he was still alive.

Later that morning, Victor Company marched to a designated LZ to meet a resupply chopper and collect ammo, water, food, and mail. They had two men who were heading back with the chopper for medical attention, but so far, they had only lost one man from Jack's section, and

Terry wasn't considered bad enough to be choppered out. Once the choppers had gone, the company commander called for a twenty-minute break while Murph distributed the mail to the men.

"It's finally arrived," Murph commented, handing an envelope to Terry.

"What has?" Terry asked.

"The letter from some chick you've knocked up."

"Very funny." Terry studied the handwriting on the envelope. "This is from my Mum."

Murph laughed. "Only a matter of time, Romeo. Only a matter of time."

Terry fumbled with the envelope, finally managing to pull out a number of pages. His mum had written two, and there was a page each from his brother and younger sisters. The coloured stick-figure people his youngest sister had drawn brought a smile to his face. He put those pages down and lit up a smoke. Then read the letter from his mother.

It was the first letter he'd had in some time, and he felt guilty for not writing. There was general stuff telling him they were all well, and about how the neighbours were being inconsiderate: playing loud music and keeping them all up. There were a few lines about the kids' progress at school, and she mentioned that several people had asked how he was getting on in Vietnam.

Terry skimmed over all this. Then at the bottom of the last page, his mother wrote that Vernon had finally asked her to marry him and she had said yes. They were having a quiet registry office wedding in two weeks' time. He flipped the envelope over and checked the postmark.

"Hey, Smokey," Terry called.

"What?" Smokey replied, preparing something that vaguely resembled food.

"What day is it today?"

Smokey studied his watch. "It's August twenty-first. Why? You got some place you need to be?"

Terry waved the sheet of paper at him. "My mother married the lodger three days ago."

"Your father know about it?"

"He left a few years back."

"So what's the new stepfather like, then?"

"Let's just say he looks after Mum and the kids, and that's all that matters."

"Ah, so you're not that keen on him?"

"Nope. And they're at it like bloody rabbits. She's up the duff again."

"Who's up the duff?" JJ Johnson asked, sitting down between Terry and Smokey and catching the last few words of the conversation. He pointed at the sheet of paper in Terry's hand. "Some chick you banged up?"

"Give it a rest, JJ."

"His mum," Smokey chipped in.

JJ nodded. "How's the hand?"

"I'm rattling with painkillers, but I think the swelling's gone down. Maybe I'm not gonna die after all—mind you, the guts ain't feeling so good this morning."

"Nice bit of fun last night, eh?"

"Yeah, that was some village. Cleaned those bastards right up though."

"Let's hope we don't come across any more like that one."

They all nodded in agreement, and Terry folded up the pages, slipped them into the envelope and pushed it deep inside his pack. He would write once he got back to camp.

The routine over the following days was monotonous. They were up before dawn, marching to a designated spot, setting ambushes, then repeating the same thing all over again the next day.

At the beginning of the third week, they were walking in formation, skirting the edge of the jungle before they headed into it. The sky filled with the drone of planes, and they all looked skywards. Three large C-123s flew over them, thick curls of mist filtering down to ground level, coating everything in a residue, including the men.

"My rifle's sticky," Smokey complained when they stopped for a ten-minute break.

"Rub some dirt on it, you can clean it later," Terry advised.

"My bloody arms are sticky too. What was that shit?" Elvis asked.

"They'll be spraying to kill the bush off or the mosquitoes."

"Hey, Boss, is that spray safe?" JJ asked their section commander.

"That's what they tell me."

"Might be good for repelling scorpions, Romeo," Blackie said.

"Might be even better for thick lips."

They all laughed.

The following week, they saw signs of it everywhere they walked. Dead and dying trees created a surreal landscape, and although there was little cover for the enemy, there was not much for them either.

With two days left to go, Terry was exhausted. His hand was back to normal, and he was off the painkillers. It was something he didn't care to experience again, and each time they stopped to dig their foxholes, he scraped the area clean first, to make sure there was nothing nasty lurking.

"Got a smoke?" Smokey dropped down beside him. Terry had skipped lunch to clean his rifle while One Section was taking a break. They were all feeling the strain from the three weeks in the bush and were longing to get back to Nui Dat and a shower, a proper bed and real food.

"Sure." Terry dug in his pocket, pulled out a packet and shook a couple loose.

"Thanks, mate. Did ya hear there's an all-girl band coming to camp?"

"No. Where are they from?"

"As far as I know, New Zealand. They're Kiwis."

"I hope we get back in time to see them."

"Yeah, I reckon it'll be worth it. Evie Hallet is one of them, and she's gorgeous."

Evelyn was coming? Terry couldn't believe it. He wondered if Jack knew, but surely Evelyn would have written to tell him.

"Yeah. Yeah, she is," Terry said as he finished cleaning his rifle and began packing his gear back into his pack. He thought about Evelyn and the concert and realised he hadn't thought about her at all for at least a month.

Perhaps he was finally over her.

Chapter 12

It took Frankie several days to get over her first assignment. She couldn't get the image of the dead soldiers out of her head. Or the blood and torn limbs and bodies that lay on the floor of the chopper. Some were men she had talked to only hours before.

She had gone back to her room and tried to wash the jungle off her: the dirt and the blood. When that had failed, she had gone down to the bar and ordered a large whisky, eventually buying a bottle to take back to her room.

Her photos had impressed the bureau chief, and he wanted to buy four off her. She had made her first sale. She should have been excited, but somehow the shine and excitement had diminished. Sixty dollars for all four images. It was the equivalent of a lottery win, and she knew what she had to do. She owed Louis for the gear he had paid for, and she needed to use the remainder to find somewhere to rent.

"I've got another job for you, Frankie, if you're interested," Bobby Miller said, noticing her reading the daily file of stories two days later.

She had been on two more small assignments and neither of them out in the jungle. She had got perfect shots both times, but nothing as dramatic as her first assignment.

"I have to find somewhere to live first. I've been staying at the Continental, but I can't afford to any longer. You don't know of anyone who might want to rent out a room?"

Bobby rubbed his chin, then called to a young Vietnamese man across the office.

"Van!"

The young man looked up and walked over.

"Van, Frankie's freelancing for us and needs a place to stay. You wouldn't happen to know of anywhere?"

"My mother's sister, she own beauty salon and have spare room above the shop. There is furniture. Maybe you stay there?"

"Where is it?" Frankie asked. She hadn't even seen it yet, and it already sounded perfect.

"It is in Nguyen Hue, in direction of river."

"Can I see it?"

"Yes. I can take you in"–he glanced at his watch–"one hour."

The room turned out to be basic, but Frankie thought it was perfect. It was on the second floor with access through the salon or from a private stairwell at the rear. Van's aunty liked to be called Miss Lilac, which was the name of the salon, and she was happy for Frankie to move in anytime. Frankie gave her a week's rent in advance and the following day moved her meagre belongings into her very own apartment. It was actually two rooms. One was larger, with a queen-sized bed, a small sofa, a television set and a table at one end. At the other end of the room was a small kitchen bench with a cooker, a jug and an assortment of cups, plates and pots, and a washing machine. A tiny room opened off the larger one and provided a shower, a toilet and a hand basin. It was cheap, and it was hers. It was all she needed.

There was a small, high window in the bathroom, but Frankie was drawn to the large single window in the main room, relieved to find it opened with ease. Leaning out, she discovered it overlooked the narrow alley that ran from the street to somewhere behind the salon and gave access to her stairs.

In the main room, there were shelves attached to one wall, and a wardrobe without doors gave her a place to hang her clothes. As soon as she had saved a bit of money, she would buy a few small items to make it homelier.

So far, she was selling one or two photos a day, and although it was a good start, she would need to earn more than that if she wished to dine in the same places as many of the other photographers and journalists. She was getting sick of eating at street stalls.

Slowly, things picked up. Bobby Miller knew the bureau chief at *Newsweek,* and they asked her to do an assignment on the Montagnard people. The hill people were lovely, and after spending three days with them, she realised they were quite different from their fellow countrymen. She was sorry to leave them–especially the children, who had formed the habit of following her everywhere, entranced by her hair. But after three days of primitive conditions, she longed for the comfort of her small apartment.

Two days later, she spent a day with a chopper pilot shooting a

'Day in the Life of' which she sold to *Time*. She was slowly increasing the number of images she was selling and learning who she could sell them to.

She had been in Saigon for just over a month when she agreed to do an assignment for the AP at a camp fifty kilometres inland from the city of Da Nang. They would chopper her in, and she would spend a week in a camp with the Marines. She was pleased to hear Louis was the journalist accompanying her, and they planned to get enough material to put together a two-page spread for the *Washington Post*. Frankie was thrilled. It was a chance for her to make a name for herself.

They were introduced to the commanding officer, and Frankie was pleased that he accepted her as the photographer on the assignment. Not everyone welcomed a female. He briefed them on the activity in the area and invited them to join several operations while they were there, which they both readily agreed to.

"Have you been out on a march since the last one?" Louis asked Frankie while they were having lunch.

"No. I have to admit I'm nervous."

"Show me a man out here who isn't nervous, and I can guarantee he's a stupid one. We'll be fine. These soldiers are some of the best. There isn't a huge build-up of enemy in this area, so the ops are mostly routine search and destroy. Quite different, no?"

"Well, I'll soon find out."

They were leaving in thirty minutes for a three-hour march, and tomorrow, would go out on a three-night patrol. Frankie was more nervous about that. The memory of the previous overnight patrol was still clear in her mind, but she knew if she wanted to get the photos, she would have to front up. She couldn't tell their stories by sitting in an office in Saigon.

Each time they stopped, Frankie made a point of chatting with the men. Although she had told herself not to get attached to them, it was hard not to. They were all so likeable and were happy for her to take their photos.

The following morning, they were choppered into a clearing about thirty kilometres from camp, to make their way back over three days, searching for tunnels, bunkers or any signs of VC activity. Frankie had volunteered to walk behind the second point man. Louis was back about five men behind her. She had her pack on her back and camera around her neck, and every so often she would lift it and take a photo of a scout. Or turn and capture the expression on the face of the man walking behind her.

She was keeping one eye on the ground and the other on the man in front of her, trying to keep her noise to a minimum.

The soldier in front of her stopped and, not noticing, Frankie smacked right into him. "You need to move back," he whispered. "Give me some distance."

"Sorry, I didn't realise I was so close."

"I like close," he replied, winking at her. "But if I stand on something unpleasant, it's likely to take you out too, and I'd hate for a pretty girl like you to get all messed up, now."

Frankie nodded, embarrassed at her blunder and thankful for his honesty. He turned and cautiously moved off, and she waited a few seconds before following him.

Several minutes later, Frankie noticed him drop to his knee and raise a fist in the air. What had he seen or heard? She crouched, waiting, heart pounding so loud she expected someone to tell her to shut up. A few seconds later, a sergeant picked his way past her to talk to the lead scout. She took another photo and waited, wondering what was happening. A few minutes later, they continued their march.

With her shoulders aching, Frankie was pleased when they finally stopped to set up camp for the night. It had just gone four, and they had at least two hours before they lost the light. Several of the young men joined her while she ate. She was light relief for a few minutes of their day. None of them knew much about New Zealand, and they had plenty of questions for her.

As dusk fell, it poured with rain, and even though she had a poncho on, everything seemed to get wet. It rained most of the night, and as she lay on her bedroll on the ground, she couldn't make out any of the usual night noises. She wondered how on earth anyone could detect enemy soldiers through the sound of the rain on the foliage. It was almost impossible to sleep. How did the men do it, night after night?

Those three nights out in the jungle were the longest nights of her life. But when they made it back to camp, the men congratulated her on how well she had coped. It had been much easier because she hadn't had to face the harsh reality of death on this trip, but her nerves were shattered, and she was exhausted. She couldn't wait to get back to Saigon.

When she returned to Saigon, everything was the same. The people, the traffic, and the habits. Nothing made sense. At the Five O'Clock Follies, the nightly media briefing, General Westmoreland told media that sixteen thousand troops had been killed so far, and almost a hundred and ninety thousand enemy troops. The numbers were unbelievable, but it was as if nobody cared, or even noticed. It was senseless. She wondered how many of the young men she had met and talked to over the last couple of weeks would have the luxury of going home.

Over the following two months, the sale of Frankie's photos increased. Her images appeared in both *Time* magazine and *Life* and were printed in newspapers in America and New Zealand.

She soon learned that the harder she concentrated on getting the images, the more she could shut out the war. It felt as if she were immune to the bullets. As long as she had a camera in front of her face, no harm would come to her. But it was taking a toll. Twice, she had arrived back at her small apartment, burst into tears and sought solace in a bottle of whisky. The alcohol helped to stop her thinking about what she had seen during the day and blurred the reality of the injustice–just enough so she could sleep.

Chapter 13

Victor Company arrived back in Nui Dat a day ahead of the concert. The arrival of a group of Kiwi girls was the talk of the camp, and all the men were keeping everything crossed they wouldn't be sent out on operation and miss the concert. There was talk about Evie Hallet too, and Terry realised Jack hadn't told anyone he was engaged to the lead singer.

By the time they arrived back in camp, Terry had decided it would be best for all concerned if he stayed away. He didn't need to see Evelyn. It was more important Jack saw her.

He was pleased to have come out of that last firefight unscathed. All he wanted right now was have a shower, throw out the clothes he was wearing and lie on a soft cot.

Twenty minutes later, after he'd taken his turn in the shower and was wandering back to his bunker dressed in his towel and jandals, he reassured himself that if he had somehow managed to forget about Evelyn over the past few weeks, then it was for the best.

Terry walked with Jack to the mess for breakfast the following morning.

"I guess you'll want to spend as much time as possible with Evelyn while she's here. I'll do your turn on the wire for you if you want." Although the whole company had the day off before they headed out again at first light, Jack's section was rostered on perimeter duty. But Terry needed to keep busy.

"Hey mate, that's good of you. I won't say no to that. You're not going to miss the concert though, are you?"

Terry nodded. "I'll try to get there if I can."

"Evie would love to see you if you can make it."

"Well, if I can't fight my way through the crowd to the stage, give her a hug from me."

"Will do!"

After Terry had eaten, he wandered over to the PX. The lieutenant was talking to one of the men and smiled when he saw Terry.

"Gidday, LT."

"Terry. How's the hand now?"

"It's back to normal, thanks. Still the worst pain I've ever experienced though."

"I'll make a note not to irritate any scorpions."

"Wise move."

Terry was back in his bunker when he heard the music. It filtered through the old rubber tree plantation and he tried to distract himself by cleaning his boots. He could hear singing, but the voices were indistinguishable. Bugger it. He'd walk along the back of the escarpment and catch the last of the show before he headed down for duty.

Luscombe Bowl was packed. Damn near every man in camp was there. Some sat on the ground, others on deck chairs, and some even sat on top of jeeps and trucks to get a better view. Terry threaded his way between a row of trucks until he could get a clear view of the three girls on the stage. There was no mistaking her. She was wearing a short dress and knee-high white boots, and every guy in that damned audience must have wished he could get her into his bed. She had them mesmerised.

As Terry watched, she cried out, dropped the microphone and leapt from the stage into the arms of one of the soldiers way down the front. For a moment, Terry wondered what was going on, then he saw it was Jack, and it made perfect sense. The embankment erupted in cheering and wolf whistles as he watched Jack kiss his fiancée, and then she led him by the hand back to the stage, where he sat on the steps watching her.

Like every other man there, Terry couldn't take his eyes off her. She had grown more confident and had a much stronger voice than when he'd heard her sing back in Foxton. That felt like a lifetime ago as he walked back to take his turn on perimeter duty.

"It's been quiet, so far," Terry updated his replacement at the end of his shift.

"Cheers mate. Let's hope it stays that way."

Terry walked over to the mess. He'd done a double shift, and he was ready for a feed and a cold beer. The place was packed. He wondered what was going on. The instant he stepped inside, he saw the reason: Evelyn and the girls. He thought they would have been long gone by now, and it didn't feel right being here. He turned to leave.

"Terry!"

Out the corner of his eye, he saw Jack heading his way, behind him

Evelyn and the girls followed. Terry slapped Jack on the shoulder and then leaned in and hugged Evelyn. It was only the second time he had held her, and now he felt uncomfortable touching her.

"I thought I might have missed you," Terry said to Evelyn.

"They were meant to fly out a couple of hours ago, but there's some trouble up country and they have to stay over," Jack told him.

"Watch those girls!" someone shouted from across the room. "Romeo's here."

Terry ignored it.

"How are you, Terry?"

Her voice snapped him out of his thoughts and back to the mess hall.

"I'm doing okay, thanks. You're looking gorgeous as usual."

Evelyn grinned. "Terry, I'd like you to meet June."

June smiled.

"And this is Shona."

He winked at June and shook the other girls' hands. "Well, girls, I gotta go to work. I'll catch you later, Jack." He hugged Evelyn again. "Great to see you over here, Evie. Girls." He nodded at June and Shona and retreated from the mess as fast as he could. As he marched out into the fading light, he heard the sound of guitars strumming. The words of the Victor Company's song, 'Green, Green Grass of Home,' followed him all the way back to his bunker.

But when he got there, his mates told him they had to do a couple more hours on the wire, in case the enemy launched a surprise attack on the camp. And as he took up his position, he realised he'd missed out on dinner.

Chapter 14

The following morning, the men of Victor Company waited on the chopper pad for pickup. They were being dropped into an area they hadn't been into yet, on another search and destroy operation.

"Listen up!" the LT yelled as he approached the men. "One Section, One Platoon, you lot are staying behind. Victor Charlie don't want your sorry arses out there this week."

A cheer went up from the eight men of One Section.

As the Hueys arrived at the LZ to pick up the men, the commanding officer raised his voice. "I'll brief you men when this lot have gone!"

When the last of the choppers had lifted, he advised the remaining men they would be going to Saigon, assigned to guard duty at the New Zealand Embassy and the home of the New Zealand ambassador for the next five days.

"Your ride should be here in"–the officer checked his watch–"ten minutes. When you arrive in Saigon, you'll report directly to HQ."

Terry let out a low whistle. Cushy job.

After their briefing at HQ in Saigon, they were split into two teams. Four based at the Caravelle Hotel, where the embassy was located, and four at the ambassador's residence. The men were told that when they weren't working, their time was their own. Terry was in the team based at the Caravelle, in the centre of the city. It seemed the Caravelle staff were being extra vigilant after a bomb had exploded on the fifth floor, killing one person.

Murph and Smokey were stationed inside the hotel. JJ and Terry were happy to find a place to sit outside and have a smoke, but after an hour in the heat, JJ declared he would take the inside duty tomorrow. The only time Terry had been in Saigon was when they'd first landed, and then they had been bundled into trucks and not seen any of the city. It felt like months ago now. A stint in the city would be a welcome relief.

The Caravelle Hotel sat on one side of the popular Lam Son

Square, which was currently bustling with traffic. At midday, the heat was intense. Rows of motorbikes were parked haphazardly on either side of the hotel, and people sat around eating lunch or sleeping. A planter box containing a large tree provided shelter, and Terry made himself comfortable as he watched the comings and goings. JJ sat on a doorstep a couple of metres in the other direction. The traffic never dwindled.

Girls approached them touting their services or trying to get them to accompany them to a bar. And kids offered them cold drinks, which they gratefully accepted until they were warned that street kids made great vehicles for delivering grenades, on the pretence of selling whatever they had to offer.

It was almost seventeen hundred hours. Soon their duty would be done for the day, and they could walk back to the bunkhouse attached to the ambassador's residence, their lodgings for the next week.

"Do you feel a little guilty, JJ?" Terry asked.

"About what?"

"Well, the comfy beds for one."

"How do you know they're comfy?" JJ asked.

"Can't be worse than sleeping on the jungle floor."

"Point taken."

"And no bloody scorpions, either," Terry muttered.

"We on bar duty tonight?"

"I'm up to—shit!" As he focused on dodging motorbikes on the footpath and crowds of people, Terry walked straight into someone. Automatically, his hands went out to steady the person he had almost knocked over.

And there she was. The woman with the copper hair. Brushing Coca-Cola off the front of her dress.

"Shit, I'm so sorry."

She held up a hand. "No, I'm sorry. I should have been looking where I was going, but I was miles away."

"I like your accent," he said, desperately trying to come up with a way to detain her for just a bit longer.

"It's the same as yours, isn't it? Aren't you a Kiwi?"

She was staring at him, and he was mesmerised by her eyes, her freckles, and her hair. She was the full package.

"God help us," someone behind him muttered, and the men laughed.

"Yeah, Kiwi through and through. From Foxton."

She looked surprised. "Palmerston North, but I was living in Wellington before I came over."

"I think I owe you a drink."

"I'd like that."

"You would?" He had seriously thought she would turn him down. He was lost for words.

"We're heading back to our digs," Murph interrupted. "We'll let him out in about an hour. Would it be convenient to meet him outside the Caravelle?"

"Sure." She turned to Terry. "I'll see you then. I need to change."

"Yeah, umm, sorry about that."

She smiled at him then turned and walked away. Terry watched her stride off towards Lam Son Square as the traffic weaved its way around her and finally engulfed her.

"Come on, Romeo." Murph slapped him on the back. "Let's get you back and spruced up."

"Don't know how you do it, Romeo," Smokey stated. "What the hell do you have that I don't?"

"I've got the whole package," Terry said with a straight face.

There was a roar of laughter, but right at that moment, nothing could put a dent in his mood.

Terry was back at Lam Son Square ten minutes early. He crossed the square and as he took a seat on the white painted steps of the Municipal Theatre, he lit a cigarette. From his vantage point, he could see both the Caravelle and Lam Son Square.

"Hello."

He turned to see her sit down on the steps beside him.

"Where did you come from?" He hadn't even seen her arrive.

"Nguyen Hue Street, over there." She pointed towards the street. It ran down the far side of the Caravelle, towards the river.

He held out his hand. "Terry. Terry Edwards. Victor Company. Royal New Zealand Infantry Regiment."

"Frankie Proctor," she said in return, shaking his hand. "I can't believe you're from Foxton."

"And to think I had to come all this way to meet you."

"We kind of met on the plane over, didn't we?" she commented, smiling at him.

Oh shit, he remembered the ass he'd made of himself. "That wasn't me. There must be someone over here that looks just like me."

She grinned at his attempted cover-up, but the smile didn't quite make it to her eyes. He wondered what she did over here that made her so sad.

"If you ever see him, tell him not to rack up any bills. Okay?"

Abruptly, she burst into laughter, and he thought it was the nicest sound he had ever heard.

"So, where would you like to go, ma'am?"

"How about Brodard's on Tu Do Street? It's a French coffee shop. They make great egg coffees."

"Lead the way." He jumped up and offered her his hand, helping her to her feet. "Do you know your way around?"

"I'm getting to know the streets and good eating places."

"Don't you eat in your hotel?" He imagined her staying in a hotel suite and relaxing by the swimming pool during the day, or out shopping in some of the boutique shops.

"Hell no. The local cafés and restaurants serve great food and are much cheaper. And besides, I moved out of the hotel. Much too expensive."

It was his turn to laugh. "So, what are you doing here in Saigon?"

"I work here."

"Doing what?" He was surprised and curious.

"I'm a photographer," she explained. "At the moment, I'm freelancing for the Associated Press. Or anyone who will buy my photos."

They walked around a group of people eating on the footpath. A woman was cooking something that involved a large wok of what looked like boiling oil.

"That smells good–do you want some?"

"Okay. I'm game."

Terry held up two fingers to the woman and pointed at whatever it was she was cooking. The woman rattled off something Terry didn't understand. He handed her some notes, and she bowed her head and smiled. A few minutes later they both walked along the street, eating something that tasted delicious but was unidentifiable.

"You know, you probably paid her way too much," Frankie chided.

"Well, if you go back tomorrow, she might give you extra helpings. Damn, this is tasty." In his haste to get back to the Caravelle to meet her, he hadn't eaten.

By the time they got to the café, it was full, and diners spilled onto the footpath.

"You wouldn't know there was a war on, would you?"

"Not judging by this lot," Terry agreed.

As they entered the café, a couple were leaving a table towards the back. Frankie ordered the coffee while Terry grabbed the table. She had argued it was her shout since he had treated her to the first course.

"I'm enjoying our evening," she said when she returned to their table.

"So am I. But I kind of feel guilty about my mates though."

"The ones you were with earlier?"

"No. The ones who didn't get picked for duty in Saigon and are out on another operation."

"I feel sorry for the thousands of young men who are drafted and sent over here, ill-prepared to fight for their lives or be killed in the field for no reason. It's a tragic waste of lives."

"We're just doing a job. Following orders." He didn't know where that outburst had come from, but he wondered where she had been since she arrived in Saigon to stir up such a reaction.

"Sorry. I didn't mean to lay that on you." She put her coffee down and leaned into him. "See the bar over there?"

Terry nodded.

"Just to the right, on the back wall, is a narrow shelf–the one with the waving cat on it. See it?"

"Yes."

"Just under that shelf is a small hole. Keep your eyes on it."

Terry watched the hole for what seemed an awful long time. Then looked at Frankie.

"No, I'm serious. Watch the hole."

He turned back in time to see a large rat edge its way out of the hole and sniff the air, then run down the wall and disappear into another room.

"Damn! That was the biggest rat I've ever seen!" Terry declared.

"Keep watching."

Sure enough a few minutes later, in full view of at least a dozen diners, the rat ran back up the wall carrying what looked like a chunk of meat and pushed its way back inside the hole.

"Well, I'll be buggered."

"And there you have it. One of the delights of Saigon."

"Do they know about it?"

"Oh, I should think so. It's hard to miss. Apparently, it does it every evening, and everyone just ignores it. It's probably lived here for years." She smiled at Terry, holding his gaze a little longer than necessary.

"I should walk you back," he said once they had finished their coffee. She nodded, and he stood up and walked around to pull her chair out for her. Together they wandered back out into the sweltering night air. It had been raining and reflections of the street lights glittered in the puddles on the road.

"Have you picked up many jobs since you've been here?" Terry asked.

"I was lucky enough to meet a French journalist who lives at the Continental. His name's Louis. He works for the AP and took me along to meet the bureau chief. My third day in Saigon, I ended up in the jungle at Chu Lai on an overnight march with the First Infantry Division. They were hunting a battalion that had attacked them the night before."

"And did they find them?"

"They did. I've never been so terrified in all my life."

"It sounds dangerous. You got some good pictures though?"

"Yes. Eventually. Which was remarkable because I was shaking so hard most of the time. I remember a couple of the young men I got to know while I was with them. One died just before the evac chopper arrived."

"Shit."

They were back in Lam Son Square again.

"Do you feel like coming to my apartment and having a drink with me?" she asked.

"Are you sure?"

She had eyes that pleaded with him, and again he wondered what things she had seen while she had been out in the field, and just how bad it had been.

"Totally. The night is still young."

They walked across the square, and after crossing over Nguyen Hue

Street, walked down towards the river. She stopped outside a beauty salon.

"This is it."

"What? You live in a beauty salon?"

"I got this through a colleague at the AP. Miss Lilac is his aunty."

They stood staring up at the signage.

"Every Friday, she does my hair and nails. Tells me I have to look good for the weekend."

"What happens on the weekend?"

She laughed. "Absolutely nothing. But Miss Lilac tells me if I look pretty, I stand a better chance of finding myself a boyfriend. And I have to admit, it's nice to put on some feminine clothes after living in fatigues all week."

They walked down the alley, and he followed her up to her room. She slipped off her sandals and took an opened bottle of whisky from the bench, and after pouring a generous measure into two cups, she handed one to him.

"To my friend Terry Edwards"–she held up the cup–"from Foxton."

It was the first time anyone had proposed a toast to him, and he'd drink to that. He raised his cup to hers, china clinked, and he watched as she took a decent swallow. He wondered if she was a seasoned drinker or whether it was Dutch courage. There was only one chair in the room, so he took that and let her sit on the bed.

She drained her cup and refilled it.

He had never met a woman who could knock back the hard stuff the way she obviously could.

"God, that feels better. Something to help me sleep tonight. Did you know I've been out in the field twelve times since I've been here?"

Terry shook his head. He had a feeling she wanted someone to talk to, and he was happy to sit and listen. She was gorgeous to look at, which made the listening part easy.

She edged back on the bed, so she was leaning against the headboard.

"It's great–don't get me wrong. It's exactly what I wanted. But it's hard, you know?" She looked down at the cup in her hands, and Terry noticed they were shaking.

He crossed to the bed in three steps, reached across and took the cup and climbed onto the bed next to her.

"I know it's hard, Frankie. It's not a job for the weak or faint-hearted. But you're here to tell a story, aren't you? To speak for those who can't tell the story themselves."

She looked up at him, and he could see the reason for the sadness in her eyes.

"There are so many though."

"So? Use more film."

She attempted a laugh, and for a moment, he couldn't tell if she was laughing or crying.

"It's such a beautiful country. With humble people, and yet we're tearing it apart."

"Hey." He shifted closer and put an arm around her shoulders, pulling her into him. "It makes your job here that much more important."

Without warning, she kissed him; he was shocked for a second by the intensity of her passion and how forward she was, and then he returned her kiss with equal passion. It was as though they both needed to celebrate being alive, to live in the moment, to bond with another human being under normal circumstances.

Just two young people who wanted nothing more than to forget the war and the courageous men dying in their hundreds every single day.

<h1 style="text-align:center">Chapter 15</h1>

When Frankie woke the following morning, the first thing she noticed was the whisky bottle. It was sitting on the nightstand beside the bed where she had left it. Except, it was no longer empty. It had a beautiful stem of orchids in it. Rolling over, she confirmed the other side of the bed held nothing but memories. He was gone.

She grinned. Oh, but he had been there all right. And the sex had been amazing and a much-needed release. She had needed to feel alive and to forget things even if just for a short while. She sat up and swung her legs over the side of the bed. Her head instantly reminding her about the quantity of the whisky she had consumed.

Pulling the sheet off the bed, she wrapped it around herself and walked gingerly over to the window. It was already open, and she couldn't remember whether she had opened it. She peered out, at the empty alley below, the smell of coffee drifting up from somewhere nearby.

She needed coffee. She walked back to the bedside table and picked up her wristwatch, squinting at it in the bright light. *Eight-fifteen!* She should have been at the AP office fifteen minutes ago. *Shit.* She pulled the sheet off, threw it on the bed and rushed into the bathroom, turned the shower on and stepped under the water.

She slipped on the fatigues that had become part of her life, left her hair wet and hurried out the door.

There was no one in the alley, but Nguyen Hue Street was packed with the usual scooters, bicycles, cars and people. She ran where she could, dodging around parked motor scooters. A wolf whistle attracted her attention, and she looked across the street to see Terry waving at her.

"I'm late! Come round tonight, if you get the chance," she called, waving back.

He gave her the thumbs up, and she returned her attention to avoiding obstacles on the footpath.

Things were busy in the AP office. Typewriters clattered, journalists took notes while talking on phones, machines spewed out reports and telex machines hummed. The room was thick with cigarette smoke, and several plates with a selection of French pastries sat on a table in the middle of the room.

"Morning," she greeted the bureau chief as she helped herself to a fresh pastry, and tried not to sound too puffed from the sprint to work.

"Ah, Frankie." Bobby Miller sat on the corner of a journalist's desk, going through a wad of papers. "I wondered if we'd see you today. Pull up a chair. I want to talk to you." He slid off the desk and walked back to his own. Frankie followed him.

"I think I've seen enough of your work to know what you're capable of."

Frankie wondered what was coming, whether he was about to tell her that her work wasn't good enough, and she should go home.

"Your images have improved immensely, and I'm impressed with your ability to cope, especially in the combat role. I want to offer you a permanent job with the AP."

"Really?"

"Yes. Don't sound so shocked. You deserve it. Here." He handed her a full accreditation pass. "Throw the other one away. This one will get you anywhere you want to go in the South.

"Thank you!" She leapt from the chair and flung her arms around the surprised bureau chief.

"You might not want to thank me. Your workload is going to increase."

"I don't care." In fact, the news couldn't be more welcome. It meant she would now have a steady income and the financial freedom to come and go as she pleased. To buy a new dress and eat at expensive restaurants if she wanted.

"I've assigned you to fly up to an orphanage at Nha Trang with Jim. Apparently, the army's running some sort of trial programme. Healthcare, education, food, the works. I want heart-rending images for this story. How soon can you be ready?"

"Thirty minutes?"

"Good."

The visit to the orphanage at Nha Trang was gut-wrenching. Frankie wanted to adopt every child there. It shocked her to learn that many of them were of mixed race, the result of men from the allied forces sleeping with local bar girls. In some cases, they were the result of rape.

Watching their cute wee faces made her want to cry. They all deserved to have at least one loving parent.

She was impressed with how the army was helping the orphanage and was pleased with the images she captured while there.

As she unlocked the door to her apartment later that night, she heard footsteps behind her on the concrete stairwell.

"Hey, Copper."

She turned to see Terry reach the landing. "Hi."

"I almost didn't recognise you in your greens this morning. Have you just finished work?"

"Yeah. A job up in Nha Trang. I've just spent the day with about fifty orphaned children. I miss them already. Then I stopped at the office to develop the film."

"If you're too tired, I can try and make it tomorrow."

"I'm tired but give me a few minutes to have a shower."

"What say I pick us up something to eat while you get cleaned up?"

Frankie smiled. "You wouldn't mind?"

"Nope." He grinned. "But I'll have no idea what I'm buying, so you're taking your chances."

"Reckon I can handle anything you throw at me."

His laugh echoed down the stairwell as she closed the door behind him. Under the shower, she struggled to wash away the images of the sad little faces she'd seen at the orphanage and eventually gave up and turned off the water. By the time Terry returned, she had changed into a cotton dress and put on the pretty pearl earrings Nell had given her, and she was feeling a little more refreshed.

"I've got crispy spring rolls and some type of beef dish." He looked at her and smiled. "Plus, I have pancake things stuffed with prawns and salad, French bread sticks, and some beers."

"It all looks delicious. Thanks." She watched as he spread the food on the bed and opened a beer. "I'm starving. So, how long are you at the Caravelle for?" she asked, biting into mouth-watering pancake.

"Two more nights. These are bloody good," he said, finishing a spring roll and helping himself to another.

"I'll be away tomorrow, overnight. But when I get back, how about I take you out to dinner? You know, just to say thanks for the meals you keep buying me."

"Can you afford it?"

"Yes. Because guess what?"

"Ummm." He swallowed a mouthful of beer. "You went totally mad today and adopted seven kids and then married the chopper pilot?"

Frankie laughed so hard she almost choked. "No! Although it's tempting, the chopper pilot was gorgeous, but I'm sure I've shocked my mother enough without arriving home with a husband and a plane full of kids." She stopped for a breath. "Miller at the AP made me a permanent member of the team today. I am now officially accredited."

"Congratulations! That's what you wanted, wasn't it?"

"Yes. And it means I can shout you a proper meal when I get back." She drained her beer and continued eating.

Terry wiped the remains of a pancake from his hands. "I reckon you have the prettiest hair I've ever seen."

"Thanks."

"And, did you know that every time you laugh, your freckles dance?"

She smiled and helped herself to another spring roll. "I hated them as a kid. I got teased so much at school."

"Those freckles are my friends," he stated.

They sat in silence, finishing their meal. She liked Terry. He seemed like a good, honest man. He made her laugh, and they had great sex.

"So, how about a bit of dancing to round out the evening?" she asked.

"What did you have in mind?"

"Well." She stood up and walked over to turn on her radio. The American Forces station was playing. "How about this?"

He stood up and walked to where she was waiting for him then reached down and took one of her hands in his.

"I have high expectations, but let me warn you, I'm not too good with waltzes," she stated.

"Well, aren't you lucky? The slow ones happen to be my speciality. Just relax and let me lead you."

With his hand on the small of her back and the other holding hers, she let him lead her around the tiny make-do dance floor, his hand pulling her body into his.

As they danced, she asked him about his family back in New Zealand, and where he'd worked before he came over.

When they ran out of slow dances, they sat on the bed talking until the small hours of the morning. Terry told her he should head back, but he was worried that if he got caught out on the street, he'd get into big trouble, so Frankie asked him to stay, telling him he could leave at dawn before the city woke.

He had no arguments.

"Where are you going today?" Terry asked, sliding off the bed and pulling on his trousers.

"I'm spending a couple of days on the Mekong Delta with the patrol boats and a group of SEALs. Don't forget our date tomorrow night."

He buttoned his shirt and tucked it into the waistband of his trousers then reached out and stroked her face. "I won't. You be careful out there."

"I will. The guys always look out for me."

"It's the guys I'm worried about." He leaned down and kissed her.

She smiled a sleepy smile at him. "Be gone." She laughed, watching him stride across the room to the door.

"See you tomorrow."

And he quietly closed the door and was gone.

Frankie could still feel his touch on her skin; she loved the way his hands caressed her as though she was the only thing that mattered at that moment. She had never felt like that with anyone before. Not even with Scotty back in Wellington.

She was fond of Terry and pleased to have him as a friend. She wondered if it would have been different if they had met back in New Zealand, whether her feelings were because of the circumstances they found themselves in, here in this place.

The two days on the Mekong were fun, exhilarating, and terrifying, all at the same time. The men treated her like royalty, thrilled to have a woman on board, and she quickly struck up a friendship with them. They teased her about her accent and the colour of her hair, but she gave as good as she got. The men enjoyed her company and were happy for her to take photos of them.

They treated her to grilled steaks, hash browns, American hot dogs and beer; all the western foods she hadn't had in a long time.

The boats patrolled the waterways, and most of the work was routine: stopping small fishing boats and checking smaller cargo boats. Occasionally, they would open fire on a boat that refused to stop, and one inspection turned up a large cache of weapons hidden under false floorboards. They had allowed her to go aboard to photograph the search. She hoped the resulting photos would make a good story. When it came time to leave, they all begged her to come back or to meet them when they were off duty, and she laughed, telling them she never knew where she would be from one day to the next.

Bobby Miller nodded to himself when he looked over the contact sheets the following day. She could tell he was pleased with what he saw. He made notes and already knew who he was sending the photos to. As Frankie walked down Le Loi Street and turned into Nguyen Hue, she was practically floating, even though she was still humping her pack on her back. So far this week, she had made a thousand dollars from her photos.

She couldn't have been happier.

Chapter 16

Terry sat on the front steps of Miss Lilac's, waiting for Frankie. He had received lots of handy tips about grooming and offers from Miss Lilac herself, which he thanked her for, but refused. When he told her he was waiting for Frankie, she said he could wait in the salon, but he politely declined that offer too. There were too many young Vietnamese girls inside, and after all the stories he'd heard, they scared the bejesus out of him.

He was thinking about those stories and watching the traffic when he spotted Frankie walking down Nguyen Hue towards him, dressed in fatigues and boots, hair tousled, hat tucked in a pocket, and pack on her back. She looked gorgeous.

He jumped up and ran down the street to greet her.

"Here, let me carry this." He lifted the pack off her shoulders. "As much as you look mighty good in one of these, I'm more suited to humping them around."

"Thanks." She rolled her shoulders and smiled at him. "You look nice."

His heart flipped, just a little, at her words. He was pleased she had noticed. He hadn't brought anything tidy with him, so he'd got his mates to cover for him while he went shopping for a dressy shirt and some smart trousers.

"How did your trip go?"

"I got some great images and had an amazing time. Riding those patrol boats was something else."

"That's good."

"What about you? No one lob any grenades at the ambassador's residence or the Caravelle while I was away?"

"Nope. No suspicious behaviour at all." He followed her down the alley and up the stairwell, waiting as she unlocked the door to her apartment.

"You're early, aren't you?"

She was right. He had knocked off early, and it was only just four in the afternoon. "I pulled a double shift. I wanted to spend as much time with you as possible." He paused and put the pack down on her bed. "I go back to Nui Dat tomorrow, and I don't know when I'll get to see you again." He was feeling slightly awkward now, like a stalker, and she might not even want to see him again, anyway. He was making a lot of assumptions.

"Perhaps I can get an assignment out at Nui Dat?"

"I doubt it. The Australians won't allow women out there."

"You forget, I've got a pass from MACV now, it gives me the right to go anywhere."

He leaned against the small bench that passed for her kitchen, watching her unbutton her shirt. "Not Nui Dat."

"We'll see."

He had never felt like this about anyone, not even Evelyn. Evelyn was a fantasy, one that would never come true. Frankie was real. She was soft, and feminine, tough and bloody beautiful all at the same time. Frankie was a whole different girl. She was older, worldly, and she was alive and full of energy, enthusiasm and compassion. And she was here with him.

She dropped her shirt to the floor and stepped out of her trousers. "I'm going to take a shower. Help yourself to a drink. Or, you could join me."

Never one to look a gift-horse in the mouth, he kicked off his shoes, and his clothes followed. To hell with going slow. Shit, either of them could die tomorrow. Right now, they were both alive, and in Vietnam, you had to live for the moment. It might just be a bit of fun for her, but it was great fun, and great sex. What the hell.

"Yeah, all right."

"So, do you think we should grab something to eat?" He'd propped himself up on one elbow, and watched her as she lay on her back, smoking a cigarette.

"Actually, I'm starving." Frankie turned her head to look at him, and he brushed her hair from her forehead. She smiled.

He traced the freckles on her face until he reached her mouth, where he stopped and removed the cigarette from her fingers. After inhaling deeply, he leaned over her and stubbed it out in the ashtray.

"I am too." He kissed the corner of her lips, teasing her, his hand following the contour of her stomach down to the inside of her thighs. He loved the way she responded to him, arching her back up off the bed, the soft moans. His lips played on the pale skin of her breasts.

She whispered his name, and he shifted his attention to her mouth, kissing her with more passion until he remembered he needed to breathe.

"I promised you dinner," she said finally, glancing at her wristwatch. "Let's go to the Rex. Or the Continental. Do you have a preference?" She sat up and swung her bare legs over the side of the bed.

"None at all." Actually, he was cursing her offer now. He could happily have stayed there in her bed for the rest of the night and not shared her with anyone. He wanted to memorise every inch of her body, so he could dream about her on nights in the bush when he couldn't get to sleep.

"Right. The night awaits."

Twenty minutes later, they were walking down Nguyen Hue. She had decided they would go to the Majestic, down by the river. She said she'd heard nothing but great things about the rooftop bar but had never been there.

Terry felt proud escorting her into the bar. She looked striking in a short sleeveless dress that accentuated her tiny waist. She was wearing lipstick too and had little pearl earrings in her ears. He loved the way she ran her fingers through her hair as they walked, leaving it tousled. She looked damned sexy.

He led her to the bar where they ordered drinks and were shown to a table. Frankie nodded and said hello to a couple of men, who he guessed were journalists or photographers, and he tried not to feel jealous. In the distance, the sky flashed white, a reminder that his world lay not far from the city.

The assignment in Saigon had been an experience, and by chance, he had met Frankie, but he was also longing to get back to camp and to the job of soldiering with the rest of his mates.

"Penny for them."

He turned away from the lights on the horizon. "I was thinking about getting back to camp. I'm a soldier, my job is out looking after my mates."

"I'll miss you."

"I doubt it. You'll be too busy with your chopper pilots, and orphanages and Marines."

Her smile melted his insides, and he could have dragged her off to the bathroom right then and there to make love to her in one of the stalls.

"Not the same. Perhaps we could meet up at Christmas? Or Tet? There are rumours floating around that the North is going to call a ceasefire. Maybe you'll get a few days R and R."

"That would be nice." He smiled back at her, then remembered Victor Company would be gone by then and felt a surge of regret as he realised that he would possibly never see her again. "I'm leaving in November. We seem to be out on ops every other day, if not for weeks on end. I doubt I'll make it back to Saigon again."

"Oh."

He didn't want to read anything into the look on her face, but for the briefest second, he thought she looked disappointed.

"Well." She held up her glass. "Here's to my Foxton Boy. I'm pleased the war brought you to me, even if only briefly."

He held up his own glass. "And to Copper, whose light will always shine brightest when I'm deep inside Vietnam." Their glasses clinked, and he smiled at her, trying to keep the mood light. They were both well aware this was their last night together in a long time, or maybe forever, if one of them was killed.

Their meals were delicious, and as they ate, they chatted about the war. Frankie told him about assignments she had been on, and he filled her in on Nui Dat and what it was like to get a scorpion sting. When she laughed at him, he noticed she attracted the attention of every man in the bar.

"I think I should get you back to your apartment before one of these men fights me for you."

"Highly unlikely, but your offer sounds like one I can't refuse."

He stood up and walked around to her side of the table and pulled out her chair for her. Terry hoped it was obvious to those watching that they were a couple. Somehow, he felt protective of her although he had no right to, as he had no claim on her. They were just good friends and would probably never be anything more.

He asked her about her parents and where they lived in Palmerston North. He told her about the New Year's Eve dance he'd been to at the Astoria Ballroom, and was surprised to hear she had also been at the dance. He couldn't believe he hadn't seen her, but she explained she had gone with a group of friends and she'd had a short hair cut at the time; a moment of teenage rebellion, she told him, laughing at the memory. She remembered Evie Hallet singing and was interested to hear she had just been out to Vietnam to entertain the men at Nui Dat. She asked if Terry knew her, he told her he did, and then changed the subject.

Back at the apartment, they sat on her bed, drinking beer and talking. He wanted to know everything about her. How long she intended to stay in Vietnam and where she would go after Saigon.

"I don't know how long I'll be here for," she said. "Probably until the war ends, or I get shot and shipped out," she added, almost nonchalantly.

He didn't even want to think about her getting wounded. Never mind killed. "You any good at running?"

For some reason, she found that funny and burst into laughter.

"What's funny about that?"

The question only made her laugh harder, and she fell back on the bed holding her sides.

He grabbed the ashtray as it bounced and shifted it to the floor. "I reckon if you can run, you'll be okay." He tried to explain his reasoning.

"I'd have to run bloody fast to dodge a bullet," she said, trying to contain herself and failing; tears formed at the corners of her eyes and spilled down her cheeks.

"I can't believe you don't have a boyfriend waiting for you, or worse, a husband."

"I just haven't found the right person." She put the radio on, and as Jim Morrison's voice filled the room, she pulled herself up and started dancing.

"Dance with me." She took his hand and pulled him into the middle of the room. He wanted to remember this moment forever. Holding her hand as they danced in her small apartment to The Doors. Two young people, living in the moment.

Terry woke the next morning to the sound of chatter in the alley below Frankie's window. Beside him, Frankie was still asleep. He looked at his watch, five forty-five. He didn't want to leave, but they were heading back to Nui Dat this morning. He leaned over and kissed her cheek.

She smiled.

"I have to go shortly."

"How did I know you were going to say that?"

"Do you think we'll get to meet up again sometime?"

"I hope so. You know where to find me. At the AP bureau. Don't forget. Across the road from the Rex, up four flights of stairs, large door at the far end of the corridor."

"Okay. I can't promise anything before November, but I'll try."

He pulled on his clothes as she sat up in bed watching him, and when he was dressed, he turned to look at her. She stood naked at the end of the bed, shrugging on her robe, and he wanted to remember that image for the rest of his life.

"Well, that's me," he said regretfully. "I guess I'd better be going."

Frankie walked to the door with him. "I've had lots of fun this last week. Thank you." She looked down as though fascinated with her bare feet.

"What for?"

"For making me forget the war and reminding me that life is for the living."

"I'll miss our dinner outings," he replied, trying to keep things light.

"Yeah, me too."

He couldn't help himself, he took her face in his hands and kissed her. Gentle at first, and then with more passion as if drinking in the taste of her. Creating a memory he could take with him. He didn't want her to forget him, but he knew she probably would.

"Keep your head down, soldier," she said, putting her hand on the side of his face.

"Yeah." He grinned. "And don't you forget–running is the answer."

She laughed and pushed him out the door onto the landing. "Remember, the AP bureau."

"I will," he yelled as he ran down the stairs to the alley.

As he made his way back to meet up with his mates, he wondered if it had all been a dream. It felt like it.

Although he had never thought about marriage before, he found himself wondering what it would be like to be married to a girl like Frankie. He decided if he ever got the guts, he'd ask her about the idea.

Chapter 17

They arrived back in camp at eleven hundred hours to the news there had been a serious fragging incident. HQ decided that it was the result of stress and long hours spent on ops, and each section was granted a three-day R and R pass to Vũng Tàu.

By fourteen hundred hours, One and Two Sections were being airlifted out for a week's patrol while Jack's section was the first to head to town.

All Terry could think of was getting hold of Frankie and letting her know he was heading to town for three days. Maybe she could get a couple of nights off. After all, Vũng Tàu was only a couple of hours from Saigon.

That week back in the bush was the longest Terry had ever experienced. The first thing he did when he got back to camp was head to the mess, to see if he could get on the run through to Bà Rịa. Twice a week, headquarters dropped off donated food to a school there. Today was one of those days, and he needed to be on that truck.

As luck would have it, the driver was happy to swap duties, and Terry, pleased to get a break from the leaky backpack, got to do the deliveries to Bà Rịa. As soon as Terry got to the school, he unloaded the containers of food and asked if they had a phone he could use. They were grateful for the donations and pointed out the building that housed the school's small office and the only telephone. He put a call through to the AP bureau, but Frankie wasn't there; she was in Da Nang covering a story. They were expecting her back the following afternoon.

He'd known there was a possibility she might be away on an assignment, but he couldn't help feeling disappointed. It seemed it was going to be nearly impossible to organise meeting up with her. With Three Section currently on R and R, he only had a few days to get hold of her. But the following day, they were told to prepare to head out for three nights. There had been some activity on a trail twenty kilometres inland. Reports suggested VC were moving large quantities of food, and the two platoons would try to slow their progress.

This trip, he found himself walking second scout in place of Smokey, who had been complaining of a guts ache all morning. Terry was careful and competent in any position, but scout required keeping his wits about him. There could be no thinking about Frankie until he got back to camp. The last thing he needed was to stand on something booby-trapped.

They located the trail half an hour before dusk. There was no sign of movement, but plenty of signs of use. Both VC and NVA favoured the hours of darkness. They knew the terrain like the back of their hands.

Operating in total silence, the men set up an ambush, and then prepared themselves for the firefight. They had carried extra ammunition and were taking no chances. Orders came down there was to be no digging fox holes, no smoking nor heating food. They were to do nothing that might give away their position to the enemy.

Sure enough, two hours after darkness fell, a Claymore was triggered. Victor Company had the trail covered and the VC, although taken by surprise, fought back with everything they had. Normally, Terry carried an SLR, but because he was walking second scout this trip, he had picked up an M16 and he let rip, leaving Smokey to help Blackie feed the M60. The fighting lasted for almost an hour before the LT called in an air strike and told his men to move back.

However, the VC took their retreat as a victory and as they advanced on Victor Company, the first incoming sounded overhead. Terry hit the ground as the earth shuddered and debris bounced off his hat. To his left, Elvis was lying prone, and on his right, JJ was also head down.

Terry lifted his eyes, scanning for movement.

"Incoming!" someone shouted, and this time the round landed closer to the Victor Company men, tearing branches from trees and hurling them over their heads. Terry wondered who was walking-in the mortar rounds. He heard his section commander yell, *"Danger close."* Then he noticed the machine gun had fallen silent.

"Blackie! You okay?"

"Got a jam! Got a jam!"

"Hold on!" Keeping his body close to the ground, he moved crab-like to where Blackie was slapping the bolt and swearing. "Here, take mine." They swapped weapons, and he worked on the M60 to get it going again. He had an uncanny knack for fixing anything mechanical, and his only threat to holding the record for the fastest dismantle and reassemble, was from his mate Jack. It took under two minutes before they were feeding the ammo back through the machine gun. Someone from their lines tossed a grenade.

"Cheers, Romeo!"

"Nest ten o'clock!"

"Someone take those bastards out!"

"Incoming!"

Collectively, their heads went down again. Terry was no religious man, but he prayed like hell the rounds weren't being walked-in any closer.

When the call to hold fire came, silence screamed in their ears. For all the fighting, no one had been killed, and only one member of Three Section had been wounded when he'd taken shrapnel to an arm.

"You okay, Romeo?" JJ asked as they walked out to set up a tripwire across the track.

"Yeah, why?"

"Looks like you blew the arse out of your strides, mate." He roared with laughter as Terry fumbled with the back of his trousers, touching skin.

"Holy Jesus, I've been shot!" He had blood on his hand from one of his buttocks.

"Too many tins of beans, more like it."

"I'm not kidding. I've been bloody shot."

"Well you're still walking mate, so it can't be that bad. Get Doc to check it out when we get back."

Terry grumbled about no one caring if he died from his wounds as JJ chuckled to himself, and they set up the wire and a couple of Claymores and headed back to their safe harbour. They had stopped the enemy once, and Terry hoped there would be no more encounters tonight. Although, he doubted any of them would sleep.

The doc took one look at Terry's backside and roared with laughter.

"I'm a bit bloody sick of being the butt of everyone's jokes around here," Terry stated, agitated by the lack of sympathy.

Doc laughed harder.

"Keep the bloody noise down, Doc!" the section commander rasped at them.

"Romeo here is sick of being the *butt* of everyone's jokes, and he's just been shot in the arse."

The boss looked from one to the other, and Terry could tell he too was trying to stifle a laugh.

"Is it serious?"

"Nope, it's just a graze. Our boy is very lucky. Might be sore sitting down for a while though."

"Get on with it then. And keep the noise down or he won't be the only one who gets a bullet up their backside. Do you have a spare pair of strides, Edwards?"

"No."

"Ask around then, someone must have a pair. Don't want you flashing your backside at us the rest of the trip."

Great. Everyone was a joker. To make matters worse, as the boss walked back to talk to the radio operator, it started to rain. Terry pulled his collar up, readjusted the sweat towel he had tucked around his neck, and went about trying to find a replacement pair of strides.

The remainder of the night was uneventful. As soon as it was light, they scouted the area for bodies and found three. There were signs everywhere that the enemy had taken a beating. Then Elvis stumbled, and Terry could hear him curse, then mutter something in Māori.

"What've you got, Elvis?" Smokey asked, joining his mate.

"Gook leg. Shit I thought it was a branch."

Smokey looked down. "Aw, shit."

"Smoke?" Terry asked, joining them.

"Yeah," Elvis said.

"Thanks," Smokey added.

Orders were to sit out another night to see what they could catch. They packed up and moved five kilometres to the east and set up again. There was still a lot of enemy movement in the area, and their encounter the night before seemed to have done little to dent the VC's enthusiasm.

The second night was quiet, but it came on to rain just after eighteen hundred hours and didn't stop all night. By morning, the men were cold and soaked-through and eager to get back to camp and eat a hot meal, but they still had one more night out.

On the third night, the jungle filled with a thick mist. Terry felt like it was something straight out of a horror movie, it gave him the shits and he found it hard to sleep, but by midnight it had lifted only to be replaced by rain. The men lay hidden wherever they could find shelter. Some tried to sleep while others took their turn on watch.

Through the heavy rain, no one spotted or heard a group of VC creeping through the bush towards them. They made it through the ambush site until one of them triggered the tripwire. Two Claymores fired, and suddenly everyone was wide awake and scrambling as the bush erupted in tracer rounds and bullets. Someone threw a grenade. The rain didn't quite muffle the screams.

After twenty minutes, the jungle fell silent, and an inspection turned up four bodies. No one knew how many VC there had been and how many had escaped. Terry was thankful it was all over. He hated firefights at night. Fighting in the jungle during daylight hours was bad enough, but at night Charlie could be anywhere, even circling back on them now, and they would never know.

Not a single member of One Section slept for the rest of the night, and when dawn finally broke, they were relieved to walk their tired bodies back to the LZ, an hour's march away. The rain had long stopped, and Terry's clothes were bone dry. Although, it wouldn't be long before they were drenched in sweat again.

Sick of playing table tennis, and after spending an hour in the pool, Terry decided to try getting hold of Frankie one final time.

"AP."

"Is Frankie Proctor there?"

"*Anyone know where Frankie is?*" the person on the end of the line yelled.

Terry was desperate to see her again, but never in his life had he chased a girl so enthusiastically. He had rung the AP bureau twice since they'd arrived in Vũng Tàu on R and R, hoping he could entice her to join him.

"Can I get someone else for you?" The question interrupted his thoughts.

"No." He had been hoping like hell this time he would strike it lucky. He guessed it was always going to be a long shot. "She's a friend, and I was hoping we could catch up."

"Hang on—she's out on assignment, bud. *Anyone know where she went? Where is she?* Oh, yeah, she's up at Pleiku. Left early this morning, apparently. How long you here for, buddy?"

"Not long. When's she due back?"

"Two days. If you're still here then, give her another ring."

"Sure." Two days too long. Tonight was their last night in Vungers. They were heading back to camp in the morning. "Thanks anyway," he told the voice.

"Do you want me to give her any message?"

"Just tell her Terry called."

"Will do."

The line went dead, leaving Terry disappointed that the chance to spend time with Frankie had slipped through his fingers. He walked back out into the bright sun. They were staying at the Badcoe Club, down by the beach, and he walked over to a table and sat down. Men were yelling and throwing a rugby ball around the swimming pool. Small groups of men were sitting around drinking. He had never felt as alone as he did right then. It was stupid to feel that way. He was surrounded by his mates, but the one person he wanted the most, he couldn't have.

"Hey, Romeo."

"Smokey."

"What're you up to?" Smokey handed Terry a can of beer.

"What does it bloody look like?"

"Looks like you need a bit of cheering up," Murph stated, sitting opposite Terry. "What's up?"

"Nothing's up. Jesus. Can't a bloke just sit here and enjoy a little peace and quiet?"

"Hell no. This is Vungers, mate, and we've only got one more bloody night of freedom."

"We're heading into town to have a few drinks before the night gets interesting, you should come along, mate," JJ suggested.

They were all sitting around the table now. Terry took out his smokes, flicked them open and offered one to Smokey, and then threw them on the table. He'd spent the last two days swimming at the beach and in the pool, watching movies and drinking beer. Yesterday, he'd written a letter to his mother then gone into town to post it and decided to look for a gift for Frankie. He didn't know why, but he wanted to get her something, and he decided on a small marble Buddha with long earlobes and a huge smiling face. He had hoped to give it to her if she came down to Vũng Tàu. But now, he didn't know when he'd get to see her next.

For all he knew, she could be seeing other guys. He'd heard how the chopper pilots always managed to pull the chicks. Frankie was always jumping on choppers, maybe one of those chopper jocks had taken a liking to her?

"Yeah, okay." Terry took a swig of his beer. "I'll come into town with you buggers. Someone has to keep an eye on you."

A cheer went up. Someone slapped him on the back, and someone else tousled his hair.

He'd go with his mates and have a good time. Forget about Frankie just for one night. Get rolling drunk, pick up a nice-looking girl, have a few laughs with the boys.

What harm was there in that? Wasn't that what every young soldier did on his time off?

Chapter 18

The group of men from One Section arrived in town late in the afternoon. They had started drinking before they left the club and were well primed by the time they hit the first bar. They formed a plan of attack on the way into town, aiming to have one beer in every bar in Vũng Tàu and see how many bars they could cover in the one night.

After the first three, their chances had diminished considerably. By the time they had hit the fourth bar, a seedy-looking establishment, they were all well lubricated and going downhill fast. Elvis was treating everyone to perfect renditions of Elvis Presley songs, which was how he'd got his nickname in the first place. Terry thought Elvis was damned good, especially with a fair amount of booze in him. The more they drank, the more attentive the bar girls became, but with Murph's help, Terry got the guys out onto the street.

"I'm bloody starving," Elvis said, trying without success to light his cigarette.

"Let's look for somewhere to have a feed. Here," Terry said, pulling his lighter from his pocket and flicking it towards the cigarette.

"I'm amazed you're still with us, Romeo," Murph commented. "I thought you'd have pulled yourself a lovely sheila by now. Let's go that wa–" he tripped on the edge of the footpath and grabbed JJ's arm.

"I'm pacing myself, boys," Terry said.

"Jesus, how many bars are there in Vungers?" Smokey asked no one in particular.

They staggered up the street and found an elderly Vietnamese woman frying meat in a wok on a crudely built charcoal firebox. She had rail-thin arms, and wispy hair pulled into a bun at the back of her head. When she smiled at them, Terry noticed she was missing a considerable number of teeth.

"I'll have five of whatever she's cooking." Elvis held up a hand, waved it around and put it back in his pocket. "Smells good."

"What is it?" JJ asked.

"Who knows," Terry answered, holding up his finger too, and then pointing to himself and each of them. "Might be dog."

"As long as it's not a bloody rat," Smokey stated, carefully inching closer to study the contents of the wok.

The woman rattled off something no one understood and held out her hand.

"I'll take care of this," Smokey stated, holding up his hand, palm facing the others. He dug in his wallet and produced some notes. "Here." He offered them to the woman.

She nodded and snatched the offered notes then, one by one, handed out leaves piled high with sticky rice and the meat.

A small crowd formed, some waiting for food, others wanting to see what the off-duty soldiers were up to.

"This is good shit," Elvis said.

"We should take her back to camp with us," JJ suggested. "She could teach those bastards in the kitchen how to bloody cook."

The old woman said something they couldn't understand and pointed to the ground.

"I think she's offering us a seat," Terry said.

"She probably wants your phone number, more like it, Romeo." There was a round of laughter.

"Or the whereabouts of your tent," Murph added.

"I prefer my women with a full mouth of teeth," Terry stated, matter-of-factly.

Smokey roared with laughter then staggered, struggling to right himself while not spilling any of his food. "I like 'em with a mouthful of somethin' else."

"That reminds me," Donny Tamihana slurred, surprising everyone. Until now, the section's rifleman had been quietly following along, getting plastered. "I want to go to The Bamboo Palace. I heard it's got hot girls."

"I'm game," Blackie answered. "Anyone know where it is?"

"Nope."

Donny staggered over to the group of locals squatting around the old woman with the food. "'Cuse us, Mrs," he said, bowing over and almost losing his balance. "Which way to The Bamboo Palace?"

There was much chatter from the group before a boy pointed down the street.

After much deliberation, it was agreed they were on the right street but needed to walk another block.

Donny bowed again, this time with Terry holding his arm.

"Lead the way," Murph ordered.

"Yeah, I'm starting to dry out after all that rice," Terry added.

"Anyone got a smoke?"

Somehow, they all made it to The Bamboo Palace, and before they had even made it to the bar, Donny had a girl on his arm. The grin on his face would have put the proverbial Cheshire Cat to shame.

The bar was busy. Most of the patrons were off-duty soldiers, and from what Terry could make out, either Australian or American. The men ordered beers and took a table. Before they had finished the first can, they had a circle of girls around them. Murph had one on his knee and was looking mighty pleased with himself. Smokey and Donny had their arms around a couple of girls, who were both laughing and chatting up the men. Blackie and Elvis seemed intent on smashing the record for the greatest number of beers consumed and on winning the bet that they could each drink more than the other. JJ was at the bar ordering more drinks for everyone.

A girl sat down beside Terry, nodded and smiled at him.

"Hello honey," Terry said, extending a hand to her. "I'm Terry."

"Mai Lihn," the young girl replied.

"Don't bloody shake her hand," Murph yelled at Terry over the noise in the bar. "Ya losin' ya touch." He chuckled and returned his attention to the girl on his lap.

"Never mind him. What are you drinking, love?" Terry asked, ignoring his mate. She looked bloody gorgeous, with her pretty silk dress cut right up to her waist, providing a tantalising glimpse of skin. Her English was impressive too.

"Special Saigon whisky," she replied.

JJ arrived with drinks and handed them out.

A guitar appeared from somewhere, and that was enough for Elvis. He decided these bar patrons needed to hear his Presley impersonation too. Halfway through, Blackie got up and left the group with a pretty, young Vietnamese girl. There was lots of drunken cheering.

Then Donny nudged Terry on the arm. "See ya later, mate." He winked and was led off by his girl.

"Two down." Terry laughed.

"Yours is a bit of all right," Smokey commented, draining a can and nodding towards the girl sitting beside Terry. "Don't think I'm going to make it back to the club tonight." The girl on Smokey's knee was running her hand up and down his thigh, and Terry laughed, he knew where that was heading.

"She'll be right mate. Don't worry about me."

"I'm not. I'm worried about bloody Elvis though." He was now standing on a chair trying to show everyone in the bar how well he could gyrate his pelvis, much to the delight of several giggling girls.

"You're bloody embarrassing, Elvis!"

"Who fuckin cares, mate!"

"Not me," Terry replied. Tonight he couldn't care less. Tonight was about letting loose and having some fun, and he was having a hell of a good time.

"You need a soft bed, Kiwi." Mai Linh's arm was around his shoulders.

"Yeah. Know where I can find one?"

"I can make Kiwi very comfortable."

"Ah, that's what I was hoping." They stood up, and Mai Linh took his hand.

"About bloody time, Romeo!"

"Bugger off. How about your girl?"

"Nah, mate, got me a beauty of a wife, I can wait." He smiled and raised another beer to his lips. "Go have some fun."

"He numba one Kiwi!" JJ shouted, and those still left at the table cheered heartily.

"Don't you fuckin' forget it!" Terry shouted and laughed. He leaned down towards Murph and slapped him on the back. "Don't wait up either. Okay?"

"No chance."

"Right, darlin'." He turned to the pretty girl waiting for him. "Let's go have us some fun."

Chapter 19

Terry followed Blackie through a patch of elephant grass. The dense, cutty blades were well over their heads. He had learned early in his tour to roll his sleeves down, or his arms ended up looking like bloody, red roadmaps.

As they snaked their way through the grass in single file, two large planes flew low overhead, a fine mist fanning out and drizzling down on them. Terry paused, looked skywards then walked on in silence.

Clearing cover, the men followed a paddy bund and took cover on the other side in a small banana plantation.

"More spray?" Terry asked as they sat having a hot drink.

"Yeah, us Kiwis are hard to kill," Murph replied.

"They were bloody low."

"What do you think they were spraying?"

"Probably one of those defoliant runs. These banana palms won't be here tomorrow. Betcha."

"Or it could be insecticide."

"I can taste the bloody stuff," Donny said, joining them.

"We've been walking through it for the last hour and a half."

"If it gets rid of these blood-sucking mozzies I'll be happy," Terry replied, slapping at his neck. "Little bastards."

"There has to be some merit in wiping out the jungle by blanket-spraying everything in sight and eliminating Charlie's hiding places," Smokey stated.

"Yeah, but what about us?" Terry asked.

"What about us?" Smokey asked, eyeing them all up for a cigarette.

"Well, think about it, Smokey. There won't be anywhere for us to hide either. They'll pop up outta their tunnels like spiders and pick us off. We'll be sitting targets."

"Jesus, neva thought about that." He shifted nervously. "Anyone gotta smoke?"

They hadn't encountered any enemy all day, although they had stumbled on a track that looked like it had been used recently, set an ambush and waited overnight, with no results. Now, they were slowly making their way back to Nui Dat.

Victor Company was now only a couple of weeks short of going home. All but five were heading home. Three were staying on in Terendak, one was transferring to a logistics unit in Vũng Tàu, and Jack had told Terry he was staying on. He'd put in to transfer to Whiskey Company.

For the last few nights, all Terry could think about was going home. He had thought about his options while he took his turn at perimeter duty. Weighing up what he would do when he got home took his mind off the shadows and kept his imagination in check. He wondered if he even still had a home.

His boss had promised him his old job back, which was great, but he had a feeling that things wouldn't be the same. As he glanced around at the guys, he realised he'd miss them, that's for sure. Murph was lying on his back with his hat over his face, grabbing some shut-eye. JJ was cleaning his rifle, and Donny was reading a book. Blackie and the boss were discussing something, and Smokey and Elvis sat hunched over their hot drinks, deep in conversation about the pros and cons of spraying the jungles.

Even though they had only been together for six months, he knew them like they had been mates for years. Each man had become an extension of the other. They had learned how to wind up each other to maximum effect for a few laughs and knew how the others would respond or react in certain circumstances. They depended on each other to stay alive.

Since Jack had re-signed for another tour, Terry had been tossing around the idea too. Joining Whiskey Company would mean another twelve months in Vietnam, but he had nothing back home. No wife and family like some of the other guys. Not even a girlfriend, and probably not even a place to sleep, unless he counted his mother's sofa or his father's spare wire-wove bed with its uncomfortable, lumpy mattress.

When he'd talked to Jack about joining Whiskey Company, they had ended up in a heated discussion. Terry had discovered his mate had fallen for some bar girl he didn't know from squat. He claimed it was the girl he'd saved from the village a few months back. Some buggers did bloody stupid stuff, but Jack wasn't usually one of them. It had to be an infatuation, nothing more. What he had waiting for him back home was twenty times more valuable than some bar girl he had fallen for over here.

And what would it do to Evelyn if she found out? It would

devastate her. He shook his head, failing to understand what on earth was wrong with his mate.

Terry's application to transfer to Whiskey was processed without a hitch, and by the end of November, Victor Company had left Vietnam. This time, both he and Jack were assigned to Three Section, in the same platoon. He was detailed to walking second scout, after Jack. It seemed word had been passed down from the commanding officer of Victor, and the consensus was that the two most experienced men were leading Three Section, and Three Section would lead the company.

Terry had been promised a week's leave prior to joining his new unit, but they were called out on a four-week operation and wouldn't be back in camp until almost Christmas. The leave had to wait.

The four weeks gave Terry time to get to know the rest of Three Section. This time, they would be together for twelve months, and there appeared to be some good men amongst them, although he wasn't so sure about the machine gunner. He seemed to have a wild streak to him and a morbid sense of humour, which worried Terry. Their section commander was a decent bloke, though. He was as short as their last one was tall. He seemed to know what he was doing, and he didn't tolerate anyone taking things into their own hands. From what Terry could tell, he made calculated decisions and seemed to follow orders to the letter. Terry hoped his decisions would keep them all safe.

Eighteen days out, Terry and Jack were taking a break; the platoon had set up a safe harbour while they stopped for lunch. They had put in a solid morning's walk and made good progress, with no enemy contacts.

"What do you think of Hart?" Terry asked Jack while he heated a can. Earlier that day, Hart, the machine gunner, had given a detailed rundown of what he would do to a VC if he got his hands on one. The men had made light of it, but Terry wasn't impressed. They were people too, no different to Hart, or himself for that matter, and this was their country. If they were going to die, they deserved to die with dignity.

"I reckon he's a bit of a surly bugger. Just don't know which way he'd jump if pushed."

"Boss'll be keeping his eye on him, I reckon."

"Hope so," Jack mumbled.

"So, what are you planning to do for your leave?" Terry asked, spooning the contents of his meal into his mouth and screwing up his face. It tasted as bad as it looked.

"I have to go into Vũng Tàu."

"You don't have to, mate. I thought about flying over to Hong Kong or Singapore for a few days, but to be honest, I can't be–"

"No," Jack interrupted. "You don't understand. *I have to.*"

"Why?"

"You know that girl I met in Vungers when I was on leave?"

"That bar girl?"

"Actually, her name's Mai Linh."

Terry's spoon stopped midway to his mouth.

"And she's pregnant."

Terry almost choked. "So?"

"It's mine." Jack's voice had dropped almost to almost a whisper.

"Yeah, and I suppose she told you that."

"Yeah."

"And you believe her?"

"No reason not to."

"There are hundreds of reasons not to. And they're probably all American, Aussie or Kiwi reasons."

"I believe her."

"Jesus," Terry finally said. He was desperately trying to think of the name of the girl he'd slept with that night in Vungers. He was sure it was Mai Linh. But how common was that name? Surely there were plenty of girls with that name.

He put the can down and reached for his tea. He needed tea, tea with a good dollop of condensed milk in it. What if they had slept with the same girl? What if he was the father? He looked at Jack. His mate was dragging heavily on a cigarette and looked like he had the weight of the world on his shoulders. The best thing Jack could do would be to walk away. Go home to Evelyn and forget about this girl. Terry's mind was spinning as it processed the implications.

"What about Evelyn?"

"What about her?" Jack hissed.

"You're not going to tell her, are you?"

"Nope. And neither are you."

"Why are you going to see the bar girl again? Why not walk away?"

"Don't be an arsehole, Terry. If it's my baby, I should help support it."

"*If* it's your baby. A baby over here's the last thing you need."

Jack tossed the dregs of his cup at the ground, hauled himself up to full height and looked down at Terry.

"What the fuck would you know?"

He walked off, leaving Terry to stare after him. Jack took things too seriously. *Far* too seriously.

At the end of their third week, Three Section encountered one small group of NVA and managed to take them by surprise, killing twelve. Then during the fourth week, Jack stepped into a wire and was incredibly lucky to notice it before he lifted his boot. He motioned for Terry while the rest of the Section took cover and waited.

The wire had caught between Jack's bootlaces, and being unable to tell exactly how much pressure had been put on the wire, Terry had to remember some of the tricks he had learned in Terendak. While the sweat poured off him, he managed to save Jack from a certain-death situation. If he had stuffed up and triggered the mine, both he and Jack would have gone sky high, and Three Section would have been picking up bits of them for the rest of the afternoon.

Just as Terry disarmed the mine, they realised there was a company of VC coming towards them, and the section sat rigid, waiting for them to pass. Once they had, the order came through to trail them. Enemy activity had increased in the past few weeks, and so far, no one could figure out what the enemy was up to.

Jack and Terry trailed them at a safe distance. They appeared to be making a beeline for the Long Hải Hills. Dodger radioed in the battalion's position, and minutes later, the ground shuddered and the sky filled with flames and smoke as three jets roared across the sky above them and disappeared. Whiskey Company was right there to pick off any fleeing stragglers, but by the end of the firefight, they had lost Hart who'd been hit by a sniper during the contact.

Reports of Terry's bravery in disarming the mine spread; by the time they had made it back to camp, he was a hero, and everyone wanted to shout him a beer. It was three days before Christmas, and on the twenty-seventh, he would get the five days leave due to him. As far as he was concerned, he couldn't have asked for a better Christmas present.

Terry didn't care if all he did was swim, lie on the beach or sleep. Since his three-day leave in September, he had been out on operations and patrols almost every day, and he was exhausted. The leave could not have come at a better time.

On the morning their leave kicked in, Terry and Jack caught a lift into Vũng Tàu. Terry was spending his week at the Peter Badcoe Club, and although Jack would check in his rifle at the club, Terry knew he would not be staying there, and he probably wouldn't see Jack again until he collected his weapon at the end of their leave.

Dressed in shorts, t-shirt and jandals, Terry headed for the bar. It wasn't yet lunchtime, but already several men were gathered at tables or outside on loungers drinking.

By the time he had eaten and had a couple of beers, he was bored stiff. Maybe he should have gone further afield. He decided to go into town to buy some postcards to send to the kids. His brother had a birthday coming up in a month, so he'd look for something to send him too.

He caught a taxi into town and was content to wander the busy streets. Children hawked cigarettes, cans of drink and sunglasses while old mama sans sold pineapples or other produce. Groups of men with cyclos, waited for fare-paying passengers. The familiar smells of street food cooking filled his nostrils, and even though it was early afternoon, girls hung around the doorways of clubs and bars touting for business.

By five, he was feeling hungry and decided to look for a restaurant he had seen earlier, advertising French cuisine. He thought it might be worth trying before he went back to the club for the evening. He had no interest in the bars or the girls, all he wanted to do was relax and do nothing.

The restaurant was quiet, three others sat at the back, drinking beer. It was still too early for most diners. Terry took a seat two tables back from the window. From his viewpoint, he could watch the street outside while he ate.

He ordered his meal and a beer and took out the postcards; he would scribble a few words while he waited. The young waitress brought his beer, and as he thanked her, something outside the window caught his eye. A woman. With a riot of copper hair. As he sat there staring at her, she stopped, glanced at her watch then looked up and directly at him. His heart skipped a beat. He couldn't believe his eyes. He was staring straight at Frankie.

Chapter 20

Frankie's stomach rumbled, reminding her she hadn't eaten since breakfast. She glanced down at her watch: twenty past five. Something smelt good. She looked up, and through the window of the restaurant she'd stopped outside. A man stared back at her. It took her only a second to register the face. *Terry Edwards!* She backtracked to the door and went in.

"Terry! Is it really you?"

Terry stood up. He seemed a little awkward, as though he didn't quite know how to greet her, so she stepped up to him, kissed him on the cheek and smiled. She felt him relax a little.

"Hello, Frankie."

"What are you doing in Vũng Tàu?" She couldn't believe, after all this time, he was standing right there in front of her.

"Having some downtime. You?"

"Combining work with pleasure. I came down to do an assignment on the nursing staff at the Thirty-Sixth Evac down here. Those women put their hearts and souls into their work, no doubt about it."

"I hope I never have to find out," he said. "Have you eaten? Do you want to join me?"

"I'd love to."

Terry pulled a chair out for her and motioned for a waitress. "You look tired. Been a tough week?"

"Every week's a tough week."

"Oh?"

"I guess I'm just battle weary. I can't believe how green I was when I first arrived in country."

"Weren't we all?"

She nodded in agreement, and after placing her order with the waitress, sat back and lit a cigarette. "You seem a little more battle weary than the last time I saw you, too."

"How can you tell?"

"I don't know." She paused as she studied him and tapped the ash off the end of her cigarette into an ashtray. "You're a little leaner, and there's something in your eyes that tells me you've been there. Seen things."

"Good guess on both counts."

What she wanted to add was that she thought he was even better looking than when she'd last seen him. He was tanned bronze from all the exposure to the sun, and his hair was bleached lighter than she remembered. She also couldn't help but notice the way his muscles flexed under his t-shirt as he reached for his beer.

"So, have you finished your assignment?" Terry asked.

"Yeah. I've got a couple of days off so thought I'd stay down here. Find out why it's called the Riviera of the South."

They talked as they ate, and she realised Terry was the first guy she'd spoken to over here who didn't try to talk her out of being a combat photographer. She was pleasantly surprised at how talking to Terry made her feel like she was catching up with an old friend.

She was beginning to make a name for herself over here, but it had taken six months of total commitment. He sat and listened to her talk about the hospital and the soldiers she'd seen there and asked her questions about her assignments, and she told him about the companies she had been out with and the attitudes of the different commanding officers.

"I think I owe you an apology," she said finally.

"Oh? For talking my leg off?"

She laughed and pretended to look under the table. "Well, maybe two apologies then."

"Go on. What's the second one for?"

"For ignoring you. You rang the office looking for me."

"Yeah. I had three nights off here, and I thought you might be able to get down for a night or two."

"I could have. I'm really sorry." The truth was, he would have been just what the doctor ordered. She'd been out with 173rd Airborne, and they'd walked straight into an ambush, suffering heavy losses. She made it out with a few scrapes and bruises, nothing serious, but she'd shut herself away in her apartment for two days, drinking herself into a stupor, trying to erase the images of the mangled and bloody bodies from her head.

"I wasn't in a good headspace, but you probably would have been a good diversion."

"Thanks. I think."

"I'm sorry. I promise I won't ignore you again."

"Apology accepted. Feel like a walk on the beach?"

"Okay."

He picked up the bill while she collected her bag and camera, and they caught a taxi to Front Beach.

"I've never been to this beach."

"It's the one the locals use, apparently. The allied forces use Back Beach, on the other side. It's portioned off, Kiwis and Aussies use one part, while the Americans use another and the Koreans another."

"I didn't know that."

"I think Back Beach is nicer, but this one has these little bars and stalls all the way along. The other beach isn't as developed. Though, I guess in a few years we might not even recognise it."

They walked the length of the beach, stopping to buy cold drinks, and then sat watching the sea, until Frankie could no longer stifle a yawn.

"God, you must be exhausted, and I'm keeping you up."

"I am," she agreed. "But I'm also enjoying this. At the risk of sounding weird, you somehow make the horrors of this war seem like a lifetime away." She glanced at him then turned back to the beach. They were sitting on a concrete step, and he was staring out across the sea to the horizon, his body silhouetted by a street light.

"You're not weird at all. You might be a little crazy putting yourself in danger over and over again just to get a few pictures, but that's not being weird."

Frankie laughed. "So that's what the attraction is. We're both crazies!" Laughing, she elbowed him playfully, and he responded by wrapping an arm around her.

It was hard to explain how she felt about him. Their lovemaking had been incredible, but their friendship wasn't just based on sex. Most importantly, he made her feel safe and protected, and she wished she could take him with her on every assignment she went on.

She had been in Vietnam just over six months now, and had seen some horrific sights. She was slowly learning to distance herself from them; if she put her camera lens to her eye, she could persuade herself it was the camera seeing the dead and wounded, not her. Sometimes it worked, sometimes it didn't. And sometimes, the camera just wasn't big enough to act as a shield against the horrors of war.

Most times, she couldn't get back to her little apartment quick enough. She would stand in the shower and cry, not for the situation she was in or for what she'd seen, but for all of the boys who were losing their lives every day. The boys she'd made friends with, who stopped and spoke to her while they were out on an operation, and who, hours later were killed by a bullet or a mine. There were five hundred thousand American soldiers in Vietnam now, and sometimes she also felt like crying for the ones who hadn't even arrived yet.

"Walk me back to my hotel?"

"Sure."

There was no curfew on the streets of Vũng Tàu, and although it was well after ten, there were still people out walking and on bicycles, though much of the traffic had died down. Vũng Tàu somehow felt distanced from the war, even though the town was full of soldiers and supported an American logistics base, an Australian hospital, and a military airbase.

She led the way down the street, away from the beach, and after crossing several streets, they stopped outside a sprawling two-storied hotel.

"Nice," he said, looking up at the windows. "Beats Miss Lilac's."

"You remember my digs."

"I remember Miss Lilac. She terrified me."

Frankie smiled.

"You're not the only one to say that. Why don't you stay the night?"

"Sure you're okay with me staying?"

Frankie laughed. "I wouldn't have asked if I wasn't." She took his hand and led him through the entrance into a large foyer. "Wait here while I collect the key."

He nodded, and when she returned, he was sitting on one of the steps of the hotel's grand, sweeping staircase.

"This staircase is seriously impressive," he whispered. "You do realise I expect to be equally as impressed by the beds."

"I'm sure you won't be disappointed." Taking his hand, she led him up to the first floor and along an elegantly decorated corridor to her room.

Chapter 21

"Aren't you supposed to be back in New Zealand?" Frankie pushed herself up off her towel, propping herself up on one elbow. She'd been meaning to ask him why he was still in the country but she kept forgetting.

Terry was lying on his back with one arm draped over his face to keep the sun out of his eyes. He had a nice body: lean, tanned and muscled, and his hair was dishevelled from their earlier swim.

"Yeah."

He didn't move.

"So, why are you still here?"

"'Cause I'm just as crazy as you." He turned his head to look at her and smiled.

"Tell me something I don't know."

He pushed himself up to rest on his elbow too, so they were the same height and their faces closer together.

"I joined Whiskey Company."

She let out a low whistle. "You just won Crazy of the Year title with that one. You had the chance to go home, and you opted to stay? Definitely crazier than me."

"Maybe." He leaned forward and kissed her.

His lips tasted salty, and his eyes smiled at her.

"How long is this tour?" she asked, after kissing him again.

"Twelve months."

"Holy shit. That's impressive." She studied his face, trying to read the reasons behind his signing up for a second tour, but his face gave nothing away. "Promise me one thing."

"For you, Copper, anything," he replied.

"Don't get yourself killed."

"I don't plan to."

"Good. Feel like another swim?"

She was up and already running across the hot sand and was halfway to the water by the time he caught up.

An hour later, they caught a taxi back to the hotel. They ordered lunch to be delivered to Frankie's room and after sharing a shower, sat on the queen-sized bed in their underwear eating their food while The Rolling Stones played on the radio.

"Want to go dancing tonight?" Frankie asked. "I have an invite to a New Year's Eve party at The Grand Hotel."

"Oh, I'd completely forgotten what day it was. Would I have to smarten up?"

"Yes, of course."

"I didn't bring anything flash."

"Well, let's go shopping and find you something."

"Will I get to wear these strides again?" Terry asked Frankie as he tried on the fourth pair of dress trousers with the shirt he'd chosen.

"Of course you will."

"I meant, with you," he teased.

"Perhaps."

"Well then, if there's a chance these are for a 'once only' occasion–" he unzipped the trousers.

"We'll take these." Frankie nodded to the little Vietnamese man, waiting with an arm draped in discarded shirts and trousers. He nodded, took the trousers and retreated. Frankie turned her attention back to Terry. "It will totally depend on how well you can dance tonight." She placed a hand on his chest and pushed him back into the crudely made changing cubicle.

"Oh, baby, you forget," he whispered huskily. "I'm dynamite on the dance floor."

She unbuttoned his shirt, desperate to remove it, and he hastily pushed her skirt up her thighs to her hips.

At that moment, they were oblivious to everything and everyone; the world ceased to exist. They made love in the cubicle with a burning intensity. If anyone had dared to open the curtaining, neither of them would have noticed, they were driven by the moment, by the knowledge that by this time next week, either of them could be killed out in the field. But for now, they were young and very much alive.

They caught a taxi to The Grand Hotel and joined all the other couples who had fled Saigon for the same reasons she had, for a reprieve from the war. Frankie spotted a couple of journalists she recognised, with their Vietnamese girlfriends, and a commanding officer from an American infantry unit she'd been out with two weeks earlier.

She explained to Terry that journalists always got invites to these things, especially in Saigon, and now she was making a name for herself, she was suddenly on all the guest lists. She introduced Terry to everyone she knew; they were interested in where he was based and told him they'd only heard great things about the Kiwis and their skills in the bush.

Frankie wore a gorgeous evening gown made of Vietnamese silk, strappy sandals, the pearl earrings that Nell had given her as a going away gift and an attractive pearl necklace she'd found to wear with them. Terry looked incredibly handsome too as he led her around the dance floor amongst the other couples. He was tall and devastatingly good-looking, with his sun-bleached hair and tanned skin. Together, they looked like the perfect young couple, and they could hardly keep their eyes off each other all evening.

They were there to celebrate the arrival of the new year, and the hotel was decorated to its fullest, with lavish bouquets of flowers, and balloons that were anchored to the tables to keep them from floating to the ceiling. There was a huge glittering ball hanging in the centre of the room, throwing sparkles of light at people as they danced, and the sound of glasses clinking could be heard above the laughter and chatter as waiters wandered the room offering drinks to the party-goers.

Seconds from midnight, the crowd burst into a synchronised countdown, and as the countdown reached four, Terry pulled her into his arms and kissed her. And as the rest of the crowd cheered and hoisted their glasses in a toast to the new year, Terry took her by the arm, and together they hurried from the room laughing.

Frankie contacted the AP office to let them know she would be staying in Vũng Tàu an extra two nights. She figured she was due a couple of extra days' leave, and it meant she could spend three more days with Terry. She had never put a man before her job; it was unheard of. But hell, she was due a break, and it would be a long time before she would get another. Unless the war came to a sudden end, and although there were rumours that General Westmoreland had pronounced the South was close to winning, Frankie seriously doubted that would happen anytime soon.

Frankie and Terry spent the following three days doing as little as possible. They lounged by the hotel pool, ate at local cafés and restaurants, and one morning got up early and went for a walk through the streets, with Frankie shooting photos of the locals. As they explored the backstreets, she took photos of Terry too and even stopped a young woman to ask if she could take a photo of them together. On Front Beach, she took photos of the local fishermen as they pulled the fish from their nets. Terry helped pull a small fish from a net and held it up to show her; she laughed at the way he screwed up his face and she clicked off another couple of photos. When a fisherman offered to take their photo, Frankie handed over her camera, hoping the photo would turn out okay.

On the last night, they ate dinner in Frankie's room, and when they thought the hotel's guests would all be in bed, they crept down to the pool and went skinny dipping, trying to keep their voices down so as not to be detected.

Before they knew it, it was time for Terry to head back to the club to collect his rifle and catch his ride back to Nui Dat, and she had to get back to Saigon; she had stories to cover and couldn't afford to spend any more time off work.

Terry was packing his gear when his fingers touched something cold in the bottom of his bag. He pulled out the little marble Buddha that he had bought for her months ago; he had forgotten he still had it.

"This is for you," Terry said, handing her the gift.

"Thank you."

"He's a happy Buddha. Whenever you're in a bad place, find him, think of me and smile." He grinned at her. "He'll look after you in my absence."

"I will. He'll go everywhere with me." They kissed, tenderly at first, but then with a passion and urgency that came from the realisation they may not see each other again for a long time, or, if luck was against them, maybe ever. They were both well aware that they had jobs that could get them killed.

She'd had a great holiday, and she kept telling herself theirs was a friendship that suited them both. They were lucky enough to be having fun in an environment where every minute of every day, hundreds of young men were dying. There were no promises to each other, other than to do their best to stay alive. Both knew that once they left Vũng Tàu, the real world would be waiting, and things would be totally different.

Chapter 22

Despite being busy, Frankie missed Terry for the first few days. She missed him opening doors for her and pulling out her chair before she sat down. Missed him laughing at her corny jokes and teasing her about the colour of her hair and her freckles. It felt like he was the one sane person in her life, and he made her feel like a woman. He didn't put any pressure on her or demand more of her than she was prepared to give. In her eyes, he was perfect, and she found herself wondering if there was any chance they might get together after the war was over. She reprimanded herself. She knew better than to make plans or think about what she was going to do when she finally left Vietnam. None of them was in a position to do that.

Her days were always full: jumping on a flight to somewhere, joining patrols or accompanying a journalist on an assignment, and when she wasn't out on assignment, she was working in the darkroom or helping one of their journalists. It was mostly in the evenings, when she was on her own in her apartment, that she thought about Terry. And on the nights when she was curled up in the jungle, trying to sleep, the thought he might be out there trying to do the same thing, somehow made her feel closer to him.

She tried to tell herself that what they had was just a great friendship, it couldn't be anything more, but she found herself talking to his photo, propped against a stack of books beside her bed. It was a crazy thing to do, but somehow it helped her feel not quite so alone. It comforted her to think he was just there, laughing at her, even if he was waving that stupid fish in the air. The couple of photos she had printed off were now her prized possessions.

As it neared the end of January, the atmosphere around the city changed, in subtle ways that went undetected by most foreigners. Rumours something was about to happen had spread through the news agencies, and although the North had declared a ceasefire, several of the journalists that had been keeping their ears open believed the Vietnamese Lunar New Year was a likely time. The city seemed somehow quieter than usual, and when they'd shared a lunch in the office three days earlier, this had been a topic of discussion. Celebrations had been banned in previous years, but President Thiệu had sanctioned them this year, and with the countrywide ceasefire, the city was gearing up for monumental celebrations.

Louis had invited her to accompany him to a party President Thiệu's wife was throwing. It was the first 'big' party Frankie had been invited to, and Louis said it would not disappoint.

He told her that everyone who was anyone in Saigon would be there.

Frankie had a new dress made, and Miss Lilac styled her hair and told her she needed to wear make-up to help attract 'the man.' Frankie laughed. These days, appearance had gone out the window, but she agreed to have her make-up done and was surprised by how feminine it made her feel after experiencing all the dust, and grime and bloodshed of the battlefields.

"Who is this woman?" Louis asked when he arrived to collect her. He kissed her on both cheeks. "You look beautiful, Frankie," he stated as he waited for her to gather her wrap and camera and lock the door.

"Thank you. I almost feel human again. The girls at Miss Lilac's have obviously done a good job."

"You must first have a good foundation on which to work."

Frankie laughed. "I feel twenty years older than I did eight months ago."

"War ages us all. I am sure I have much more grey hair now than when I first arrived."

"Ah, but that makes you look so much more distinguished, Louis. Grey hair only ages a woman."

"Not always, *ma chérie*. Grey hair can be very elegant on a woman." He frowned at the Leica she had over her shoulder. "Do you never stop working?"

"No." She grinned. She had learned quickly that in Vietnam, anything could happen in the blink of an eye. The evening might not provide an opportunity for photos, but these days she never went anywhere without her camera.

Lights from the palace flooded the entrance, silhouetting the military police and palace guards. Once inside, Frankie could see they had spared no expense. Large floral arrangements, which towered over Frankie, lined the foyer and filled every room they entered. A small orchestra played quietly at the far end of the main ballroom as guests mingled and introduced each other. Frankie noticed a room to one side especially set up with tables that overflowed with every kind of food Frankie could think of with more lavish floral art centrepieces.

There were several journalists from the different agencies circulating, and naval officers and high-ranking army officers with their wives or girlfriends, too. She recognised a couple of President Thiệu's cabinet ministers, and although she didn't know as many as Louis did, she was beginning to connect names to faces.

Louis guided her around the room, introducing her to various guests, most of whom he had interviewed at some stage. She thought the New Zealand ambassador was lovely and his wife equally so. They told her they were flying to Tokyo in two days' time for a week's holiday, and they were looking forward to sampling the Japanese food.

Between introductions, Louis took great pleasure in filling her in on all the gossip. As they drank their way around the room, the band began to play a waltz, and Louis took her glass and deposited it on a passing tray then led her to the dance floor where he bowed graciously to her.

"I'm no good at waltzing." She laughed, recognising she had probably had enough champagne for one night.

"Follow my lead."

He held her firmly, and she let him lead her around the floor. At the end of the dance, he complimented her on her footwork, and she knew she had Terry to thank for that. By the third waltz, the commanding officer of a unit she had been out on an assignment with cut in on Louis, and he looked devastated. It felt like she was in a fairy tale. She was Cinderella at the ball, dancing alongside all these women dressed in their beautiful dresses, partnered by some of Saigon's wealthiest and most handsome men.

Frankie's dress had a tight bodice and a long, flowing skirt and, like many of the dresses here tonight, was made of the finest silks Vietnam had to offer. It had cost her a small fortune as had the strappy silver sandals she had bought to wear with it.

As the night wore on, the music changed to rock and roll numbers. This time, Frankie took Louis by the hand and pulled him out onto the dance floor, and it was his turn to tell her he felt uncomfortable and complain that he couldn't dance to this. However, after a while, he relinquished his inhibitions and lost himself in the music, along with all the others on the dance floor, as the staff circulated with silver trays of canapés and more glasses of champagne. At two-thirty in the morning, they all flooded out onto the manicured gardens to watch the fireworks.

Men threw endless strings of crackers, and everyone was laughing as they toasted Saigon and each other with cocktails, champagne, or beer.

"Why do they light crackers?" Frankie asked Louis over the noise of the exploding fireworks.

"It's always part of Tet celebrations. They drive out evil spirits."

Frankie nodded.

"The fireworks display is also a show of rank and wealth," he informed her as he put his arm around her to keep her warm. At that moment, Frankie realised how much of a friend he was to her. They had covered many assignments together, and he was like an older brother.

A couple of blocks away, the American Embassy was also due to light a spectacular display of fireworks. Then, right on three o'clock, Louis pulled her to one side.

"What's the matter," she asked, sensing he was worried about something.

"Listen," he said.

She could see he was straining to hear something above the sound of fireworks that now engulfed the city.

"What is it?" She couldn't hear anything except the overwhelming noise of the fireworks exploding.

"Come on," he said, grabbing her arm.

"What's wrong?" She almost had to run to keep up with him.

"I am sure I heard grenades."

"What?"

"Yes. Get your things. We must leave. Quickly."

Frankie rushed to the cloakroom to retrieve her wrap and camera. When she returned, Louis was waiting for her at the main entrance.

Outside, things still looked normal, although Frankie thought there seemed to be a bigger military presence than when they arrived. Louis took her by the hand, and they ran across the lawn towards the large double gates, but when they got there, they found they had been locked, and they were directed to use a smaller side gate that was unlocked especially for them.

"Why don't we take a taxi?" Frankie asked as they ran out onto the side street where she saw bright flashes of light that didn't look like fireworks explode across the sky.

"Because I have a feeling something is very wrong."

Just as he finished speaking, red tracer bullets crossed the street, and there was an almighty shudder as a rocket hit a target somewhere nearby.

"Oh, my God! What's going on?" Frankie whispered.

"They're attacking the city," Louis said. He crouched down, trying to keep a low profile as they made their way along the street. "Keep low and stay against the wall."

"Who's attacking?" she whispered, remaining close behind him.

"The NVA. Probably with help from VC guerillas."

As they moved up the street, keeping behind parked vehicles and trees, Frankie could smell the cordite. Another grenade exploded somewhere close by.

"The American Embassy is on Thong Nhut Street. We should try to get as close as possible," Louis said, just loud enough to be heard over the explosions.

"I'm right behind you," Frankie said. She was pleased she had worn flat sandals rather than heels. She lifted her dress and tucked it into her pants and hung her camera around her neck. It was much too dark to take photos. It was hard to see anything at all, except when the brilliant flashes of light filled the sky.

They moved up the street to the corner, protected behind one of the beautiful old trees that lined the road.

"If we head down there to the end of the street." Louis pointed up the street. "We should be about three hundred metres from the embassy."

Moving slowly, Frankie heard the whine of the next rocket before she felt it. The ground rumbled as it struck, and the street lit up like huge floodlights had been turned on. She made a lunge for the nearest tree as she tried to take in the scene that was unfolding before her.

"Come on," Louis yelled at her, and together they sprinted down Tu Do Street, past the Roman Catholic Basilica. There were military police behind trees and vehicles, and every few seconds, bright bursts of rifle fire illuminated the air before everything was plunged into darkness again.

They moved from tree to vehicle down the street, trying to make themselves as small as possible. From somewhere to their left, gun fire pinged against metal. Rapid machine-gun fire and grenades answered it, and Frankie was sure she could hear screaming.

As they got closer to the embassy, the end of the street was criss-crossed with tracers; for a brief moment, Frankie thought it looked like a giant neon cobweb. A jeep drove past them and slowed, then over the noise of the gunfire, she heard the sound of the motor rev then the crunch of metal. When the sky filled with light again, Frankie saw the driver slumped over the steering wheel. The attack was constant, and it seemed to be directed against the American Embassy.

Another flash further down the street indicated more mortar attacks, and they ducked behind a vehicle, waiting to make a dash for the other side of the street, to the protection of the embassy wall. There must have been VC everywhere.

There was no time to think or to feel scared. In the field, she always felt protected by the men around her, but here, they were on their own. Rockets stuck the embassy. It was still too dark to take any photos, but Louis would be able to file an accurate report of what had unfolded here. The palace, where they had come from, would be on lock-down, and she supposed most of the guests would be protected inside. They might not have got out either if Louis hadn't thought he heard grenades.

What looked to be a Citroën drove past with its headlights off and came to a halt not far from them. They were on the opposite side of the street to the embassy now, and Frankie could clearly see flashes from gun barrels inside the grounds. She wanted to get across the street; she wanted to be up against the wall, so she could get a better view of what was going on. As bullets hit the side of the parked Citroën Frankie thought she could duck behind the car and then make it safely to the wall. It would make a great vantage point.

Grabbing her skirt and holding it tight, she made a run for the car, hoping she wouldn't be seen. Once there, she crouched by the tyre and took a deep breath as she counted to five, then made a break for the embassy wall where she landed safely, flat on the footpath to avoid detection. Her heart raced in her chest. It was a terrifying firefight.

"Louis, I can see VC in the grounds!" There was no reply, and when she turned, Louis wasn't behind her. "Louis!" she hissed. Nothing. "Louis! Where are you?" She had followed him until she had broken cover and made a break for the car, and then the embassy wall. When she ran, she'd thought he was following her.

She strained to see if she could make him out on the other side of the street. It was still too dark. He may have found a better vantage point. While she was wondering where he was, a rocket hit a building about one hundred metres away. The blinding flash of light was enough for Frankie to make out a body lying on the road behind the Citroën. Instantly, she knew it was Louis.

"Louis!" she screamed, picking herself up and running towards him. He lay in a crumpled heap. She grabbed him under his arms, trying to drag him off the road. "Louis!"

He didn't respond. She looked around, but she couldn't yell for a medic; she was on her own. "Come on Louis." Tears began to spill from her eyes. "Come on, damn it. Don't die. Please." Her tears flowed freely now. "Don't die here, not like this."

She knelt in the dust and debris in her beautiful silk dress, with the man who had done so much for her when she first arrived in Saigon. And she couldn't find a pulse. She ran her hand over his face and hair as tears blurred everything around her. He was her closest friend, and he couldn't die.

"Lady! Lady!"

She had no idea how long she had been cradling Louis's head in her arms, but when she looked in the direction of the voice, a young soldier crouched beside her, his frame outlined in the murkiness of the dawning day. He reached out and took her arm.

"You need to move, lady."

"No. I can't leave Louis. He's been injured."

He knelt beside Louis and checked for a pulse.

"It's too late to save him, ma'am. He's dead. We gotta get you outta here."

"No. I'm press." But she didn't have her press card or any ID she could show him; then she remembered her camera.

The soldier hesitated.

"I'm Frankie Proctor from the Associated Press, and I want to get some photos. I've been here since the fighting started." She gently put Louis down, and the young soldier helped her up. If he noticed what she was wearing, he didn't comment. She must have looked a mess. The skirt on her dress was ripped, she had blood smeared on her bodice, and her hair and face were caked in concrete dust.

"Follow me," he said, sounding reluctant to let her anywhere near the embassy gate or building. "And stay down. We're still taking fire from the embassy."

"They've got inside?"

"Yes, ma'am, it looks like we've got several inside."

"How did they get into the compound?"

"Blew a hole in the outer wall down there." He nodded towards a hole further down the wall.

She and Louis had come from the other direction and had missed it.

"What about my colleague?"

"He's not going anywhere, ma'am. We'll take care of him when this is over."

He ran towards the front gate, and as they got close, he pulled her in behind the cover of the military police hut at the main gate, in time to see a dozen Hueys come in low over the surrounding buildings and treetops towards the embassy. One landed on the embassy roof, and Frankie watched as soldiers jumped down and scattered. At the same time, several of the Hueys opened fire on the grounds around the building, and an MP shoulder-charged the embassy's front door, allowing a group of soldiers to rush in. The resulting noise was deafening as grenades exploded inside the building drowning out the gunfire.

There was so much happening, and as wedges of daylight filtered through the dust to the street and the grounds before them, she took as many photos as she could. There was rubble everywhere, and everything was riddled with bullet holes. Men were running in all directions, and when she looked down, two dead soldiers were lying at her feet. She gasped as the reality of the situation hit her, and she remembered Louis.

A wireless crackled, and she heard the muffled voice of the operator.

"What's going on?" she asked, desperate to get in and get some close-up photos of the damage.

"We got 'em all, ma'am, except one little gook who's still inside."

For the briefest moment, there was silence, and then another volley of shots rang out, and the wireless crackled once again. Frankie took a photo of two military policemen as they hurried across the front lawn of the embassy, a wounded soldier between them. As soon as she heard the all clear on the radio, she was up and running towards the embassy building.

"Lady!"

But she was too quick for him as she bolted for the covered walkway up to the embassy door. All around, there were bodies of dead VC, each wearing a red armband, and blood was splattered across walls and on the large concrete planters that lined the front of the building. Death was everywhere. The lobby of the embassy was a tangled mess.

Frankie rushed from the main entrance of the building to the side gate where bodies of dead military police lay, and then headed to get photos of the hole that had been blown in the wall. She had two shots left, so she headed back to the main gate where she took a photo of the two dead soldiers and another of the choppers coming in. She had counted nineteen dead VC and five dead American soldiers. And Louis.

"I've got to get back to the office."

"It's not safe out there at the moment, ma'am, the whole city is under attack, and snipers are everywhere."

She nodded, her mind working faster than she could logically process information. She wasn't far from the bureau. She ran over to Louis. In the daylight, she could see his body was contorted and crumpled like a discarded rag doll. He had dried blood all over his mouth and down his chin, and he was covered in concrete dust.

As she studied his body, she discovered a gunshot wound in his chest, and his clothes were torn and blackened by the explosion. Through tears she searched through his pockets, until she found his wallet, flipped it open and found what she was looking for: his press card with his name and photo on it. She took it out, rolled him slightly and tucked the ID card inside his back trouser pocket, and then slipped his gold watch from his wrist and onto her own. If anyone tried to loot his body for valuables or money, they would find nothing; she would make sure his family got his things. She kissed his forehead.

"I'll miss you, Louis."

"If you wait, I'll find someone to escort you," the young soldier said, appearing at her side.

"Thank you. I'll wait with my colleague. He was a journalist with the Associated Press."

The soldier nodded and walked back towards the gate. The air thundered with the sound of more choppers as soldiers checked the bodies that lay around the grounds and escorted the two prisoners they'd captured away. General Westmoreland stepped down out of one of the choppers. He had arrived to inspect the damage first-hand and soldiers ran around ensuring he was safe.

In the midst of all the activity, no one noticed Frankie slip from behind the Citroën and disappear.

Chapter 23

Frankie woke to the sound of banging. It took her a minute to remember where she was as the thumping continued. She swung her legs out of bed and staggered towards the door.

She had come home from the AP bureau exhausted, locked herself in her apartment and stepped out of her dress and into the shower in an effort to erase the events of the early hours of the morning. All attempts to do so had failed and all she could see was Louis's battered body and his face covered in blood and dust.

When the shower failed to offer any solace, she carried the whisky bottle to the bed and fished in her bag for the Marlboro packet she knew was there. She found the pack, and with trembling fingers, she flipped the lid and removed a pre-rolled joint. Out in the field, men died all around her, but she didn't know any of them; this was different, Louis was someone she'd known well, someone who had taken her under his wing and helped her get a job, and she had loved him dearly. She resorted to smoking the joint and downing several glasses of whisky to help stop her brain reliving the morning's events.

It was January thirty-first: the first day of the Lunar New Year and Louis was dead. Beautiful, kind, Louis. She owed him everything.

"Who is it?" she asked, worried it might be VC, and that the city might have fallen.

"It is Miss Lilac."

Frankie unbolted the door, and it flew open as the overbearing figure of her landlady pushed her way in.

"I not seen you for days!" She bustled across the room, flung open a window then turned to Frankie. "Your boss, he look for you. You need shower and come down to salon. My girls make you beautiful again."

Frankie shook her head.

"Thank you. I'll be fine. I just needed to sleep it off."

"You need go to work, so you can pay rent to Miss Lilac." She glanced around the apartment. "Leave key with me. I will get cleaner to clean room."

Frankie smiled and nodded her thanks. "I will. Thank you."

The photos Frankie took during the attack on the embassy made the front page of the *New York Times, The Washington Post* and almost every newspaper in America, Australia and New Zealand. South Vietnam was still reeling from the surprise attack.

"We suspect this attack will have an impact on the support Westy and LBJ get back home." The bureau chief had called a briefing to update everyone. "As you know, there's a seven o'clock curfew in place, and there are still pockets of resistance throughout the city. Cholon was hardest hit, and in the North, Hue is still under siege. George, I want you and Frankie to head up to Hue and cover the fighting there. Ed, you get what you can in the Chinese quarter, find a family, relations, something first-hand. Westy went live only a couple of weeks ago telling everyone that the fight was winding down, that there was light at the end of the tunnel, but this has blown that theory right out of the water."

While Frankie had been sleeping off her drug and alcohol binge, General Westmoreland had shown up at the Five O'Clock Follies and declared that the attack on Saigon had been a ploy to distract from the NVA attack on Khe Sanh. But it was more than that. It had been revealed that the NVA and VC had attacked every major city in the South, and if nothing else, it confirmed the allied forces had no show in hell of winning this war. The war effort was rapidly losing the support of the men in the field.

Frankie flew up to Hue and found the same scenario. Both sides were taking a battering, and the body count was climbing rapidly. In the past week, Frankie had seen a lifetime's worth of death and destruction.

It was so far removed from anything back home; it was a whole other world. And as she sat huddled in the rubble outside the ancient city walls, she reached into her bag and felt amongst the film canisters at the bottom for the little marble figure she knew was there and felt comforted when her fingers finally curled around it.

After three days in Hue, George and Frankie flew back to Saigon. She was relieved to be away from the constant barrage of mortars and

RPGs. Relieved to put on a dress and feel like a woman again. She knew she needed to take a few softer photo assignments.

Just for a few days.

Chapter 24

Terry made himself comfortable for the night on the patch of ground he had prepared for himself. The supply chopper had not long left, and the men all had their packs full again and were enjoying a hearty feed. The months were running into each other, and the missions outside the wire were becoming more dangerous.

He'd received two letters with this last drop but hadn't had a chance to read them yet. Jack had also received mail, and as usual, he seemed to disappear into a hole of depression as he read it. Terry was worried about him and was sure his moods were related to the bar girl in Vũng Tàu that he had got pregnant.

Terry admired Jack's sense of loyalty, but as far as he was concerned, all Jack's loyalty should belong to Evelyn, not some girl from a knocking shop. Jack had received a letter from Evelyn to say she was making another trip to Vietnam, and Terry knew he was worried about seeing her again. The only thing Terry worried about was Jack doing his duty and keeping his mind on his job. Jack could spend all the time he liked worrying once he was back inside the wire. Terry knew he needed to keep an eye on his mate.

Jack got up and disappeared, and as Terry sat eating, he studied the writing on his envelopes. The first was from his brother, Simon; he recognised his writing, but the second he didn't recognise. He dropped them on the ground while he finished eating his meal, then, after a quick rinse of his cup, he filled it with water to make himself a cuppa.

Letters were few and far between, but then he had never been good at writing letters either. He opened the envelope from his brother, revealing two pages. Simon had drawn a picture of Terry with his gun and what looked like dead bodies lying on the ground. Flames were coming from the gun barrel, and he had drawn little speech bubbles with words in them, just like in the *Commando* comics. Terry grinned; it was clear he was into all this soldier stuff.

There wasn't a lot of news. A bit about his birthday and a 'thank you' for the present Terry had sent him. He had a new baby brother whom they'd named Tristan. Terry winced, poor kid, where the hell did they find that name? Simon told him he was playing rugby at school, and they had won every game so far this season. At the bottom of the second page, he had written that everyone sent their love. Obviously, his mother had told him to add that. Terry made a mental note to write to him as soon as he got back to camp.

Terry added a squeeze of condensed milk to his tea, stirred vigorously then took a sip, feeling the hot liquid slide through his body. It was thirty minutes until stand-to. He picked up the second letter. It wasn't his mother's handwriting, or his sister's or father's. He studied the stamp. Vietnamese. Strange.

He flipped it over and opened it. Inside, there was a single page, written in tidy handwriting.

> *Dear Terry,*
>
> *I'm keeping my fingers crossed this letter finds you. If you're reading this in camp or out in the field, well, I guess it means you're still alive and doing your best to help Whiskey and the great American machine stop the NVA and VC.*
>
> *I was thinking of you tonight, and I decided to write to you, for no reason other than it somehow makes you seem closer—and I'm lonely. Silly, I know. It's worst at night. When I get back to my apartment, the loneliness screams at me, and I'm afraid that my tendency to look at the bottom of a bottle is becoming a too-frequent habit. I hate falling asleep because of the things I see. It's like experiencing everything twice. The whisky makes everything go away. For a while. I'm sure you understand what I mean.*
>
> *Work is busy, which I'm thankful for, especially after Louis was killed on the morning of Tet. I keep telling myself not to get involved with anyone, or make friends, because if you get too attached to someone, you risk losing them.*
>
> *Everyone in the office is in shock over the death of Bobby Kennedy, and they'd only just got over Martin*

Luther King dying.

How many times can a heart break?

Sorry, I probably sound morbid!

I've taken to keeping a journal to record my thoughts when I'm sent on assignments.

It's hard to write in it sometimes. But I'm told it's good therapy, although I can't help but wonder if it doesn't make the nightmares last longer. Who knows, maybe one day I'll write a book. (funny idea)

I hope you don't mind me writing to you, and I hope I haven't made myself sound pathetic. But you know me, I can talk the leg off a chair!

I was at the Majestic the other night and as I stood and watched the fire flashes north of the city, I wondered where you were and what you were doing. I remembered how I felt safe and protected when you held me, and how I felt that the world could have ended, but you would still have kept me safe. Then I thought about you and wondered who was keeping you safe. But I guess your mates in Whiskey are doing that job.

He flipped the page over.

I think I'm starting to ramble again! Anyway, keep your head down and don't be anyone's hero. And I have my smiling Buddha here to keep me company every day.

If you get a chance, let me know you're okay. xx

Copper.

She had written to him. He reread the letter then carefully folded the page, and tucked it and his brother's letter deep into his pack for safekeeping. He sure missed her.

With butterflies singing in his heart, he gathered his gear and joined the others.

Chapter 25

Terry noticed Jack had been assigned to look after Evelyn while she was in country. He was gone for almost a week, and Terry wondered if their commanding officer had got wind of the business with the bar girl in Vũng Tàu.

Not long after Jack got back, he returned to Vũng Tàu. Terry later found out that the girl had given birth, and Jack had been given permission to visit her and the baby. Terry thought he was only digging a deeper hole, but in the end, it wasn't any of his business, unless it interfered with Jack's job as a soldier.

Since the Tet Offensive at the end of January, patrols had been relentless, and Terry, like many of the others in Whiskey, was feeling the strain of being constantly alert to everything and not having enough time inside the wire at Nui Dat. Even the shitty jobs like being on spraying detail were a welcome relief these days.

The only thing motivating the men was the news from the commanding officer that each platoon would be allocated three nights leave on rotation when the company returned from this operation. As Terry sat in the chopper watching the patchwork of lush green and dead jungle pass below, he wondered if he could get hold of Frankie to let her know.

He had replied to her last letter when he got back to camp. He'd written a single page thanking her and telling her just knowing she was thinking of him, was enough to keep him safe. His reward was a further two letters, one each month. Although it was almost the end of July now, and he hadn't had a letter from her in a while.

He watched a Huey draw level with his chopper, and as they dropped down closer to the LZ, the door gunner swept his machine gun from side to side. He wondered why she hadn't written. Had she been injured? He couldn't allow himself to think about her being killed somewhere out in the bush. No, he realised if anything had happened to a female photographer, the news would have spread like wildfire. Especially if she was a Kiwi.

He had four months in country left, and then he was done. There was no sticking around for a third tour. He had to go home. But he would have to leave Frankie here. She had a job to do. Someone nudged him with their elbow, and he turned to see his section commander give him the thumbs up. Terry nodded. They were getting close to the LZ. Terry glanced across at Jack. He was miles away. Terry kicked the underside of his boot and tilted his head at him. Jack grinned. Terry studied the faces of the men inside the crowded cabin of the chopper. He wondered what each one was thinking about at that moment.

He missed Smokey, Murph, and Blackie and wondered what they were all up to these days. Maybe he would catch up with them when he got home.

The chopper landed in a cloud of swirling green smoke, and the men quickly jumped out and ran for cover. They would start walking shortly and harbour up some ten kilometres away. It was stinking hot, and already the sweat was running off him. They had received news that back home they were having snow storms in the South Island and thousands of livestock were dying. What he wouldn't give for an hour in the snow.

It was their third day, and the company had stopped for a lunch break.

"This is the best damned cuppa I've ever had," Terry stated to no one in particular. It was good to get his pack off and sit down for a while, and the hot, sweet liquid was just what he needed.

"Could go a beer," Rusty Taylor commented.

"Me too," Jack added.

Terry lifted his cup to his lips, and as he did so, something hit the ground near his boot, sending up puffs of dirt. *Shit.*

"Sniper!" In one quick movement, he dropped his cup, made a grab for his rifle, and dived for a small clump of scrub. Around him, everyone was scrambling, trying to find cover.

"Where's it coming from?" the LT yelled.

"One o'clock," Terry yelled back.

"Got one at two o'clock!" someone else yelled.

There was silence, and then a machine gun opened up.

"Someone take out that gun!" the boss yelled.

Eddie Dunstan yelled back and tossed a grenade. Shockwaves from the explosion eliminated two VC and a machine gun, but they were still taking fire.

"Coles, Edwards, eleven o'clock, yours. Rusty, Lewis, five o'clock. Let's get these bastards."

Little puffs of dirt sprayed into the air around Terry. He hugged the ground and snaked his way towards a clump of trees. The bullets stopped then resumed from another direction. Terry knew they were up against AK-47s and from what he could tell, it sounded like at least half a dozen. Jack signalled he was going to break cover and fire; Terry would provide his cover. They managed to hit two more VC. From several feet away, Lewis tossed another grenade, and as suddenly as it all started, it was over. The bush fell quiet again.

The boss sent a team out on reconnaissance; it looked like a small group of VC had walked into them. Terry was gutted he'd lost his only decent cuppa of the day, and the boss ordered everyone to head out in ten minutes. Orders from HQ were to head in the direction the VC had come from.

However, this time Three Section didn't take the lead, they were further back in the formation, and when they came under attack again, they held their position and waited for One Section to call them up. The LT wasn't mucking around this time, and he called in an air strike. Thirty minutes later, they were at their harbour site for the night.

They encountered no more NVA or VC for the rest of their operation, and when it was over, they headed back to their designated LZ to await the choppers.

They had two nights back in Nui Dat on camp detail, and then they were to go out on day patrols for the next four weeks. HQ wanted the men relatively close to the camp while the sections took their allocated leave.

Terry was on patrols during the day, and at night he manned the bunkers on the wire until it got dark. On his first night, he took paper and a pen with him.

Hey Copper,

A quick note to you while I'm sitting in this bunker on perimeter duty. Just to let you know, we're getting three nights out of the place soon. I know this is a long shot, but is there any chance you could get to Vungers in two weeks? If everything goes to plan, I'll be there on

*Friday 16th August. Or maybe I could find a way to get
to Saigon.*

*It's been a hard slog lately, and I miss your
freckles.*
Let me know if you're going to be around.

Terry read the letter over and finally signed it, *Your boy from
Foxton.* He folded it, slid it into an envelope and pushed it into his breast
pocket.

In the morning, Terry rushed to the postal office and mailed his
note to Frankie, sending a silent prayer skyward she would get it in time.

"What are you up to this early?" Rusty Taylor asked, joining him
on the way to get breakfast.

"Wanted to mail a letter."

"Wife?"

"No. A friend." He hadn't told anyone about Frankie, not even
Jack. If he told people, it would make the relationship seem real, and
besides, they didn't even have a real relationship. Neither of them could
afford to, they were just good friends. "How about you? Got a wife back
home?"

"Yeah. Her name's Sharon. We've only been married a year."

"I bet she's missing you."

"She'd better be." Rusty grinned. "I won't be able to get home fast
enough in November."

They walked into the mess and joined some of the others eating
breakfast.

"Letter for you, Edwards," Jack said, tossing the envelope onto the
end of Terry's bed.

"Cheers, mate." It had been exactly five days since he had posted
his note to Frankie, and he knew without even looking at it, she had sent
him a reply. He was cleaning his rifle. He would read it when he was on his
own. He folded it in half and slipped it into his pocket.

"Well?"

"Well, what?" Terry looked up from his cleaning.

"Aren't you going to open it? Must be important, it's got an AP stamp on the top of it. What's AP stand for?"

"The Auckland Pussycats," he said casually, fitting his rifle back together.

Jack scratched his head.

"Haven't you heard of the Pussycat Club in Auckland?"

"Nope."

"Well, I joined up. It's probably my membership card. I'll be hitting that place as soon as I get back. Full of beautiful girls in nothing but bikinis."

"Yeah, right. What's with the Vietnamese stamp?"

"Perhaps they have a branch over here for us boys."

He could tell Jack didn't know whether or not to believe him, but he wasn't ready to tell him about Frankie. He knew if he did, it would be all over camp in no time. Rusty and Eddie joined them, and they sat and played a few hands of poker before Terry had to take over on perimeter duty.

In the last of the light before stand-to, Terry unfolded the envelope. He studied the writing then turned it over to rip it open, wondering what Frankie had to say. There was one sheet of paper. He was almost afraid to read it in case she was writing to tell him she couldn't make it.

It was now or never. Unfolding the sheet of paper revealed a brief note scribbled in blue ink, and the Associated Press bureau address in the top corner:

> *Terry,*
> *If you can get to Saigon, I will be in town for two nights.*
>
> *Flat out—on my way out now, heading up to the DMZ. I'm joining a recon team with the 1st Marine Division. Hope it doesn't get too rough.*
>
> *Go to the Continental. I've paid for a room for us. Room 22. Let's catch up in style. If all goes to plan, I should be back by the time you arrive.*
> *See you soon, and I miss you too!*

Love Copper

He punched the air with sheer joy. It was the best news and more than he had dared hope for. All he had to do now was get himself to Saigon. Then she would be all his, for two glorious nights.

Chapter 26

Terry hitched a ride to Tan Son Nhut Air Base with an American chopper pilot he'd become friendly with, and from there, caught a taxi to the Continental. It was Friday, and not yet four. He headed to the reception desk at the Continental and asked for the key to room twenty-two.

"Room twenty-two." The young woman repeated, handing the key over. "Please let us know if you require anything during your stay," the young woman stated as he signed the registration document.

"Certainly will. Thanks." He had obviously arrived before Frankie. "Actually"–he hesitated–"where could I buy some flowers?"

"There is a shop selling flowers on the corner of this block, sir, or we can buy some for you and bring them up to your room."

"I'll get them. Which direction?"

The woman pointed up the street in the direction of the Rex Hotel.

"Thank you."

Orchids. Frankie would love them. He headed down the street and found the small shop, which sold all kinds of flowers. He chose a bunch of pretty stems and headed back to the hotel. Taking the stairs two at a time, he climbed two floors and walked down the hall until he found room twenty-two. The room was quiet, confirming Frankie still hadn't arrived.

He looked around. Four-thirty. The queen-sized bed looked so inviting. Windows looked out over Lam Son Square, and he remembered most of the buildings from the time he had been posted to guard duty at the Caravelle.

He lay the flowers on the bed and dropped his bag on a chair. Perhaps he should get a drink at the bar while he waited. There was a knock on the door. His pulse leapt, and he looked in the mirror to check his hair and shirt. He felt like a nervous teenager on a first date. *Come on Terry, mate. Pull it together.* He hurried to open the door for her.

The woman from the reception desk stood there. She handed him a vase.

"I thought you might like this to put your flowers in. Would you like me to arrange them for you?"

"Umm, no. Thank you. I can manage."

She smiled at him and nodded then turned and hurried down the hall. Terry heard the elevator doors click shut.

He took the vase, filled it with water and sat the flowers in it. He looked around and decided to put them on a small table beside the bed. They were pretty, colourful and even smelt good. He sat on the bed and gave it the bounce test. Nice. It was soft and had crisp, white sheets on it and four voluptuous pillows; man it looked comfortable. He glanced at his watch. Ten to five.

He checked the fridge and found several cans of beer. He took one out and opened it. There was a television at one end of the room, and he wandered over and fingered the controls. It was something to fill the time. Five-thirty. He wandered to the open windows, leaned against the window frame and lit a cigarette, content to watch the evening traffic. She had probably been held up.

When Terry checked his watch again, it had gone six, and his stomach was rumbling. He decided to go downstairs and get something to eat. They could go out for a proper meal when Frankie arrived, or better still, get something sent to their room.

The restaurant was busy. He ordered and found a table for two at one end of the room where he could keep an eye on dinner guests coming and going. He expected her to waltz into the restaurant at any moment and tell him she was starving. But it didn't happen, and by eight-thirty, she still hadn't shown, and he was getting worried.

He paid the bill and walked back up to their room. It was just as he had left it. He grabbed his bag and rummaged through it until he found her note. He ripped it from the envelope and reread it, just to make sure he had the details right. Maybe she was waiting for him at her apartment or maybe she'd been held up at work? His mind worked overtime trying to work out a reason why she might be late. He didn't want to consider she might have been injured, or much worse, killed.

He knew what it was like out in the bush, and if the Marine Division she had gone out with had come under attack, they might not be able to get anyone out. After grabbing another beer from the minibar, he shucked off his shoes and pulled up a chair to the window. While he waited, he'd watch Saigon go past and hope like hell she was okay.

Terry woke to the sounds of the Saigon traffic. Somewhere, someone was singing, and a dog was barking. It took him a couple of seconds to remember where he was. He was still dressed in his civilian clothes and lying on top of the bed where he had fallen asleep. A quick glance told him the other side of the bed was empty.

He told himself it was okay. The Marines would keep her safe, and nothing would harm her. She was level-headed and wouldn't put herself in unnecessary danger. Yes. They would make sure Frankie was safe. She'd turn up sometime today. They would only have one night together, but hey, one night was better than none.

He got up, took a shower and went down for breakfast. When he got back up to their room, he scribbled a note:

> *Frankie, in case you arrive and I'm not here,*
> *I've gone over to make sure you aren't holed up in your*
> *apartment.*
> *See you soon,*
> *Love T*

He crossed the square and walked towards the Caravelle, once there, he crossed the road and headed towards the river. He stopped outside the dusty, painted signage of Miss Lilac's. It was open, but the girls were busy, and he didn't want to go into the salon, it was a woman's domain. He followed the alley to the stairs and climbed them two at a time. He tried her door. It was locked. He knocked and listened. Nothing. No sign of life. He put his ear to the door and listened for any noise. Nothing. He turned and ran down the steps again.

Miss Lilac was standing on the doorstep of the salon.

"You look for Miss Frankie?"

"Yes. Have you seen her?"

"She was here–" She turned to the girls inside and rattled off something he couldn't understand. "Four days ago. But no sign of her now."

He thanked her and hurried off before she could offer him a haircut, manicure or facial. He walked back up Nguyen Hue Street until he reached Le Loi Street, and there on the corner, right across the street from the Rex Hotel, was the Associated Press office. He walked further down. What had she said? Something about being up several flights of stairs and the door at the end of the corridor?

At the end of four flights of stairs he found the corridor, and there at the end of it, he could see the large, distinctive door Frankie had described to him. Behind the door, the office was a hive of activity. Men were hunched over typewriters, phones were ringing, and a machine was spitting out sheets of paper into a wire basket. There were smaller offices off the big one.

"Excuse me."

A man looked up then went back to the paper he was reading.

"Yeah?"

He had an American accent, and Terry wondered if he was a journalist or a photographer.

"I'm looking for Frankie Proctor."

"She's out on a job."

"When will she be back?"

The man put the paper down and looked to one of his colleagues, then back at Terry. "You need to go talk to Bobby. That's his office over there. He's the boss."

Terry nodded his thanks. He was beginning to get a bad feeling.

He walked across to the open door, knocked lightly and walked in. "Good morning, sir, Terry Edwards." He offered his hand. "I'm looking for Frankie Proctor. She was out on a job, but I believe she's late, and I wondered if you'd heard from her?"

"Come in, son, sit down." The bureau chief got out of his chair and came around his desk to sit on the corner. "She was on an assignment up in Quảng Trị Province with the First Marine Division."

"Yes, she told me she was heading up there, but she was supposed to meet me yesterday. Where exactly is this Quảng Trị Province?"

"It's up near the demilitarised zone. Did you hear about what happened at Khe Sanh?"

"Yes, sir." He had. The North had launched a massive attack on a Marine garrison on January twenty-first, and it had lasted seventy-seven days. There were reports that the Marines had lost five hundred men. He couldn't even begin to imagine what it must have been like for the men caught in the middle of it for such a long time.

"The Marines are caught up in another firefight up there. She should have been back midday yesterday, but they were coming under heavy shelling and couldn't get choppers in or out."

"Are they still under attack?"

"Yes. As far as we know."

"There's no word she's injured though, is there?" It was the question he had wanted to ask as soon as he stepped inside the office, but one he didn't want to hear the answer to.

The bureau chief shook his head.

"Nothing has filtered back to us."

Terry stood up. "Thank you. I guess there's nothing we can do but wait."

"She'll be fine. Are you a soldier?"

"Yes, sir."

"Then you know how volatile these situations can be."

"Can't you stop her from taking these jobs?"

"How?"

"You're the boss, aren't you?" Terry had no idea how the AP worked, but surely this man could give her safer assignments.

"No, I can't. She's a damn good combat photographer, and I don't want to lose her. If I suddenly tell her she's covering the soft stories, she'll just find another news agency to work for, and they'd take her without question. She's a force to reckon with and from all accounts has earned the respect of the men she's out in the field with. She's one of them."

Terry had never felt so helpless. What would happen if the Marines couldn't get enough reinforcements in, or failed to get Frankie out? What if the VC overran them? It didn't bear thinking about, and Terry didn't feel reassured at all. The two men shook hands, and Terry turned and left. There was nothing he could do. He was here in Saigon for another night, and he could only hope and pray she might turn up.

Lost for something to do, he wandered down the street back to the Continental hotel. He sat in the bar and ordered a beer.

All he could do was wait.

Chapter 27

Terry was sitting in a perimeter bunker, manning the gun and enjoying a cigarette in peace when Rusty wandered over.

"Mail for you, Romeo," Rusty Taylor said, handing Terry an envelope. "Looks official too."

"Thanks, Rusty." His heart stopped when he saw the AP logo on the envelope, and the address had been typed. "It's from a friend in Saigon. Nothing official."

Would it be from Frankie, or was it from her boss with news he wouldn't want to read? He flipped the letter in his hand and tapped it against his leg a couple of times while he plucked up enough courage to open it.

He was immensely relieved to see the note was written in Frankie's handwriting.

> *Dear Terry,*
>
> *I am so sorry I missed you in Saigon. We came under heavy fire, and there was no way they could get me out. I was helping an injured soldier and happened to be in the wrong place at the wrong time. I suffered a concussion and a sprained wrist when a mortar round came in and landed a few feet from me. As soon as they could get a dustoff in, they choppered me to Da Nang Hospital for observation. I think they were overcautious, but I'm back in Saigon now, and apart from still being a little sore, I'm fine.*
>
> *Hope you weren't too disappointed and managed to find something to do while in the city. I hope you enjoyed the room too, especially that big comfortable bed! Only sorry I wasn't there to share it with you.*
>
> *I miss you so much.*
>
> *Keep your head down,*

Copper x

"So?" Rusty asked. He had been watching Terry as he read the note.

"All good. Thanks for dropping it over though. I appreciate it."

"No trouble, mate." He turned and wandered back to finish his detail.

Terry folded the envelope and stuffed it into his trouser pocket. He wondered if she had told him the whole truth, but Frankie was alive and back in Saigon, and that was a huge relief after not knowing anything. The front line was no place for a woman, especially a beautiful one like Frankie, but there was nothing he could do about what she did for a living.

That afternoon, he wrote back telling her he would be leaving Vietnam in a couple of weeks, the date was set for November the fourteenth, and he didn't think there was any way they would be able to see each other again before he left. The thought depressed him. Frankie had come to mean much more than he had bargained on. What they had was special, and he didn't know what to do about it, or his feelings. He had no idea when she would return to New Zealand, or if they would ever see each other once the war was over.

Three Section had been assigned to perimeter duty for the past two days, and before that, general maintenance duties in camp. The men were all itching to get back out beyond the wire, and they were rearing to go when word finally came through they were to head out the following morning.

They were choppered out to an area sixty kilometres north of Nui Dat where there had been reports of heavy VC movement, and Whiskey Company was expecting trouble. With eleven days to go until they went home, every man in the company was counting down, except Jack. Terry didn't think he'd made up his mind what he was going to do about the baby yet. Lately, it seemed to be the only topic of conversation every time they were on their own. In his opinion, the man was mad to even think about the girl or the baby.

Today, Terry had swapped positions with Davis. Jack wanted the machine gunner up front in case they ran into trouble. He had told Terry he was expecting it, and he wanted some heavy firepower up front with him.

If they were going to run into trouble, Terry was happy walking at number five. He was treading carefully, and when the message came back to stop, he automatically crouched to wait as Jack made his way back down the line. Every one of them had nerves wound as tight as guitar strings, and he had no idea why they had stopped. Perhaps he had seen something? It wasn't standard practice to break formation.

As Jack drew even with Terry, the air erupted in shrapnel and debris. Terry hit the ground.

There had been no gunfire, only a blood-curdling scream. It had to be a mine, or a tripwire. Jesus, he hated them.

"What's going on?" Terry yelled across to where Rusty Taylor was lying on his stomach.

"Mine."

"Who was it?"

"Davis, I think."

"Shit."

There had been no follow-up fire and no sign of the enemy, but it was enough to spook the men and notify every Charlie in the area of their whereabouts. Terry didn't get a wink of sleep that night. Not many of them did. They were expecting an attack, and it came the following day.

They were walking in single file, in complete silence, when an AK-47 opened fire on them. Like dominoes, the line of men hit the ground. There had been no warning, no mines. Like many of the previous times, they had been ambushed.

They had a platoon each side of them and the support if they needed it. It took only a matter of minutes to determine they were up against a sniper, probably more than one.

Damned snipers were a pain in the arse. Almost every time they'd been out lately, they had encountered a sniper somewhere. They were bloody lucky they hadn't lost more men than they had.

Terry saw Jack crawl away to his right. He looked over to his LT and received his orders. He and Butler were to follow Jack in case he needed back up. Terry knew his mate would be in his element, stalking his prey through the undergrowth. He could see him lining up a shot. Watching and listening. Terry heard Butler come up behind him. They lay still. Waiting. He heard two shots: Jack's M16. Terry stood up and moved around slowly, covering Jack.

"Butler!" Terry hissed. "Sweep that way." He did the hand movements to show where he was going.

When Terry got to Jack, green smoke floated around the small clearing, and he could see Jack crouched over a body. Worried he might be injured, he rushed across to his mate.

"Hey, Coles, you all right?" Jesus, he was bleeding from his shoulder. Then Terry noticed Jack was holding one of the VC snipers. On closer inspection, he saw it was a woman, and she looked very much like the bar girl from Vũng Tàu. It couldn't be, not all the way out here. "Go back and get the boss, Butler. Tell him Jack cleaned them up. Get the medic too."

Jack wasn't in a good way. He hugged the body, muttering, "why" over and over. Terry could have sworn his mate was crying. He had no idea at all how to help the poor bugger.

They loaded Jack into the dustoff chopper together with two wounded men and the body bags containing Davis and Mai Linh. A solemn mood descended over Three Section. Their best point man had taken a hit, and they had lost three others. For the rest of the patrol, Terry took over as lead scout. The commanding officer put One Section out in front, and Terry's section followed.

At the end of the patrol, they were choppered back to camp without any more contacts. Like everyone else in Whiskey Company, Terry was relieved to be back, the last few days were always the worst.

"Listen up," the CO said, addressing the company on the parade ground the following morning. "You have one overnight tomorrow, two days in camp, and then we head out again on one final op. We have some roads to patrol this time. Should be easy enough, but you'll need to be alert. I know you are all short and wanting to go home in one piece, so don't make any mistakes." He dismissed the men and walked back to his office.

As usual, Terry had been on spraying duties. He had sprayed from the back of a truck this time, dealing to the scrub and weeds around Luscombe Bowl and the runway. He had finished for the day and was heading back to his bunker to get cleaned up, thinking about the cold beers waiting for him in the mess.

"Edwards."

Terry looked up to find his section commander striding towards him.

"Sarge."

"Got a minute?"

"Sure. The beers can wait a bit longer."

"The LT has arranged for you to go into Vũng Tàu tomorrow to see Coles."

"Is he okay?" Terry wondered if something had happened, or if Jack's wounds had been more serious than they looked.

"He's fine as far as I know. They operated on his shoulder, and he's recovering as well as can be expected, but there's this thing with the woman."

"So, what can I do?"

"I have no idea. But he's asked to see you before we send him home. So go and see him, will you? You can stay overnight at the club, and I want you back here the following day."

"Will do. Did you hear any more about the woman?"

"Only that she was a high-ranking officer in an NVA regiment."

Terry let out a low whistle. "That's some heavy shit to get tangled up in. She must have been pumping our boy for information."

"At a guess, I would say so. That's probably why she let him live."

He stood watching as his section commander walked away. Of course he wanted to see Jack, but what the hell could he do to help?

By the time Terry got to the hospital late the following afternoon, Jack was pretty worked up about finding his daughter, Angel, and begged Terry to help him. Jack had no idea where she was, and each day he was stuck in the hospital was a day closer to being sent home. Angel was four months old, and she could have been left anywhere.

Terry sighed. "I'll give it a go. But I reckon she'll be out in a village somewhere, being looked after by relatives. Besides, I don't even know where to even start looking."

"Just try, will ya mate? Go to the bar, The Bamboo Palace. Someone there must know about the baby."

"Yeah, all right." He stayed and talked to Jack for a while until one of the nurses came and ushered him out. He'd start looking in the morning.

And he'd start in the obvious place.

Chapter 28

"You want! You want!"

A wiry Vietnamese woman thrust her sinewy, brown hands towards Terry, offering him mangoes from her selection of produce.

Terry shook his head and quickened his pace. He sure as hell didn't want any mangoes, pineapples, coconuts or anything else she might have. He didn't need any distractions. The street market was a hive of activity; he couldn't afford to drop his guard.

The calls echoed after him as he threaded his way through young men leaning on motorbikes, stalls of trinkets, and women cooking food he didn't recognise. Street markets made him nervous, especially as he was on his own, with memories of Tet still fresh in his mind. Any of these people clustered in doorways could be Viet Cong, or their sympathisers. Why he had agreed to try to find the child for Jack, he didn't know. He also had no idea what finding her would achieve. There was nothing either of them could do. Jack was in no position to take care of a small baby, and the army wasn't about to help.

He tried to remember the landmarks even though he had been drunk at the time. The buildings, window shutters, doorways, even trees or gardens. Anything that would help direct him to the dirty, pink two-storied house he was looking for, or the bar he had visited; a sign hanging out the front with a large, faded smiling sun on it. As he began to doubt he was on the right street, there it was: the sign, and next to it, the street he had taken once before.

Terry hurried, slipping away from the main thoroughfare. A glance over his shoulder confirmed no one was following him. A puppy bounced out from a doorway and ran after him for a few steps before losing interest and turning back. The small street came to a T-junction. Terry looked left before heading right.

Motorbikes littered doorways, and birds chattered from cages hung alongside windows. On the other side of the street, an old Vietnamese man squatted on a doorstep, cigarette burning in bony fingers, a rooster in a cage beside him. The pungent smell of fish sauce from a nearby kitchen permeated the street. A woman cycled past, partially hidden under her conical hat.

Terry knew where he was going now, as he'd been here before, but he hadn't told Jack that. It was something he didn't feel particularly proud of, but hell, he'd done a few things he wasn't that proud of. That was the nature of a war. You did things on the spur of the moment, or after one too many beers. And sometimes he'd done things simply because he was young and stupid and didn't know any better.

Terry's pace slowed as he scanned the upper-story windows. The facade would be recognisable from the street.

Then he saw the painted shutters with bright, patterned fabric restrained by thick metal bars. Next to the door sat an battered old table, a chipped china bowl offered burning sticks of incense, connecting the living with the dead. He didn't need two guesses who they burnt for.

He knocked and waited. He knew eyes watched from the shadowed interiors of the surrounding buildings. Impatient to get this over with, Terry pulled at the ironwork grill, it opened, and he stepped into the dimly lit interior, his eyes taking a second to adjust.

"Hello?"

Footsteps hurried across the floor above his head. Turning towards the stairs, he called out again. Who was living here now, and what would they know? A young woman appeared at the top, a mixture of alarm and anger flashed across her face before she burst into speech. Nothing Terry could understand. Was she related to the bar girl?

Terry wondered who else was in the house, then realised just how vulnerable he was. Shit, he did some bloody stupid things at times. This had to be one of those times.

He held up his hands to show he was unarmed. "I'm looking for a baby." He made a rocking motion with his arms as if he were cradling a tiny infant.

The woman stopped talking and stared at him.

"I'm looking for a tiny baby." He had no idea if she understood any of what he was trying to communicate, but she hurried down the stairs and pushed past him. He turned to follow her, and for the first time, noticed a baby sleeping in the far corner of the room.

"My sister baby."

She understood all right. "Is your sister here?"

She shook her head. "Sister dead."

Terry swallowed hard.

"Can I look at the baby?" He didn't want anything to do with this damned baby. It had caused enough problems already, but he had to be sure.

The woman nodded, suddenly enthusiastic.

"You take baby!" she said, becoming animated.

It would take him five seconds to tell if this was Jack's daughter. He gently pulled the cotton blanket away. The baby was cute, he had to give it that. It had a little button nose, and long eyelashes that lay on perfect creamy cheeks. A tiny hand clenched tight. He could see why Jack was so smitten with her. But it was anyone's guess who the child's father was. For all he knew, the kid could be his. Jack wasn't the only one Mai Linh had slept with, but there was no way anyone could prove that.

The baby stirred and screwed its face up as though somehow it was reading his mind. Terry carefully lifted the tiny arm and there, right where Jack had said it would be, was the birthmark.

"You take," the woman urged. "You take."

Before he could say anything, the woman scooped the child from the sofa and thrust her at him.

"No." He shook his head swiftly. "I'm not the father. I can't look after a baby."

She looked panicked.

"Kiwi baby! Kiwi baby!"

He held his hand up. "No." All he could think of was protecting Evelyn and Jack. And perhaps even himself. None of them needed this baby.

"You take!"

He dug in his pocket and from his wallet, pulled out a handful of notes and dropped them on the sofa. It wasn't much, but it was all he had. "You look after the baby."

Then, before she could see the guilt in his face, he turned and fled.

Chapter 29

Five days after she should have met Terry at the Continental, Frankie checked out of the hospital in Da Nang and caught a chopper back to Saigon. She went back to her apartment and packed her stuff. She was done living alone.

Since Louis had died, she had become close friends with a journalist who was working for *Life* magazine, and he had asked her to move in with him. Christopher Sands had pleaded the case that it would be safer for her if she lived with someone, now that the city wasn't as safe as it used to be. There were pockets of NVA sympathisers all over the city, and the government had imposed a curfew, but she suspected it was more a case of him looking for someone to help with the outrageous parties he was known for hosting.

They had covered a few assignments together and worked well as a team. Chris had arrived in Saigon from New York five months before her, and he had a reputation for being ruthless in his search for a story. Frankie liked that about him. He'd told her he had a spare room and asked her to think about moving in, and she'd had plenty of time to think about his offer while she was lying in a hospital bed under observation. Her assignment with the Marines had cost her cracked ribs, a sprained wrist, bruises, and shrapnel wounds, plus a concussion. Everything would heal, but she was battered and sore and would be moving slowly for a while. She was just pleased that Terry couldn't see her; he would have been upset and probably have asked her to consider going home.

Chris came to help shift her gear. There hadn't been much to pack: a couple of cases with her clothes and shoes, linen, her camera gear, a small collection of books, a radio and a few personal belongings including the framed photos she kept by her bed. Bobby had given her two weeks off work and told her to take it easy and rest up. She would rest after she had shifted.

As she was leaving, she stood at the door to her small apartment and looked around the room. If she closed her eyes, she could hear Terry's voice as they sat on the bed eating spring rolls and drinking beer. These walls had witnessed a lot of tears and emotion. And love. She locked the door and walked down the stairs for the last time.

Miss Lilac rushed to the front of the shop when she spotted Frankie and made her promise to come back and see her. Frankie nodded, and Miss Lilac cried and hugged her, telling her she was like a daughter and she would miss her. Frankie suspected she would miss the money more.

Chris's apartment was much nicer. Everything was bigger, with large windows and a balcony. It even had a proper kitchen and access to the roof. And she no longer had to climb two flights of stairs, she could take an elevator. They were nothing but friends, and Frankie was happy to keep it that way. She wasn't interested in getting involved with anyone else.

"How ya doing?" Chris enquired as he stood at her bedroom door.

"Almost unpacked, thanks."

"I thought you might like this." He handed her a bedside lamp.

"No, I can't take that, what will you use?"

"I've got two, and I don't need both to be able to find my way around a woman's body. Would you like a glass of wine? I think we deserve it after the shift."

Frankie smiled. "Thanks, but I'm taking painkillers and knocking back the wine probably isn't a good idea right now."

"Coffee then?"

"I think I'll lie down for a while. My ribs are killing me."

"Sure." He turned and then stopped. "Do you mind if I cook tonight? I'm learning how to make Vietnamese dishes, and I need a guinea pig for my recipes."

Frankie laughed and then clutched her ribs.

"That was your plan all along, wasn't it? Lure me into your apartment and then feed me on experiments."

Chris shook his head. "I was hoping you'd never figure that out."

"I look forward to dinner."

He turned and closed her door, leaving her to rest.

She picked up the black and white photo of Terry and studied his face, as she had done so many times before. Bloody fish.

Easing back against the pillows, she reached out to the little marble Buddha that was sitting on her nightstand, grinning at her. She couldn't help but smile, despite all the bloodshed that was going on around them.

So far this year, fifteen thousand Americans had been killed in

South Vietnam, and although Westmoreland was telling the world the South was making a breakthrough and the war was starting to wind down, he was asking for more men, and they were being sent over in the thousands. Frankie was keen to get out to the airport to capture the innocence of those fresh-faced young boys as they arrived. There were so many more stories to tell.

Every time she closed her eyes, she was back with the Marines in the middle of the firefight. She had been with a platoon of men separated from the rest, and the NVA had taken the opportunity to go on a killing spree. Frankie had been terrified, the courage those Marines had shown had impressed her. Every single one deserved a medal for bravery.

One young Marine had been badly wounded by an incoming mortar, and Frankie had crawled over to where he lay and attempted to drag him to cover, but as she did, a mortar round had landed a few feet from her. Frankie had been thrown through the air, and although her injuries hadn't been life-threatening, she had lost a lot of blood from shrapnel wounds. The medic, a young man with the kindest eyes, had given her morphine and patched her up until they could get her out and to a hospital. He watched over her for thirty-six hours while she faded in and out of consciousness as the heavy shelling from the NVA continued all around them.

Frankie screwed her eyes shut then opened them again. Her hands would always be covered in the blood and dirt of that Marine. His fingers limp in her hands, on arms that were no longer connected to a body. It played over and over, like a broken record she couldn't take off the turntable.

She returned her gaze to the photo of Terry in its cheap bamboo frame–he had that familiar grin plastered on his face, one hand draped over Frankie's shoulders–but this time she just felt sad. Sad that she had missed spending more time with him. Sad that he couldn't protect her from what she had been caught up in; from the bloody horror of this war. A tear rolled down her cheek. Damned fish. With the frame clutched to her body, she closed her eyes and relived the memories again.

A week later, Chris announced he was going to throw one of his famous Saigon Tea parties. It was to be on the fourteenth, and there would be no tea involved. She was looking forward to being back at work but would cover the easy assignments in Saigon for a few weeks. Her ribs were still sore, and they would take a few more weeks to fully repair themselves, but otherwise, she was feeling more like her old self and was bored silly. Even her wrist was stronger, and unless she knocked it, it gave her little trouble.

Chris claimed the party was a welcome party for Frankie and ignored all her protests that she didn't need one. He was arranging everything. It was bigger than his usual intimate dinner parties for a handful of friends or colleagues, and as news spread through Saigon that one of Chris's famous parties was happening, Frankie was seriously worried how they would fit everyone in.

"Trivial details," Chris stated one evening as they sat in the lounge of the apartment smoking a particularly good joint. The large double balcony doors were thrown open even though the rain was sheeting down outside.

"If they want to be here, they'll find a way to make it to the drinks table," he said casually, passing the joint to Frankie who was lying on the floor, head on a cushion. "If they have to, they can use the hall outside. No one will care."

He wouldn't let Frankie do anything for the party, but on the day, she finished work early to help. Instead, he sent her off to shop for something 'fun' to wear and to get her hair done. Everything was being catered, from the food to the drinks, and people came and went delivering flowers and decorations for the apartment.

Frankie wandered down Tu Do Street, looking in shop doorways and at mannequins dressed in bright-coloured dresses and ao dais. She wondered if she would look any good in an ao dai, and on a whim, decided to try some on. They looked pretty, and in the end, she purchased one with emerald green silk trousers and a pale green silk tunic. She thought it made her look very Irish with her red hair. Then she walked the three blocks to Miss Lilac's beauty salon, wishing Terry could see her in the ao dai.

Miss Lilac was surprised to see her and made a fuss. She wouldn't let anyone else do Frankie's hair and ordered that one of the girls paint her nails while another got her coffee. As Frankie was leaving an hour later, Miss Lilac seemed to remember something suddenly and pulled an envelope from a drawer, handing it to Frankie.

"I forgot to take to AP office. Very sorry."

Frankie looked at the envelope. It was from Terry. She couldn't quite make out the date.

She stepped out into the afternoon sun and tore open the envelope as she walked. Then she stopped. It had been written after he had got her last note, and at the bottom, he had told her he was flying home on November fourteenth.

That was today! She looked around, trying to think what she could do. Stuffing the letter into her bag, she ran across the road, dodging vehicles as a stream of horns followed her. She didn't care. By the time she got to the AP bureau and up four flights of stairs, her ribs were aching.

"Anyone have contact details for the New Zealand HQ?" she yelled, storming into the office. "I need contacts at New Zealand HQ!"

"I know a desk jockey over there, any help?"

"Yes! I'll take anyone."

"What's up?" one of the stringers asked.

"Whiskey Company is flying out today, and I need to catch them before they leave Saigon."

"Here." The stringer handed her a piece of paper.

With shaking fingers, she took the paper and dialled the numbers.

Whiskey Company was indeed leaving the country, and their flight was scheduled for sixteen hundred hours. Frankie glanced at the clock on the office wall. It was quarter past three. She had forty-five minutes to get to the airport.

She had to catch Terry before his flight left. She couldn't let him leave without saying goodbye.

"Need a lift?" an American journalist by the name of Flores, asked. "I've got a jeep downstairs."

"I need to get to Tan Son Nhut as quickly as I can."

"Come on then." He grabbed the keys from his desk, and the pair of them ran down to the vehicle.

Frankie felt they were travelling at a snail's pace. "Can't we take a back street?"

"You know what the streets are like. If I take a back street and it's blocked for some reason, we'll never make it."

He sat on the horn and wove in and out of taxis, cars, cyclos, motorbikes and people as Frankie held on to the door with one hand and her ribs with the other. It seemed the whole population of Saigon was out on the streets this afternoon.

When they arrived at the airport gates, there were planes everywhere.

"Thanks!" she yelled to him as she made her way through the vehicles and MPs. And then she saw a convoy of army trucks pulling up to a Royal New Zealand Air Force Hercules about two hundred metres away. That had to be Whiskey Company! She ran across the tarmac, hoping like hell she had the right plane. There would be no time to check others.

"Is this Whiskey Company?" she shouted at a soldier over the noise of the airport.

Soldiers were climbing down off the back of the trucks, and a young man looked her up and down then nodded.

"Are you the farewell party?"

"Is Terry Edwards here?" she asked, ignoring his question.

"Edwards?" the soldier asked, repeating the name as though he had never heard it before. "Sure. He's on one of these trucks."

"Thanks." Frankie ran to the back of a truck where the men were sorting their bags and getting ready to board the plane. None of the faces were familiar. She ran to the next one.

"I'm looking for Terry Edwards," she said to whoever was listening.

"Romeo? He's in that truck." A soldier pointed to a vehicle two further up the line.

"Thanks." She rushed through the groups of men to the truck and when she rounded the back, of it found a group who were lifting bags onto their shoulders, all except a man who had his back to her. He appeared to have his arm in a sling and was carrying his bag in his free hand.

"Terry?"

He turned at the sound of his name, not realising who it was at first.

"Frankie?"

"Terry! I was afraid I'd missed you! Jesus, what happened to you? Are you okay? Were you shot?"

"You're a sight for sorry eyes, girl. Come here." He dropped his bag and embraced her with his good arm. As she looked at him, she couldn't help herself, her tears flowed freely and the need to kiss him, one last time before he left, overwhelmed her.

In the background, she could hear his mates whistling and cracking jokes, but it didn't matter. As Terry kissed her with everything he felt for her; she didn't want to let him go. At that moment, they were the only ones on the tarmac.

"Come up for air, mate," someone close to them said.

"Trust Romeo to have his own farewell party."

"What the hell's he going home for, with a bird like that here?" someone else commented.

"What happened to your arm?" Frankie finally asked again.

"Broke it. It's okay. I wasn't shot. A bloody rubber tree fell over on my bunker, and I happened to be walking out the door at the time."

Frankie laughed, then sniffed and wiped at her eyes. "Sorry, it's just that with everything that's happening in the middle of a war, and you out there facing death every day, and a *tree* falls on you and breaks your arm?"

"Shut up and kiss me," he demanded, and his lips were on hers again.

"I was so worried about you up there with the Marines last month," he finally told her.

"I'm fine."

"God, you smell so good, and you look gorgeous. I almost want to stay here."

"No, go home, soldier. Before your luck runs out."

He caressed the side of her face with his free hand. "When am I going to see you again?"

"I don't know. I'm not ready to come home yet. There's still so much the rest of the world needs to see." She had no idea when she would go home, and she couldn't look him in the eyes as she spoke.

Around them, the men were filing onto the plane.

"Will you write?"

"If you want me to. Hang on–" She rummaged in her bag and pulled out a well-thumbed notepad and a pen. "What's your address?"

"Shit, I don't know. Send it to my father's, and I'll write you as soon as I'm sorted." He dictated his father's address to her.

"Cut it short, Edwards," his section commander said, walking past.

"I love you, Terry." Tears streamed down her cheeks now, at the realisation this might be the very last time she ever saw him. Then they kissed again, and she could tell by the fierce passion in his kiss he was thinking the same thing.

"I love you too, Copper. For God's sake, don't get killed, all right? And promise you'll fight off all those other guys and come home to me."

He ran his thumb over her cheek, trying to erase the tears.

"I will."

"Good." He looked around him, most of the men were already on board, and the trucks were moving out. "I gotta go." He took her in his arms one last time. "I'm gonna miss you, Copper. So much," he whispered in her ear.

"Me too." And now she was crying openly and didn't care who saw. "Write and let me know what it's like back in the real world."

"I will."

Then they were yelling at him. The trucks had disappeared, and he was the only one left on the tarmac.

She kissed him briefly, and stroked his hair, then kissed him on the side of his face. "I love you, Terry Edwards."

"Not as much as I love you, Copper."

Then he walked towards the steps, and as he got to the top, he turned and waved, and she waved back, before he was swallowed up by the Hercules.

"You need to move back, ma'am."

She nodded absently. Terry was gone. She walked back towards the main terminal. The one person who'd kept her sane in all this madness was about to leave the country.

She had never told anyone she loved them before and doubted she ever would again. Certainly never with the same passion as she loved Terry. But she couldn't commit to anything or anyone, not while she was living in a country at war and working as a combat photographer. Life here was a fine balance between being smart, careful and lucky. She could be killed tomorrow. That was the reality.

Watching the Hercules taxi out onto the runway, she couldn't stop the flow of tears. She cried for all the pain and hurt she had witnessed during her time in South Vietnam, for the anger at how fruitless this war was, for the young Marine she had failed to save up in Quảng Trị Province, for the death of Louis, and for the loss of the best thing that had ever happened to her: Terry.

As the lumbering Hercules lifted off the ground and propelled itself skywards, Frankie turned to look for a taxi. She couldn't watch the most important person in her life disappear, not knowing if she would ever see him again.

PART TWO

1975

<h1 style="text-align:center">Chapter 30</h1>

After adjusting the bag on his back, Terry lifted a leg over the frame of his bicycle and pedalled down his drive and out onto Victoria Street. It was still early, and the street was empty. For the middle of March, the mornings were still mild. He turned into Park Street. This morning he felt a whole range of emotions: from fool-hardy and excited to scared shitless and perhaps even a little heavy-hearted. This weekend was going to be *the* weekend. The weekend he finally popped the question.

It had been seven years since he got back from Vietnam, and two years since his best mate, Jack, had taken his own life. Jack had married Evelyn as soon as he got back from Vietnam, but he couldn't cope with what had happened over there or the loss of another baby when Evelyn miscarried. Terry had watched him sink lower and lower, and although he had tried to help, tried to keep him safe; in the end, he had failed. He felt heartbroken for Evelyn and guilty he hadn't been able to do more.

It had been Terry that Evelyn had turned to for help when she couldn't find her husband, and it had been Terry who had found Jack's body. The memory of discovering his mate in that tramping hut never left him. It was worse than anything he had witnessed back in Vietnam, and he felt guilty every single day that Evelyn had lost her husband because he hadn't seen it coming.

After the funeral, Terry called by once a week to mow her lawn or do repairs if she was home, but all he wanted to do was take her in his arms and apologise, tell her time would heal the wounds. He wanted nothing more than to protect her from the hurt she was feeling.

Over the past two years, they had become close friends, and Terry had finally decided to ask her to marry him. They were a great couple and had lots of fun when they were together. They were also both still single and getting married made sense.

He hadn't heard from Frankie for almost six years, although every now and again he spotted a photo or an article in a paper that had Associated Press on it, and he couldn't help wondering if Frankie was still working for them. She had long ago stopped replying to his letters, and he could only assume she had chosen to move on with her life. He doubted he would ever forget her, but after Jack had died, he had decided it wasn't healthy to live in the past.

The first six months back in New Zealand had been the hardest. He'd left the army and tried to settle back into life in Foxton. The Returned Services Club, where he'd thought he could go for a friendly drink with other veterans, had not welcomed any soldiers returning from Vietnam, and refused to serve him. No one seemed to support the men who still put their lives on the line in Vietnam either, and there were protests everywhere. He'd found a place in Victoria Street to rent and started back at his old job.

He spent most of his spare time with his old mates, drinking or out hunting. He didn't like big crowds and preferred his own company to socialising.

His mother and Vernon had shifted, he had another little half-brother he didn't know, his mate Ron was engaged, and Matt had got himself married. So much had changed in the eighteen months he had been away.

The week before the Christmas of sixty-eight, he had received his first letter from Frankie. He couldn't open it fast enough. She wrote about the places she'd been working in. She had been back to Khe Sanh, An Khe and Da Nang and was heading to Pleiku for four days with an infantry division. She'd also spent a week with the civilian doctor she had met on the plane over from Singapore. He was doing great work up in Bing Dinh Provincial Hospital, treating civilian casualties and training Vietnamese nurses. Terry read how she had sold photos to *Life* magazine and *Rolling Stone* and was doing a series of photos for *Time,* in addition to her assignments for Associated Press.

She told him she had shifted into a new apartment with a journalist from *Life* magazine who she had been out on several assignments with. She said his name was Chris, and he was American, and he was renting her his spare room. The apartment was much larger, with a proper kitchen, and she wasn't so lonely and felt safer there. Terry wondered if something was going on between them, but if there was, there was absolutely nothing he could do about it.

Although Frankie's letters became less frequent, he continued to write for almost a year, until he received that final letter. Two pages in her distinctive handwriting:

Dear Terry,

This is such a hard letter to write. I have started it so many times, and each time, thrown it in the trash. I've come to the conclusion that there is no easy way to say it, so I'm just going to come straight out with it. I think it's time I let you go, so you can move on and try to forget me.

Yes, I feel miserable, but I also feel selfish. I really want to keep you all to myself, but it's unfair of me to hold you to the possibility of a relationship that might never eventuate.

Terry remembered every minute he had spent reading the letter. A *Dear John* letter, shit, she had written him a *Dear John* letter, and they weren't even going steady. He read on:

For the past year, I think I've led you to believe that when this war is over, I'll come back to NZ, and we'll be able to start again where we left off.

But the truth is, I don't know when I'm coming home. I plan to go to Cambodia for a while. If I survive Saigon. It has become a dangerous city now. And I want to go to Paris and also spend some time at the AP offices in New York.

As much as I love you, I can't expect you to wait and put your life on hold for me.

You deserve the chance to have a normal, happy home. To find a wife, have a house-full of children and to make something of yourself.

It's what you deserve.

When things get tough out in the bush, I reach into my bag and hold my little smiling Buddha and find myself thinking of you, when I should be concentrating on what's happening around me. It's a distraction I can't afford to have out in the jungle, and I'm sure you'll understand what I mean.

Increasingly, I find the war exhausting and an extravagant waste of precious lives. As much as it drains every ounce of my morality, my sense of common decency and integrity, and it makes me want to run and hide, it also seduces me like a temptress behind a veil. Vietnam is in my blood.

You're a lovely man, Terry Edwards, and I will never forget you or what we had over here. Please believe me when I say I hate the thought of you finding someone else, but I owe you your freedom because I love you.

I can't keep on living this way, feeling guilty for what I'm causing you to miss out on.

I wish you every happiness,

Frankie

She hadn't even signed it 'love Frankie.' How the hell did she know what he wanted? Or what was good for him? He had reread the letter, trying to make more out of it than she had written. But he couldn't.

He wrote back, asking her to not to do this to him, asking her to wait, see how she felt in six months' time. Hell, he could wait longer if he thought she was coming home to him. He reassured her he was interested in only her. She never replied to his letter.

To distract himself, he spent long hours at work, went to race meets and out on hunting trips with his mates. He helped Evelyn repaint her house. He wrote two more letters, but still, she never replied, and he worried whether she had been hurt, or if she just wasn't answering. And he didn't even know where she was. For all he knew, she could have been in

Paris, or the States, or even back in New Zealand.

The saddest part was all he had to remind him of her was a handful of letters. He didn't even have a photo. All he knew was that he didn't want to give her up, but she had left him no option, and now, after six years, he was finally moving on. He was ready to take that huge step and ask Evelyn to marry him.

He cycled up Main Street, waving to those he knew who were also on their way to work. Crisp morning air rushed past his face as he thought about Evelyn and what their life together would be like. He couldn't help breaking into a smile.

The following morning, Terry was up early and drove to Evelyn's home on the farm up at Himatangi.

After tapping on the door, he pushed it open and stepped inside. Evelyn was packing things into a cane basket, and she looked up and smiled at him. That smile always reminded him how young she was, and it felt contagious. They had been close for the last two years, and sleeping together for the past three months, and he didn't want to wait any longer. He was finally going to ask her to marry him.

"Good morning, Mr Edwards," she greeted, with a cheeky grin.

"Good morning, yourself. You're very chipper for this hour of the day."

"It's going to be a great day," she said, closing the lid on the basket and pushing it across the table towards him. "I've been looking forward to this concert in Wellington all week."

"Let me put this in the car." He grabbed the basket and headed out to the car.

"Give me two minutes to grab my coat," she called over her shoulder as she disappeared from the kitchen.

They managed to find a car park within easy walking distance of the park, and while Terry carried the picnic basket, Evelyn walked beside him carrying a rug. Although they blended into the crowd of concertgoers, as they looked for a spot close to the stage to spread the rug and sit down, Terry noticed a few people staring at Evelyn. It wasn't until they were walking back to the car that a photographer from *The Wellington Daily* asked if he could take their photo.

Evelyn looked at Terry, and he nodded. They didn't go out in public much and he wasn't used to the attention she generated. They usually went to the movies, or the beach, or had a meal at her house or his. But if she was happy to have her photo taken with him, he didn't mind at all.

"You realise that photo will be all over the papers now, don't you?"

"I hadn't thought about it. Do you mind?" he asked.

"No. I'm used to it."

"I was thinking more about being photographed with me. And the headline," he said as they reached his car. "I mean, are they going to jump to conclusions and think we're a couple?"

"Does it matter?"

He held the door open for her. "Not as far as I'm concerned."

"Then they can say whatever they like."

They stopped at Paraparaumu and got fish and chips, and then sat in the car down by the beach to eat them. By the time they got back to her place, it was almost eight. While Evelyn unpacked the picnic basket, Terry lit the fire for her.

"I had a great day today, thank you for taking me."

"I did too," he replied. He took a deep breath. He would ask her to marry him as soon as she finished unpacking.

"I've got something to tell you," Evie said as she stopped unpacking to fill the jug with water and plug it in.

Terry leaned against the bench. "What is it?" She suddenly looked serious and was fidgeting with the lid on the jar of coffee. He began to worry something was wrong.

"I've decided I'm going to Saigon."

Silence.

"What?"

"I'm going to Saigon, to try to find Jack's daughter, Angel."

"What?" he repeated, not believing what he'd just heard. It had to be a joke. And a bad one at that. Didn't she know how dangerous it was over there at the moment?

"No." Terry crossed his arms over his chest. "The hell you're going to Vietnam."

"I've made my mind up."

"Why, for Christ's sake?" He threw his hands in the air. "The NVA are marching through the South towards Saigon. You'd be mad to go there now." He paced across the room and back. Everything he had read in the papers lately predicted that Saigon was close to falling to the communists.

"I made a promise to Jack."

"I don't care about any promises. What makes you think you'd be able to find her?"

"I don't know. I might not be able to."

"You'd be looking for a needle in a haystack."

Evie spooned coffee powder into two mugs.

"Look," he said, taking her by her arms and turning her to face him. "It's a dangerous place. Why not wait until the war is over?"

"The place was dangerous eight years ago when I was there singing for the troops. What's changed?"

"Everything," he answered quietly. He released her arms. "Jack wouldn't have wanted you to put your life at risk because of the child."

"I'll be careful."

"She might not even have survived."

"I've made my mind up, Terry. I'm going."

"When?"

"In three weeks."

"*Three weeks?*" he echoed, trying to process the implication. Three weeks! She had to have been planning this for months, and she was only telling him now? There would be no way he'd be able to stop her either. She'd been to Vietnam twice, entertaining the men, but that had been different. Those times she was an entertainer, a VIP, and as such, had protection wherever she went. Now, she would be just another foreigner on the street.

And what would her parents think? His head was spinning. The last place on earth he wanted to go back to right now, was Vietnam, but he couldn't let her go on her own. He was the perfect person to help protect her, but as he watched her fill the mugs with boiling water, his marriage proposal was long forgotten.

Chapter 31

From the chair by the window, Terry looked out over Lam Son Square. Unable to sleep, he'd got up and showered, and wearing only his briefs, he sat smoking in the dimly lit room. He had only just managed to organise his travel documents in time, and while he was sorting those, Evelyn had organised everything else. He looked at her, still sound asleep in the bed opposite him. The situation felt like a nightmare, playing out in slow motion.

From the taxi, he had stared unbelievingly at the Continental Palace. Of all the hotels in Saigon, Evelyn had booked a room here. He had forced himself to follow her to their room, but had come to a complete standstill outside the door, horrified to discover they were staying in room twenty-two. He wondered how he would be able to step inside. How could he stay in this room without thinking of Frankie every waking minute?

He had finally closed his eyes and taken the step. From somewhere inside the room, Evelyn had been talking to him. He had opened his eyes, glancing around at the tidy, but tired, interior. The room was exactly as he remembered it.

The air was a little cooler tonight, and it felt good on his bare skin. It was always a relief to be able to take his clothes off and let his skin breathe. Every time he worked up a sweat, or his clothes got wet, he broke out in rashes. He had no idea why but wondered if it had anything to do with the chemicals he had used in the backpack sprayer at Nui Dat. It wouldn't worry him, except they were as itchy as all hell. He had used calamine lotion, but the most soothing relief came from standing under a lukewarm shower, or in summer, just wearing as little as possible.

Terry rested his feet on the railing of the small balcony. Air heavy with temptation flooded his nostrils, and he recalled the nights he had spent with Frankie in her little apartment. He remembered the smells, the food, and his first real love affair. There were so many good memories in this city too. He stared blankly out the window, his gaze fixed only on the past.

It was early evening, and the darkness hid the dirtiest corners and doorways. He watched the cars and motorbikes, and the people walking under the streetlights. It felt like he had stepped back in time and was witnessing the same locals trying to flog off whatever they could to make ends meet, the same people squatting on the footpaths, the same bustle.

Brilliant flashes of light illuminated segments of the sky and the rumble of explosions could be heard over the street noises. War on a large scale was coming to Saigon, of that he was sure.

Looking across towards the Caravelle, Terry remembered the week he had been detailed to guard duty and how he'd run into Frankie on the street and spilled her drink all down her front. He smiled as he remembered the guys giving him hell, and how he'd waited for her on the steps of the Municipal Theatre, nervous as all hell–it had been their first date.

He wondered if she was still working out of the AP bureau here in the city, or if she was now out of the country. He hoped she was somewhere else, preferably state-side or Paris. He'd read that even Cambodia was no longer safe. He was aching to walk up the road to the office and ask after her.

What if she was still here? What if she was walking on the street somewhere in Lam Son Square right now? He focused his attention on the people, just in case she was out there. What if she was eating in a restaurant nearby? Or meeting friends downstairs in the bar?

"Terry?"

What if he walked out of the hotel door in the morning and walked straight into her?

"Hey, you all right?"

"Yeah," he replied, Evelyn's voice dragging him back from his thoughts. "Let's go get something to eat."

The following days were filled with an endless routine of finding someone who would drive them to another orphanage or school. Terry felt sorry for Evelyn; he could see the hopelessness of the search was starting to take its toll on her. The New Zealand Embassy had given them a list of all the orphanages around Saigon and out as far as Củ Chi, Bà Rịa, and Vũng Tàu. They had also been told that hundreds of orphaned children were being airlifted out to America, Australia and New Zealand, most of them already adopted by waiting families. The more Terry heard, the more it sounded like an impossible search.

At Evelyn's request they had gone out to Tan Son Nhut Airport; she was anxious to see if they could check any of the children before they boarded flights out of the city. While there, she had witnessed the crash of a huge Galaxy loaded with children and babies. She was shocked and devastated and praying that Angel hadn't been on that plane.

Evelyn was still in shock when they returned from the airport. He ran a shower and made her get under it while he went down to get them something to eat and drink. As he took a seat in the bar and ordered a beer, he overheard two men next to him talking about Nha Trang and how it would fall to the communist troops overnight. He glanced casually in their direction.

"I'm a bit worried about Frankie," an American voice stated.

"Well, mate, you know as well as I do, that she's one capable woman."

"What if they take prisoners?"

Terry's heart stopped, his beer paused midway to his lips as he listened. There could only be one Frankie.

"The only chance she has is if she's already heading back to Saigon."

Terry put his beer down. Frankie was still working in Vietnam. She wasn't in Saigon, but she was still in country. He wondered how well these men knew her. Was she out of her mind putting herself in danger like that? She ran a huge risk of being captured.

"Excuse me," Terry heard the barman interrupt the American. "Mr Sands?"

"Yes?"

"You have a phone call. You can take it at the end of the bar if you would like."

"Thanks."

"You all right, sir?" the barman addressed Terry.

"Yes. Yes, fine."

The men seated next to him at the bar knew Frankie, and he so desperately wanted to grill them about her. Find out how she was.

The American reappeared, and the topic of conversation moved on; the men were now talking about the president and the impending evacuation of his family as a precaution.

"Excuse me."

The two men stopped talking and turned to look at Terry.

"Yes?"

"Sorry to interrupt, but I couldn't help overhearing you mention Frankie. Is that Frankie Proctor?"

"Yes."

"I wondered how she was these days."

"You know her?" the American asked.

"Yes. I met her when I was over here in sixty-seven, sixty-eight."

"Sounds like you're a Kiwi," the Australian commented.

"I am."

"She's one of the best damn photographers in Vietnam," the American, Mr Sands, said.

"We arrived over here on the same plane in sixty-seven, and I wondered what she was up to these days," Terry added, and then felt embarrassed in case they thought he was stalking her. "I hope she makes it back from Nha Trang okay."

"So do we. She has an uncanny way about her though. She's like a homing pigeon." The American laughed at his own characterisation of Frankie.

"I should be going." Terry drained the last of his beer and slipped off his stool as the barman relayed the message their meals were ready. "When you see her, tell her Terry said hello."

"Sure thing," the American said.

"Thanks." He hurried through to collect the food he had ordered. Evelyn would be waiting upstairs.

Chapter 32

By Sunday April twentieth, it was feeling like an impossible task. They had now been in Saigon for almost three weeks and were no closer to finding Jack's seven-year-old daughter, Angel.

Each day, the city seemed to swell with new arrivals from the country villages, all seeking the safety they believed the city offered. In many cases, whole families were trying to leave the country by whichever means they could. It was now common knowledge that evacuations had started, and Terry was worried they wouldn't make it out of the country in time.

Reports were coming in every day of villages on the outskirts of the city that had been overrun by the NVA or VC, even some of the villages where they had visited orphanages.

"I think we should think about going home," Terry suggested as he lay in bed watching the ceiling fan spin above him. "I know you don't want to, but we can't stay here forever, and I need to get back to work." He turned his head to see Evelyn watching him. It was the first morning she hadn't been up early, ready to go out searching.

"We've spent every day so far, going from orphanage to school to orphanage. We'd be better off planning how we're going to get the hell out of here. I'm starting to worry whether we'll get out in time." He brushed strands of hair from across her face and lifted himself up to kiss her forehead. "But a day off might be nice."

"I'm sleepy."

"Really? Have I told you what I love doing to sleepy women? Especially when they're in my bed and sexy as hell?" He was propped up on an elbow now, studying her face. Their relationship had long ago progressed from good friends to lovers, but he still hadn't asked her to marry him. He'd wait until they got home now. If they ever made it out of this hellhole of a country.

"Nope." She had mischief written all over her face. "Please don't tell me, I'd rather you showed me."

"You asked for it," Terry responded, happily.

When they eventually got up, they spent the rest of the day being tourists. Terry noticed the increased tension on the streets, and as they walked along the footpaths, he kept an eye out for anything suspicious. In a city like Saigon, it was a hard ask, and by the time they got back to their room, he was exhausted, and all he wanted to do was get on the next flight home.

"We should think about going home," he prompted again as they sat down to dinner.

"Okay," Evelyn agreed. "Let's go home."

"I think we should go to the embassy first thing tomorrow and see if we can get on a flight," he suggested.

"Okay, we've done all we can. That's the main thing."

"You've gone above and beyond."

When they'd finished eating, Terry leaned over the table towards her. "You look beautiful tonight, Evelyn. I love that dress." He had bought it for her when they had gone shopping that day, and it looked wonderful on her.

"The dress is beautiful," she agreed. "Thank you."

Her eyes lit up as she smiled flirtatiously at him. Right now, he didn't much care for the dress. Right now she was making him feel horny as hell.

"I bet the dress would look even better on the floor."

She smiled, pushed her chair back and stood up. "Shall we find out?"

Chapter 33

"The Long Hải Hills? Evelyn, come on, even if we managed to get to the Long Hải 's, and that's a big *'if,'* by the time we got back, the NVA could have taken the city, and then we'd be fucked." She was the most infuriating, stubborn woman he had ever met, and he wasn't mincing words; she needed to know just how dangerous it would be. "They're just outside the city now. We can't afford to go off on another wild goose chase."

They had run into journalists at breakfast who had told them about a bunch of nuns looking after some kids. Now Evelyn had got it into her head that she had to check them out.

He remembered the times he had patrolled through the area with Victor and Whiskey; those hills were riddled with bunker systems and tunnels. They were thick with VC who came and went, causing havoc in between times. And now, Evelyn wanted to go there. Of all the crazy ideas. This took the cake.

"It's far too dangerous, Evelyn." Why the hell did those guys have to tell her about the nuns? Why couldn't they have kept their bloody big mouths shut?

"I'll go on my own."

Aw, shit. "Don't do this." He took out his cigarettes and lit one. "How the hell can I keep you safe if you're fucking traipsing all over the bloody countryside? I'm fucked if I know." He stood up abruptly, tipping his chair over. Faces in the restaurant turned in their direction. He was angry with Evelyn and angry at the journalists and pissed with the city and the whole country. "I'm not going to get killed in this shithole of a country, and I'll be buggered if I let you get killed either!" With that, he turned and stormed off.

Terry unlocked their room and paced from one end to the other and back. This was just what he'd feared, and on top of everything, he had a splitting headache and heat blisters under his arms and down his sides from sweating in the stinking heat. He sat on the edge of the bed, and took a couple of deep breaths, then lay back and stared at the ceiling. He couldn't let her go on her own; how would he live with himself if anything happened to her? Not to mention he'd have to face her family and probably Jack's old man too.

As if it wasn't bad enough that he knew Frankie was out there somewhere, putting herself at risk, now Evelyn wanted to as well. Bloody women.

The door to their room opened, and Evelyn stepped inside and closed the door behind her.

"I'm sorry," she said, unzipping her skirt, tossing it to one side and stepping into a pair of shorts. "I shouldn't have involved you in this. I've no right to put your life at risk too."

Terry heaved himself up off the bed. "Do you realise how damned hard it is, just being back here? Hearing the gunfire, living on your nerves? The smells, the stinking heat. The fear of death. This place gets inside you, it's like a disease. It takes you over, and the funny thing is, you want to let it, you crave what it has to offer." He ran a hand through his hair, his head pounding. "Every inch of your body, every nerve ending, is running on high octane, ready to run or fight. This place has the potential to kill you if you drop your guard for a second. I escaped it once, what happens if I'm outta luck this time? What if the chopper gets shot down or we get caught at the orphanage? What then?" He turned and walked over to the window and stared unseeingly out. He turned back to face her. "Please tell me you're not going to do this."

"I'm so sorry."

It was barely a whisper, but it was as if she had yelled it at him.

"I don't want you to come."

"Christ, the child might not even be there."

"I know. She might have died years ago. But she might also be living with those nuns. I know how strong you've had to be to come back here, and I can't ask you to put your life at risk for me." She crossed the room to where he stood and kissed him on the cheek and then took a step back to look into his eyes. "I'll be back as soon as I can." She turned and walked towards the door, opening it and closing it behind her.

Come on, Terry, you've got a woman to protect, mate. It took him a moment to gather his thoughts. He couldn't let her disappear into the Long Hải Hills; if they were going to get killed, he'd go down fighting to protect her. He grabbed the Colt he had picked up not long after arriving in

Saigon. He'd kept it hidden in the bottom of his bag, and now he shoved it into the waistband of his trousers and ran after her.

"Evelyn!" She was walking towards the hotel door with a soldier, and she turned at the sound of her name. "If you're that determined to go, then I guess I'm coming with you."

"Thank you," she said quietly and put her hand in his and squeezed.

He thought she looked relieved, but she didn't say anything more. "Thank me if we make it back alive."

They walked out to the jeep where Evelyn introduced Terry to the driver. As they navigated the streets of Saigon, Terry thought there were more people than ever crowded onto the streets. The driver took them out to the airport and the American compound where a Huey sat waiting. The pilot handed them helmets and asked if they knew how to use weapons.

"I was over here in sixty-seven, sixty-eight. I can use anything you throw at me," Terry informed him.

"Good. I want you by the door," the pilot responded. "We're going to come in low to avoid being shot down. Do you think you can handle that?" He pointed to the door-mounted machine gun.

Terry nodded. He had used a machine gun countless times.

"Good. Don't use it unless I tell you to. We don't want to draw any more attention than we have to."

"I've always wanted to have a go on one of these," Terry said to Evelyn, winking at her, trying to make light of it all.

The pilot instructed Evelyn to strap herself into the back and told Terry where the weapons were, telling him to take what he needed. There was plenty of ammo too. He told them what he was doing and gave them instructions on how to find the convent when they landed.

"You have thirty minutes from the time you jump out of this chopper. If you are not back in thirty minutes, I am gone. With or without you. Understand?" The pilot looked at them both. Terry nodded.

The pilot checked Evelyn's lap belt and pointed to Terry's helmet; his voice crackled in Terry's ear. Terry gave him a thumbs up. He checked under the seat. There was an M16. He'd take that. There was also a wooden box, he opened it and helped himself to two grenades. He hoped like hell he wouldn't need any of it, but if they were stranded on their own, he'd probably need a lot more than he was able to carry.

Terry's heart hammered in his chest as the chopper vibrated and the earpiece crackled. He was as ready as he would ever be. He braced himself with a foot against the doorframe and the other against the machine gun mount. His hands gripped the gun; knuckles almost white. He was sweating like a pig, and his skin was itchy as all hell. But he couldn't scratch it; he needed to concentrate on everything around him.

The Huey lifted, its nose tilting down, before it swung out over the city and headed south. In all his trips in choppers, Terry had never felt this nervous. He felt sick to his stomach, and it was worse because Evelyn was in the chopper with him this time.

He had never been a religious man, but he was praying now. *Jesus, if you're watching out for anyone, watch out for Evelyn.* And Frankie. He looked to the heavens and prayed they would make it back. That they wouldn't get hit or attacked. Or captured.

The land gave way to the waterways, and for several minutes, they flew out over the South China Sea. Terry took a deep breath and hoped he wouldn't throw up.

Suddenly, the pilot was telling him he could see tracers, and they banked and swung back over the land again, coming in low. Terry felt like he could have reached out and touched the treetops as he swung the gun left and pointed it down towards the ground, ready to fire if he was given the order.

Then the pilot told them to get ready to get off, and Terry grabbed the M16 and another Colt and a spare clip. The skids rocked as they touched down, and the pilot told them they had thirty minutes. Then they were running. The feel of the weapon in his hands, the paddy field with puddles in it, so many memories. It was terrifying, exhilarating, and he was running on pure adrenaline.

He scanned the palms and shrubs on the side of the road; there was no sign of movement. Evelyn? Where was she? He looked over his shoulder. She was right behind him.

"Follow me," he murmured. "It looks abandoned, but we're being watched." He pointed to a gate surrounded by bamboo up ahead. The directions the pilot had given them were spot on.

They ran through the gate to a large, neglected building, and Evelyn rushed up to the wooden door and knocked. Terry checked his watch as the door opened. A nun greeted them in fluent English. He heard Evelyn talking, but he had his back to them and was watching the path they had just come down and what he could see of the road.

As she stepped inside, Terry followed.

"This is no place for guns," the nun addressed Terry in a firm voice.

"I'll wait out by the road. Be as quick as you can, Evelyn. And if you hear me yell or hear gunfire, it means we need to leave, and you need to run."

Evelyn nodded and followed the nun. Terry rechecked his watch and made his way back out towards the road. Every sense was heightened as he strained to hear any unfamiliar sounds. There was nothing. He glanced at his wrist again. He was back in soldier mode. Right back in nineteen sixty-eight, except now he didn't have the backup of the others. This time, he was on his own.

How was Evelyn getting on? Ten minutes had passed. Jesus, he was practically shitting himself. He rubbed his arm and felt the grenades shift in his pockets. Partially hidden in the bamboo, he looked one way then the other. Still no sign of life. It was eerie, and he didn't like it one little bit. Fifteen minutes. *Come on, Evelyn.* What if they got back to the chopper and the pilot had been killed? His mind was spinning all sorts of scenarios.

Several feet away, the bamboo rustled. Terry swung the M16 in that direction and held his breath. He'd be lucky if he didn't suffer a heart attack. A scrawny chicken wandered out and pecked at something on the ground. Nothing else moved. Twenty minutes! *Jesus, hurry up, Evelyn!*

He heard footsteps and swung around to see her running, and she had a child with her. *Surely not?*

He crouched down and the child climbed on his back. They had little more than six minutes to get to the chopper, or it was all over. They ran. Evelyn carried the child's bag, and the girl had her arms around his neck, and he sprinted. The pilot already had the rotors spinning, and he was waving at them from his seat, to hurry.

Evelyn scrambled in, and Terry pushed the child at her, yelling at her to get strapped in and hold on to the child. He then ran around to the gunner's door, pulling himself in as the pilot lifted the Huey off the ground and swung it back towards the sea. Terry pulled his helmet on and gripped the gun as the pilot flew low over the fields and plantations before hitting the sand dunes. Then they were out over the sea again, and he closed his eyes for a few moments and let the air rush over his face. He could feel tears on his cheeks, and he didn't know if they were from sheer relief, exhaustion or joy. He wiped his arm over his face and watched the boats pass under them.

When they landed back at Tan Son Nhut, the pilot helped Evelyn and the child out of the chopper and wished them all well.

"If I were you," he said to them, "I would get on the first plane out of here."

"Oh, believe me, we will be," Terry replied. He'd had enough of stunts like this to last a lifetime. And if Evelyn didn't want to go, he'd drag her onto the first plane out anyway.

When they got back to the hotel, the staff rushed to help the New Zealand couple who had made friends with everyone, and by some miracle, had finally found the orphaned girl they had been looking for. They sent a staff member out to buy some clothes, shoes and toiletries for the child. The whole time, the child clung to Evelyn, terrified at everything that was happening around her. She was only seven and had spent her whole life in a convent.

Terry looked at her in wonder. It must have been a traumatic few hours for Angel. Hell, it had been a traumatic few hours even for him. If they made it back home, she would be a very privileged child. Evelyn would see to that.

They ordered dinner to be delivered to their room, and the staff set up another small bed next to theirs, especially for the girl. She fell asleep lying next to Evelyn on the bed as Evelyn stroked her hair from her face and held her in her arms.

"So, how does it feel to be a mother?" Terry whispered.

"I don't know. None of it feels real."

"I can't believe you found her." She was the prettiest child he had ever seen. "Jack would be proud right now." He put an arm around Evelyn and squeezed her.

"I know this trip has been tough on you, but I will never be able to thank you enough for what you did today, for Jack and for Angel. It means a great deal." She watched him peel off his shirt. "Are you okay?"

"I need to make peace with a few demons, but I'll be fine."

"Promise me, Terry, if you ever need help–you know, if things get bad, you'll let me know. I don't want to lose you too."

He could see she was genuinely worried about him, and he leaned into her and kissed her on the forehead. "Don't worry. You won't." He stood up and walked silently to the open window. "Get some sleep. I'll be awake for a good while yet. I'll wake you if Angel stirs."

He stripped down to his briefs, lit a cigarette and leaned against the window frame, watching the bursts of light and listening to the explosions on the outskirts of the city. Today had taken him to places he didn't want to go, but he was pleased he had helped Evelyn do what she had come to do. Finally, they might be able to put Vietnam behind them and start afresh. Together.

He looked over at their bed. Evelyn was sleeping. He hadn't even noticed her climb into bed. He walked over to where Angel slept. If he married Evelyn, they would have a ready-made family. He hadn't thought about that. Maybe he would adopt Angel?

He crouched down and gently brushed the hair back from the little girl's face. This was the baby he had last seen asleep on the sofa in Vũng Tàu. The baby with the perfect fingers and long eyelashes that caressed perfect creamy skin. Her arms were free of the covers, lying on the pillow above her head. Terry peered closer. There it was. The birthmark.

He stood, staggered as if slapped by guilt, and then walked to the bed and sat down. They had found the baby he had fled from all those years ago. In the quiet space of the darkened room, as he sat begging his mind to shut down, even just for a few hours, he realised the odds of finding her had been almost zero. The odds of her surviving in this harsh environment had been equally low. But she had.

The sound of shelling somewhere on the outskirts of the city made him think about Jack. Jack and Angel. Somehow, by finding her, it had lifted some of the guilt he had carried with him all those years, as though he had finally paid off his debt after leaving her as a four-month-old baby. He couldn't bring his mate back, but he could sure as hell make sure Jack's daughter was well looked after.

Chapter 34

Frankie woke with a start. The room was shaking. Her first thought was an earthquake. She'd been dreaming about being back in Wellington, and Terry was swimming at Oriental Parade while she sat on the beach; then she remembered where she was. She tried to read the time on her bedside clock, but it was still too dark. She picked it up and held it closer. Oh God, it had only just gone four. She picked up the framed photograph and clutched it tightly.

A few days ago, when she'd arrived back in Saigon from Nha Trang, she was running across the tarmac to her car when she noticed an official-looking black sedan drive through the main gates and head for a large Bristol freighter. It looked like an embassy car, and she wondered who was in it. Whoever it was, they were smart if they were getting out now. A man stepped out, hurried around the car and opened the door. Frankie watched as a woman got out with a Vietnamese child. The three of them hurried to the plane and disappeared inside. They had almost no baggage. It was not an unusual sight. Everyone was leaving, especially officials and their families, but for some reason, the man had reminded her of Terry. She didn't know why. Maybe it was his walk, or the way he opened the door for the woman. Or perhaps it was that she had been thinking of him again during the chopper flight.

She was wide awake now. She pushed the sheet back and climbed out of bed, slipping a robe over her t-shirt and underwear. When she opened her bedroom door, she noticed the light on in the kitchen. Chris was making coffee.

"Hey–"

"Shit!" He jumped, slopping hot brown liquid on the bench.

"Sorry, didn't mean to scare the living daylights out of you."

"My poor heart." He patted his chest. "As if all this shelling isn't bad enough."

"There's nothing wrong with your heart," she said, giving him a playful punch on the arm. "They're getting close, aren't they? Has it been going on for a while?"

"Not long. I guess they're about a couple of miles or so from Saigon. Want a coffee?"

"Yes, thanks." She walked across to the plush leather sofa and sat cross-legged in the darkness.

"Here," he said, handing her a mug. "Want some lights?"

"Nope. I think I'll go up to the attic and watch the sun come up." 'The attic' was on the roof of their building. They had carried some timber up there and built a lean-to, adding a couple of chairs and a coffee table made from a small wooden box. Frankie had added a couple of pot plants, and they often went up to watch the sunset or sunrise and see which area was being shelled.

"Do you think today will be the day Saigon falls?" she asked.

"Maybe. I thought the North would have bombed the crap out of us by now. You sure you don't want to get the hell out of here?"

"Nope. I want to stay as long as I can. This is history in the making, and there's no way I want to leave. Anyway, I've seen way too much to run at a few bullets or flames."

"It could get nasty."

"Are you leaving?" she asked, sipping on her coffee.

"No chance. There are still stories to tell, and besides, I gotta make sure I get the story through before you guys at the AP."

"It'll never happen." She loved teasing him, and he always took the bait. "You coming up?"

"Lead the way."

From the attic, they sat looking out over the city in stunned silence. The sky above Tan Son Nhut Airport was a blaze of flames, and it appeared one end of the airport to the other was burning.

"Looks like it's begun," Chris said.

"Hope anyone who was planning on catching a flight out has left."

Chris put his arm around her shoulders. "Gotta say, girl, you've got guts. There will be a helluva lot of journalists who run."

"I would too if I had a family."

"Why don't you?"

"What?"

"Have a family. And kids. Most women your age would have been long married and have at least a couple of kids by now."

"I do have kids. I've spent the last eight years looking out for them.

The ones in the orphanages who have been given up in the hope of them being adopted by a family in another country, and the children whose skin is peeling or deformed because their village was Napalmed. The kids in their late teens, who have no idea what the world is about, who were told to pick up a weapon and start fighting for their country. I've cared about them all. And I've cried when they were killed for no obvious reason, other than some power-hungry world leader wanting to assert his ideology on a nation that has a history of winning against every country that's ever tried to overthrow them in the past."

"Okay, okay, sorry I asked," he said, laughing at her.

But he was right. She would be thirty-two this year and still hadn't married or had kids. Two years ago, one of her journalist friends had got married to a soldier in Da Nang, and they had both shipped out when his tour was over. But for Frankie, there had only ever been one man. And he was long gone. She drained the last of her coffee.

"There was a guy. A few years back now."

"Not the guy in the photo? Terry?"

"Yeah. He was a soldier. Did two tours and went home." She paused. "How did you know his name?"

"I saw him a few days ago," he said, casually. "Twice, actually. I forgot to tell you."

"The guy in the photo? You can't have. He's back in New Zealand."

"No. He was in the bar at the Continental. He overheard me talking about you with Ken Lester and asked after you."

"What?"

"Said to say hello. And the next morning when I was waiting for someone in Lam Son Square, I saw him again."

"When?" She couldn't believe he was here in the city, and if he was, what was he doing here?

"Twenty-fourth or maybe twenty-fifth."

"Was he alone?" she had to ask.

"He was drinking alone in the bar, as far as I know. But I saw him outside the hotel with a woman. They got into a jeep and were driven off. Didn't see him again after that."

That must have been the day she had arrived back from Nha Trang. She thought back to the black car she had seen and wondered if that had been Terry. She looked across towards Tan Son Nhut. Thick, black smoke draped across the airport, covering it like a heavy blanket. What had he been doing here? Was he with his wife or a friend?

As they sat in silence, a South Vietnamese Caribou rose through the dense smoke and before their eyes, broke in two then burst into flames. Before either of them could react, a second Caribou did the same thing.

"I need to get dressed and get to the bureau," Frankie said. "I should be out there getting photos of this, instead of dwelling on the past."

"Sometimes, it's good for our souls."

"I'll stop and think some more when this is all over," she replied as she dashed to the stairs.

Chapter 35

When she arrived at the bureau, Bobby Miller was still there. He was ashen and drawn, and she wondered when he had last left the building or even slept.

"Frankie, I thought you'd be home packing your bags," he greeted her when she walked into the office.

"Why?"

"Because I want you out on one of the first airlifts this morning."

"If you're staying, I'm staying."

"The hell you are."

"I want to. You can't do this on your own, and they're not going to throw us in prison. We're not dealing with the Khmer Rouge. I'll wire the New York office and tell them they need a photographer on the ground. I'm here. I'm familiar with the streets, and I'm known in the city. We're documenting history, and I'm not leaving now. Besides, I don't have a husband or kids like most of the others do."

The phone rang, and Bobby sighed. "Saved by the bell." He picked it up and listened to the caller then hung up. "Hughes has been out to look at the airport. He's issued a statement, no more flights in or out of the airport. The runways are now inoperable. It'll be helicopter pick-ups only from now on."

Hughes was the American ambassador, and he was refusing to leave Saigon before the rest of his staff. He had issued an order for the airlifts to start. When the Armed Forces Radio station played Bing Crosby's "White Christmas" over and over, it was the signal to evacuate, and personnel waiting to be airlifted were to head to one of the thirteen pickup points located around the city.

"Do we have the list?" Frankie asked. "I want to get out on the street and record what's happening," she said as she composed the message to the New York office.

"Yes. Somewhere," Miller said, shuffling through the papers on his desk. "Here."

"Right, I'll be back in an hour or so."

"Frankie–"

She turned to see what he wanted.

"Be careful."

"I will!" She ran down the four flights of stairs to her little Citroën. She'd bought it for a song two years ago, and it had served her well. Once in the car, she edged it out into the traffic.

The population of Saigon had now swelled to several million, many living on the streets or wherever they could find shelter. Many had gathered around the airport or the port hoping to find a way out of the country. People with any links at all to the Americans or the South Vietnamese Army were particularly vulnerable.

Frankie headed towards the port. As she parked the car and jumped out, she could see it was a hive of activity. With her camera around her neck and several rolls of film in her pocket, she made her way through the scores of people. Boats of all shapes and sizes were leaving, making their way down the river, each one crowded with people.

She had never seen anything like this. When she returned to her car, she decided she would head for the American Embassy, to see what was happening there. It was harder manoeuvring through the packed streets and it got worse the closer she got to the embassy. It was almost midday, and Frankie could see a large crowd had already gathered around the gates, shouting and pushing to get closer to the gates and walls. There would have been several thousand, and they were well aware that their only chance of getting out of Saigon was to get on one of the choppers that were landing on the embassy roof.

She parked the Citroën well clear and climbed onto the hood to watch the crowds. It was a good vantage point for taking photos. Marines stood guard inside the perimeter wall and at the gates. Two Marines even stood on top of the wall, watching the jostling crowd below. Frankie thought it wouldn't take much to swell this group to unmanageable and turn it into something ugly. In time, they would breach the gate and flood the embassy building. One of the Marines noticed her and motioned her to come closer. She clambered down off the hood and struggled through the crowd. There were insults and protests as people realised the western woman was being let into the compound. The crowd surged behind her hoping to push through with her.

"Do you want to come in, ma'am?" he yelled at her over the heads of agitated locals when she was close enough.

"No." She shook her head.

"Stand back then, ma'am," he yelled at her.

Frankie nodded, and as she turned to walk back to the Citroën, the young Marine threw a canister. She heard it hit the ground, the clatter of metal against the road, and within seconds the area was a cloud of white as people ran through it, yelling and clawing at their eyes. From the midst of it, a child was screaming. Frankie grabbed her camera and clicked off a couple of shots and then ran for the car, her shirt partially covering her face. She could feel her eyes sting and her throat felt like she had swallowed fire. This was definitely not a good situation. She drove past the palace, tears streaming down her face as she rubbed at her eyes, trying to clear her blurred vision. There was an increased military police presence, but otherwise, all was quiet at the palace.

She pulled the car up under a tree and sat for a few minutes. Somewhere on the floor was a canteen of water. She fumbled awkwardly for it and spun the cap off, pouring it over her face, trying to wash the chemicals from her eyes. Thirty minutes later, her vision wasn't so blurred, and she decided to visit some of the evac points on the list.

The driving was even slower now, as the streets overflowed with people carrying small bags, boxes or sacks with their most valuable possessions in them. Some pushed bicycles overloaded with boxes or pieces of furniture. Some stood in the street staring at the choppers as they passed overhead. Compassion stirred deep inside her. There were now thousands of homeless in Saigon, and only a select few would be able to flee the city. It was a tragedy for the families facing the onslaught of the invading North.

When Frankie returned to the office, she found Bobby Miller chewing the end of his cigarette, his head down as he typed. He lifted his head to look at her, and his eyes widened.

"Jesus, what the hell happened?" She knew she must look a mess. Her eyes and face were rubbed red, and the front of her shirt and her trousers were soaked.

"Got caught in a crowd control exercise." She rubbed at her eyes. They still stung, but at least she could see more clearly now. The water had helped. "I need coffee."

She filled him in on what she had seen.

"Well, it seems the lines of communication are not working as well as they should have," he said. He followed Frankie to the coffee pot and held out his mug for a refill. "Some of those thirteen evac points haven't been used. It's leaving a lot of people confused and vulnerable, especially the Vietnamese who were working for the CIA."

Reportedly, there were only about two hundred Americans left in Saigon now, and half of them were Marines, CIA and journalists. The rest were Vietnamese staff from the embassy.

"Where's John Wayne and Ramirez?" Frankie asked, looking around the office. There were only the four of them left at the AP bureau now. Miller had sent everyone else home. John Wayne, as he liked to be called, otherwise known as Hong, was their Vietnamese interpreter. He was a devoted John Wayne fan, and one of the journalists had put a poster up on the wall for him; he had been delighted.

"Ramirez headed over to the American Embassy just before you arrived back. He's going to spend the night there. They're expecting it to cut up rough." He sat on the corner of his desk and drank his coffee. "I have no idea where John Wayne is. He disappeared about half an hour ago."

"I might take my coffee up onto the roof, to see if I can get an idea of what's going on." She grabbed her camera and climbed the stairs.

Across the skyscape, the light was fading fast. The city had made it through another day, but they all expected the city to fall at any moment. She put her mug down and started taking photos. A chopper passed overhead, it was close enough for Frankie to see the pilot look in her direction, and she lifted her camera and took his photo before he was just a blur. There was still smoke in the sky in the direction of the airport as the sun set. When Frankie had finished taking photos, she sat down cross-legged on the roof and stared out into the night. She could just make out the shapes of choppers still ferrying people from evac sites out to the waiting ships.

It was a sad sight. She thought about her naivety when she first arrived in the city and all the assignments she had been on, the young men she had befriended, and the officers who had trusted her and let her accompany them on operations. She remembered how safe the city had been in the early years. She thought of Miss Lilac and the girls who worked for her. She remembered Louis who had lost his life doing the job he loved. And Terry. He had been such a big part of her life here in Vietnam. She wondered if that had been him at the Continental, or if Chris had been mistaken. She seriously doubted it was. Surely he wouldn't have come back here, and he wouldn't have come back to look for her. Hell, he wouldn't even know if she was still here.

All she knew was that she couldn't give him the things a man like him needed. Deserved. She'd had to do the right thing and let him go, so he could find someone and make a decent life for himself. Be happy. Have kids. There was no telling where she would go after Vietnam, or even if she would make it out alive now. The chances of getting out were almost nil. She hoped he had found someone. Hoped he had settled down and was making something of himself.

"Hey! Frankie!" Bobby's voice carried across to where she was sitting.

Frankie rubbed at her eyes.

"You all right up here?"

"Yeah." She followed him back inside. "I'll stay here with you tonight," she told Bobby when they got back down to the office.

"You don't need to. Go home and get some sleep."

"I feel safer here," she replied. "I'll go and find us something to eat." She turned and left the office.

They ate noodles and drank Cokes, and Frankie cleared a desk off and turned it into a makeshift bed.

"I'm not sure how the communists will run the takeover, and I don't want you to feel you have to stay," Bobby said to her as they were checking the last wire feeds for the night.

"I want to stay."

"What I'm trying to say is that it might get ugly."

"I've coped with ugly almost every day since I arrived."

"You've been one of the best photographers the AP could have employed, Frankie. And a good friend. I just want you to know you've done a bloody good job for us. And I will always consider you a close friend."

Frankie walked over to Bobby and put her arms around him. He had been like a father to her during her time in Vietnam, and it had been kind of him to give her the break she needed to secure a job as a combat photographer.

"Thank you for giving me that opportunity all those years ago." She kissed him on the cheek and climbed onto the desk that was now her makeshift bed.

At five-thirty the following morning, the telex machine started humming, and when the phone rang, Frankie heard Bobby answer it. She sat up, stretching an aching body. Sleep had been almost impossible, her own bed would have been much more comfortable, but she wanted to be here at the office, even if for no other reason, than to get any news updates.

Bobby hung up.

"Well, two hours ago, the American Embassy staff destroyed all their communication equipment, and half an hour ago they evacuated Hughes. It sounds like the embassy is on the verge of falling."

Ten minutes later, Ramirez burst in through the office door.

"The embassy is almost empty. They've got a Sea Knight coming in at six to collect the remaining staff and Marines. Then it's all over as far as they're concerned."

"Do you want to get on that chopper?" Bobby looked at both him and Frankie. "Either of you?"

"Nope, I'm staying," Frankie stated.

"Same here," Ramirez agreed. "I just came back to get some coffee and more rolls of film. Thought I might go for a wander." He looked at Frankie. "Coming?"

"Sure."

It was still early, but the streets were already alive. In Lam Son Square, they witnessed a group of about twelve people fighting and haggling over a king-sized bed.

"Shit I hope that's not mine," Frankie said, pointing her camera in their direction.

"The looting has begun. Do you want to call past your place, check everything's okay?"

"Wouldn't mind."

They walked to Chris's apartment. It was on a popular street, and although they had a small courtyard out the front, the building didn't look French or ostentatious on the outside. Frankie tried the front gate, but it was locked.

"Follow me." She led the way down the side of the building, the gap between the building next door and theirs was only just wide enough to walk through in single file. Towards the back, a small hole in the wall revealed a door latch. Frankie lifted it, and the door swung open.

They found the apartment empty. Chris was probably out chasing a story. Ramirez waited while Frankie threw her few prized belongings into her army-issue pack, along with a change of clothing, just in case the apartment was looted, then they hurried back down to the street. They heard a lone chopper approach, watched it hover and then land on top of the CIA building, and from the street below, they could see people clambering up a ladder trying to get on board.

"There's no way they're all gonna fit on that," Ramirez stated.

"What's the time?" Frankie asked, shooting more photos.

"Seven forty-five."

"Let's head down past the cathedral to the embassy."

They heard the chopper before they saw it and arrived in time to see the large Sea Knight helicopter lift off from the embassy roof, circle around to the left and fly away.

The scene before them was unbelievable. Frankie took photo after photo of the joyous crowd now left to loot the building. Some people cried–the choppers had been their only hope of leaving the city–while others carried furniture out of the building. An elderly woman dragged a fancy chair while others carried food items looted from the kitchens. Anything that wasn't bolted to the floor or wall was being taken.

They pushed through the chaos to see what was happening inside. It was even worse, and as they walked through the rooms taking photos, Frankie noticed someone had taken a sink bench from a kitchen.

"Hey, Frankie! Come look at this." Ramirez was looking at something on the ground.

"What is it?"

"It's a bronze plaque with the names of the men who died during the Tet attack on the embassy. Do you think we could carry it back to the office? For safekeeping?"

Between them, they carried the plaque back to the office, thankful they didn't have to fight anyone for it; it would have been worth a small fortune had it been melted down. Frankie was exhausted. With little sleep the night before, it was going to be a long day.

"I see John Wayne is back," she commented to Bobby as she helped herself to a Coke from the fridge.

"Turned up about twenty minutes ago, says we need to listen to the radio"–Bobby checked his watch–"in three minutes."

The radio was on and tuned into a station broadcasting something in Vietnamese, which no one there except their interpreter could understand. Frankie put down her pack and pulled up a chair. It was easy to tell what the radio was broadcasting by the look on John Wayne's face.

He suddenly sprang from his chair and flung his arms in the air.

"It is surrender!" John Wayne shouted. "President is announcing complete capitulation! It is now official."

Bobby was out of his chair and straight through to the teleprinter room to message the New York office. John Wayne was full of smiles and repeating the words, "It is surrender! It is surrender." Frankie wondered which side he was batting for. She grabbed her camera and ran downstairs. Outside, small groups of young men dressed in their black pyjama-like uniforms, rode the streets in jeeps, cheering and waving flags. Frankie couldn't understand what they were chanting, but she knew enough to tell the guns they were carrying were Russian AK-47 rifles.

In Lam Son Square, a huge communist flag was being unfurled from an upstairs window of the Caravelle. She took several photos and then turned towards the Continental. People were everywhere. To one side, a South Vietnamese general saluted a statue. She took his photo and then rushed to get a little closer. She wanted to capture the look on his face. As she focused the lens, he pulled out a pistol, held it to his head and fired, blowing his brains out. He crumpled to the ground, almost at her feet. She staggered back, shocked. He had given his life for South Vietnam and freedom and wasn't prepared to live under communist rule. She wondered if he had a family. A wife or children somewhere, waiting for him to come home?

She ran across the square and down towards Miss Lilac's. The doors were closed, and there was no sign of Miss Lilac or her girls. Around her, Frankie noticed young South Vietnamese soldiers discarding their uniforms as they ran. They were throwing their weapons in doorways and kicking off their shoes. Trying desperately to rid themselves of anything that would identify them as soldiers in the South Vietnamese army. It was eleven, and she had almost run out of film. She decided to head back to the office. A Russian tank covered in soldiers rumbled up the street towards the square, one of the soldiers holding a communist flag.

"We made it," Bobby told Frankie as she stepped into the office.

"Made what?"

"We got the news through to New York that Saigon had fallen before the UPI or any of the others," Bobby gloated. "Beat 'em by a whole five minutes." He looked pleased with himself.

Competition to file the news stories was always tight between the different agencies, and a five-minute break in a story the whole world was waiting to hear, was huge indeed.

"John Wayne translated that the president has now been arrested. Apparently, he surrendered in order to stop further bloodshed," Ramirez reported to Frankie.

"A wise man."

"And then John Wayne fled the office. I doubt we'll see him again," Ramirez said with a chuckle as the office door opened and an NVA officer stepped inside.

Frankie glanced at Bobby. Had they come to shut the place down and arrest them? She could feel her hands shake. Bobby stood up and casually walked over to the officer.

"Welcome to the Associated Press office. I'm Robert Miller, the bureau chief." He put his hand out to shake the officer's.

"Good afternoon," the officer replied, in excellent English. "I am Major Van Ho Pham." He stepped further into the room. "I take it you have heard the news?"

"Yes, we have. We are running with a skeleton staff as you can see, Major. This is Frankie Proctor." He gestured towards Frankie. "And this is Alberto Ramirez. Have a seat."

The officer shook their hands and smiled.

"So, this is where the news is fed to a waiting world?"

"It is indeed. I'd like to congratulate you on a peaceful victory. If you can call it that? Would you join us for a cold drink and something to eat?"

They sat in the office for the next thirty minutes, chatting to the major while they all drank cold Cokes and ate whatever they could find in the small kitchenette in the office. Frankie was surprised at how casual the officer was and impressed that he hadn't come to march them all away and lock them up.

Bobby asked him about what their plans were, and although Major Pham divulged some information, Frankie felt he was playing his cards close to his chest. He knew who he was talking to.

As soon as the major had left, Ramirez and Bobby started to write up what he had said, and Frankie retreated to the darkroom. She was keen to see some of the images she had captured and eager to get them out of the city, now it lay in the hands of the North Vietnamese. An hour later, she had five contact sheets and on them were images that would open the eyes of every news agency in America.

"I've got some great–"

Bobby was sitting behind his desk, head in his hands, and Ramirez was leaning back in his chair, drawing on his cigarette, his long legs stretched out on the desk in front of him.

"What's happened?"

"It's over, Frankie," Ramirez stated.

"What?"

"We got the stories out and four of your photos, but that's it. The authorities have pulled the plug. The AP wire from Saigon is now down and out. It's time to go home."

PART THREE

1975

Chapter 36

The nights Terry couldn't sleep were the worst. He had been thinking about his mate Jack lately. Sometimes, just for a fleeting moment, Terry got a sense of how Jack must have felt, when things just got too much. It seemed like Terry felt crook all the time and everything ached. He was covered in blisters, and now, the doctor was finding skin cancers all over him.

But Terry didn't have the guts to do what Jack had done.

A noise outside the hut attracted his attention. Terry rolled over and stared into the darkness. The hunter's hut was small, and from his sleeping bag, he could make out the window and the treetops silhouetted in the moonlight. The remnants of the fire still held a little warmth, but not for much longer.

He tried not to think about Vietnam and the things that happened over there. Or Frankie. It always came back to Frankie. She was a distant memory now, but one he couldn't give up either. He kept her to himself, a special treat for the times he spent on his own. He didn't want to forget her features: her coppery hair and the way her freckles danced on her face when she laughed, but it was getting harder these days to remember. Too much time had passed.

At home he always left the radio on at night, the volume turned down low; there was always music playing, or a talk show. And if he woke, the noise dissolved the dreams and brought him back to the present. In the jungle, he had come to like the sounds at night; it had been the silence that terrified him, and occasionally it still did. He'd lost count of the number of times he had found himself straining to hear the crunch of a footstep, the snap of a twig. Dawn in the bush seemed to take forever, yet the moment you nodded off, some bugger was nudging you awake.

Terry's guts rolled and refused to settle. He'd been feeling off colour for several weeks and ignoring it. Maybe it was time he saw a doctor. He swung his legs over the side of the bunk and hauled himself up. Pulling on a cotton t-shirt, and then his jacket, he threw a couple more bits of wood on the embers, poured water into the billy and sat it on top of the fire. Opening the door of the hut, he peered cautiously out into the bush. Listening, watching the shapes and shadows. The air was crisp, and nothing moved, not that he expected it to, but he always checked. Every night, no matter where he was. A habit he had to thank his time in Vietnam for.

A steer roared from the other side of the valley. The boys would be pleased about that, but to be honest, he didn't care so much for deer stalking any longer. It wasn't the same without Jack. Even using the rifles held little appeal. Now, it was more about spending time with good mates, telling some stories, having a beer or two, and a few laughs.

As he sat on an old wood stump on the deck, he lit up a cigarette and inhaled. He held the match to his wristwatch. It was almost three. He inhaled again and flicked the match, watching it arc out over the deck, die and disappear in the darkness.

Once again, his thoughts drifted to Jack, as they always did when he was out in the bush. He had never gone back to the hut up on the ridge after finding his mate's body there, and he never would. Shit, he missed Jack.

His thoughts turned to Evelyn and what she had been through. She had miscarried not long after she and Jack married. It had shaken her, and she had been left to cope on her own while Jack resorted to alcohol and drugs to help him come to terms with the loss of two babies. In the end, Evelyn had packed her things and left. It had taken almost two years for them to get back together, and in that time, Jack had cleaned himself up. And then he had gone and fucking topped himself. No warning. One day he went out, and simply never came home.

Jack had been his best mate, and he should have seen the signs. Something. Evelyn had been inconsolable. It broke his heart. Vietnam was killing them all one by one, one way or another. He would be happy if he never laid eyes on the place ever again. Especially after the trip back to get Angel.

The first thing Evelyn had done when they got back from Saigon was change Angel's name and lodge adoption papers. She renamed her Jackie in memory of her father, and everyone thought the name fitted her perfectly. To everyone's amusement, Jackie took a shine to Terry and followed him everywhere. Terry still carried guilt over leaving her behind in sixty-eight, and for having all the things Jack didn't: his wife, his daughter and even his house once they were married. At times, he felt like an imposter living someone else's life.

The hut door opened, and a finger of lamplight rushed the deck, narrowing and fading as the door closed again.

"Problem sleeping or are you just excited about spending the weekend with us?" Ron asked.

"Got sick of listening to you snore, more like it."

"Get this down ya," Ron said, handing Terry an enamel mug of steaming hot tea.

"Cheers, mate."

"You're not back in the jungle are you?"

"Nope."

"You looked like you had that thousand-yard stare."

"I was thinking of Jack. It's been two years since we lost the bugger."

Silence fell between them.

"You been doing okay?" Ron asked.

"Yeah. Nothing to worry about." Terry took a sip of the steaming liquid. "Nothing at all."

"How are the wedding plans coming along?"

"As far as I know, everything's falling into place. You're going to come, aren't you?"

"Wild horses wouldn't keep me away, mate."

The wedding date was set for the first weekend in June, and it was now two weeks away.

"Hope I'm doing the right thing."

"Yeah. I reckon every man who's two weeks out from tying the knot says that. Evelyn knows her own mind. She's not about to get married if she doesn't want to." Ron sat down beside Terry. "Let's face it mate, look at her. She's a total babe. She could have anyone."

"Thanks for the morale boost."

"Where are you going to live? Her place?"

"I guess so. Well, for the time being, anyway. She owns her own place, and I'm only renting. I pretty much live there as it is." He sat thinking about everything they hadn't talked about yet and realised he didn't know how his future wife felt about a lot of things. It made sense for him to shift in with her, but he needed to talk to her about shifting closer to town. Come to think of it, he had no idea if she was going back to work either.

"Right, I think we should get some food cooking and have a feed before we head out."

"Right-o mate."

Matt was up and busy stoking the fire when they went back inside. Steam gushed from the blackened billy, and he was sorting through food supplies on the hut's modest table.

"Stand aside," Ron said, muscling in beside Matt. "You can hunt it and kill it, but I don't want you bloody cooking it–it doesn't need to die twice!"

Terry laughed. His mates were just what he needed right now.

They cooked up sausages, bacon, eggs, and tomatoes while Matt toasted bread over the fire. After breakfast, they sorted their packs and rifles then headed out for a day stalking the stag Terry had heard bellowing on the other side of the gully.

By the end of the day, they had shot a boar, and had followed a couple of trails, but had seen nothing of the stag, and Terry was exhausted and sore where his pack rubbed the skin on his shoulders. He complained to the others he was getting too old for chasing deer, and they laughed at him and told him he was getting old before his time.

He was only twenty-nine, but at times he felt like an old man. When he got home the following afternoon, he felt like he had been living rough for the last month. His body ached, and he was breathing heavily, he was bloated and had cramps and felt like he could do with a bloody good feed, even though they had eaten well on the trip. Perhaps he was coming down with something, but he had no idea what.

They held the wedding in the little Anglican Church on Seabury Ave at Foxton Beach. It was the church Evelyn had married Jack in and where they had held Jack's funeral. Evelyn's sister, Joyce, and Terry's mate Ron were their official witnesses. Matt and his wife, Helen, were present, along with Terry's sister Judy and her husband. His mother and Vernon sat at the front of the church with their sons, and his father sat a couple of seats further back with a blonde woman Terry hadn't seen before. He wondered if they were an item, or if his father had brought her along to show his ex-wife he was still able to pull the birds. It was the sort of thing his father would do.

Evelyn's parents and Ray Coles, Jack's dad, sat at the front of the church too. Everyone turned as Evelyn entered the church and started her walk up the narrow aisle.

Glowing in a beautiful short satin dress and lace overcoat, she held Jackie's hand as they walked side by side. Evelyn and Jackie both carried small bouquets of miniature rose buds sprinkled with gypsophila and tied with matching satin ribbons. Terry's two younger sisters followed behind, carrying tiny baskets of confetti.

As Evelyn stood next to him, he thought his heart might burst with love and pride. He took her hand as they said their wedding vows. When they were pronounced husband and wife, he kissed her while all around them the room filled with applause.

They went back to Hallet's Hotel at the beach for the reception. The hotel, owned by Evelyn's parents, was closed for the private function.

By the time they got back to the house on the farm, everyone was feeling sleepy and sated. Terry carried Jackie inside, and Evelyn carefully changed her into her pyjamas and tucked her into bed. She was sound asleep almost before her head hit the pillow.

Evelyn sat on the side of Jackie's bed.

"You okay?" Terry asked, kissing her on the top of her head. It had been a big day for all of them.

"Yes. I'm fine. Just thinking about everything that's happened in the last couple of months."

"I'm going to lock up. We'll leave the wedding presents in the car. I'll get them in the morning."

"Thanks."

He turned off the outside light and stepped outside, then dug in his pocket for his cigarettes and tapped one free. It was the perfect, crisp winter night. He shouldn't be smoking; it didn't help his breathing in the winter. He sighed, it was another thing to worry about. He walked around the side of the house and across the front lawn towards the letter box. The fog had rolled in, and the moon bathed everything in a mysterious, pearlescent glow. He inhaled, blew the smoke out, coughed, and finished his perimeter check.

From the direction of the house, he heard Evelyn call him. He tossed his cigarette butt to the ground and strode back to the house.

Evelyn was standing on the bottom step, her arms wrapped around herself. She was slowly learning his habits.

"Everything okay?"

"Yes, ma'am!"

She reached out to take his arm.

"You looked so beautiful today." He kissed her gently on the lips, and then bent and scooped her up.

"Terry!"

"I'm carrying you over the threshold. It's traditional."

"You're a wonderful man," she said, staring up at him.

"Don't you forget it." He grinned, placing her down in the kitchen.

"I feel like I haven't even had time to tell you, what with organising the wedding and getting Jackie sorted and into school."

"You don't need to tell me. It shows in your eyes when you look at me." He shut the door and locked it.

"Personally, I thought you looked pretty smart yourself today. And Jackie did a fabulous job of walking me down the aisle." She unbuttoned his shirt as she spoke, and he removed his tie as they backed towards their bedroom.

"She did."

When he stood in his underwear and socks, she turned so he could unzip her, and as the zip reached the bottom, the dress slipped from her shoulders and fell gracefully to the floor. She stooped to pick it up and lay it on a chair. And he reached up and pulled the pins from her hair, letting it fall to her shoulders then unfastened her bra and peeled it from her. She was beautiful. Every inch of her. Just as he had imagined all those years ago. He lifted her and placed her on their bed.

"Hey, you've got that rash back."

"I know. It's fine. Don't interrupt me, woman!"

Evelyn laughed. It was cold in the house tonight. No one had been home to light the fire, and as he pulled the bedding up around them for warmth, she leaned into him and kissed him.

"I've got something to tell you."

"What is it? You changed your mind and want a divorce?" he joked.

"I'm pregnant."

"What?" He was going to be a father? He was speechless at first, and then he had so many questions he wanted to ask.

"That's wonderful news! When? How far gone are you? Do you

know what it is? How long have you known?"

"Whoa! Slow down, cowboy. I'm only five weeks." She was laughing at him now. He grabbed her and pulled her on top of him, and as their bodies pressed together, he asked if he could still make love to her with his baby growing inside her.

She nodded and told him it was perfectly fine. As their lips met, he gently made love to her. It was possible that right at this moment, he was the happiest man alive.

Chapter 37

Evelyn wanted to get Jackie a pony for her eighth birthday, but Terry didn't think it was such a good idea. The subject had come up more than once, and this time Terry wasn't in the mood for an argument. He had just arrived home from work. He'd had problems with a customer's car and had worked late to try to get it finished. He'd been feeling crook for several days and had been putting off making an appointment to see the doctor, and now Evelyn was harping on about getting Jackie a pony.

"We live on a farm," Evelyn stated.

"What if we shift from here? What do we do with the bloody thing then?"

"We aren't going to shift from here," Evelyn stated, matter-of-factly.

"That's something we haven't discussed yet." He pulled his boots off and closed the door behind him. And that was another issue he had been pussy-footing around. They needed to shift out of Jack's house. It held too many memories, and he suspected that was one of the reasons Evelyn wanted to stay.

"What do we need to discuss? It's a perfectly good home."

"A perfectly good home Jack built for *you*."

"Oh, for goodness' sake."

"Where's Jackie?"

"She's gone with Ray to feed the calves. I'm sure he wouldn't mind keeping her pony, if need be."

"That might be the case, but we shouldn't have to ask him."

"It's just a pony, Terry."

"It's not *just* a bloody pony," he argued, stripping out of his overalls and throwing them in the general direction of the laundry. "That child is spoilt rotten. She is not having a pony. What about something more manageable for a child, like a puppy?"

"She has her heart set on a pony."

"*You* have her heart set on a pony. At least she could look after a puppy herself."

"We'll see," she replied, dismissively. "I'm throwing a birthday party for her on Saturday. Do you want to tell your mother? She could bring the children out for the day."

"I'll call in and see her after work tomorrow." He stalked through to the bathroom and took two paracetamol tablets and a shower, leaving her to her plans. Since they had brought Jackie home from Vietnam, Evelyn had done nothing but spoil her. It wasn't the child's fault. She was only a kid, for Christ's sake. It was Evelyn. She was set on providing everything and anything she thought the child wanted. He understood Jackie had suffered a lot in her short life but spoiling her wasn't going to help.

The following night, he called in to see his mother to organise picking up the kids and bringing them out to the farm for Jackie's birthday party. His mother told him she would make some plates of food to help out. The smell of their dinner cooking made him feel sick, which reminded him he had forgotten to make an appointment to see the doctor again.

It wasn't until he pulled up outside Matt's place he realised he'd forgotten to tell his mum about the baby, and he felt disappointed. He'd tell her on Saturday.

He knocked on the door and waited. Helen answered.

"Hello, Terry, come on in."

"Thanks, Helen. I won't stay long, just wanted to ask Matt something. Is he home?"

"Be home in"–she checked the clock on the wall–"five minutes. Would you like to stay and have some dinner with us?"

"No thanks." He shook his head. "Evelyn's expecting me. But I'll have a cuppa, if you're boiling the jug."

Five minutes later, they heard a car pull up in the drive and a door shut.

"Terry, mate, how's it going?" The two men shook hands. Helen placed another mug of tea on the table for her husband and went back to preparing their evening meal.

"Good. I'm not staying, just wondered if you knew of anyone who might have a puppy for sale, one suitable for a child."

"For that wee girl of yours?"

"Yeah. It's her birthday in a couple of days, and I thought she'd enjoy a pet."

"I've got a mate over in Shannon whose wife's bitch had a litter. They'd probably be almost a year old now, though. Not sure how many she's got left though. Any good?"

"What breed?"

"Springer Spaniel."

"Yeah, perfect. Can you give me their phone number? I'll go over and take a look."

Matt wrote the guy's name, number and address on the back of an envelope and handed it to Terry.

"How's Evelyn?"

"She's good. She's expecting."

"That's great news, mate! Congratulations."

"I must go see her sometime," Helen said, putting the potato peeler down. "Is she keeping okay? No morning sickness?"

"Not that I know of. She wants to start working again. Singing at the odd local gig, and the occasional trip to Auckland. It seems her manager's keen to get her back up there."

"What will she do with Jackie?"

"Evelyn's mother can mind her after school. I'll pick her up after work, and she'll be all right at home with me on weekends."

"You're okay with this?"

"Evelyn's a strong-willed woman. She'll do what she wants. Besides, Jackie's a great little kid." He drained the last of his drink. "Well, I better be getting back. Thanks for the tea, Helen."

"Any time. Give Evie my love and tell her to give me a ring if she needs any help on Saturday."

"Will do."

The weather wasn't good on Saturday. The forecast was for showers. Evelyn had told Jackie they were having a special party to celebrate her birthday and the child was excited. She had never been to a party before and didn't even know when her birthday was.

The house wasn't big, and the thought of being trapped inside with a dozen noisy children was less appealing than Terry liked to admit. He helped Evelyn hang crepe-paper streamers in the sitting room and rearrange the furniture, so the children could all sit in a circle on the floor with plenty of room to play pass the parcel, pin the tail on the donkey, and other party games.

Evelyn's sister, Joyce, arrived, along with his sister Judy and her daughter. Helen was arriving shortly. She had offered to bring Terry's sisters out with her to save Terry the trip.

Terry retreated to the garage. It was his safe haven, and he had spent numerous hours lining one side of it, shifting his tools in, and making it his. It didn't make much difference, every time he opened the door, it reminded him of Jack. It was Jack's shed, and always would be in his mind. He had picked up a second-hand sofa and rigged up a make-do bar at one end. A piece of plywood on some old tyres made a great table. On the other side, he was working on restoring an old 1952 De Soto Model Six. It kept him busy, and he would probably sell it when he had finished. Now and again, the boys would get together out there to have a drink and talk cars, rugby or hunting.

He had his head buried under the hood when Jackie appeared beside him.

"Hello, kiddo." He stood up and stretched. "How's the party going?" He picked up the rag he had sitting on the engine block and wiped his hands.

"It's the best party. Evelyn said to bring you this." She offered him a plate.

He took the plate from her and walked over to the sofa and sat down. Jackie followed him.

"Thank you, love. Is this a piece of your birthday cake?"

She nodded. "Yes. It is very big and looks like a caterpillar, and it even has legs!"

"Impressive. Thank you for saving me a piece."

She sat on the edge of the sofa and watched him take a bite. "I like living with you and Evelyn."

"That's good because we love having you live with us." He winked at her and grinned. "How do you like being eight?"

"Eight is a good age to be."

Terry finished the piece of cake.

"Would you like some more?"

"No thank you, kiddo. But a little bird told me you have sausage rolls and cheerios. I might come and get a couple. They're my favourites."

Jackie looked puzzled. "Do you have a talking bird?"

Terry laughed. "No. How about I come with you, and we get something else to eat?"

She took Terry's hand and led him back to the house.

The rain had stopped, and the sun was out. Terry noticed Ray walking across the paddock towards the house. He was wearing his oilskin coat with the collar pulled up, and he was leading a small pony. He waved out. Damned Evelyn. Terry being polite, waved back.

"Well, look who's heading this way." He should have known Evelyn would get her own way.

Jackie was jumping up and down, still holding his hand.

"Hello, Jackie, happy birthday!"

When Ray got to the fence, he tied the reins to a post.

"Can I have a ride?"

"I don't see why not. He's yours. His name is Oscar. Let's go open the gate, and then your friends can have a ride too."

"I'll get the gate," Terry offered. "You can handle the influx of kids." He wasn't impressed with Evelyn.

Jackie was beside herself with excitement. She ran inside yelling for Evelyn and returned pulling Evelyn with her, followed by a stream of children. Evelyn glanced at Terry, and all he could do was shake his head. He left them all to it and disappeared back inside the garage.

"How's my little brother holding up?"

"Hey, Jude, how's things with you?"

She was carrying two mugs of steaming tea. She put them down on the workbench, and he stopped what he was doing and gave her a hug.

"Good. Just taking a breather. I always forget how much work these kids parties are."

Terry chuckled.

"The kids are pretty impressed with Oscar. They're going to want to come out here every weekend," she said.

"Don't get me started on the bloody horse."

"He's lovely."

"He may be, but he's a bit over the top for an eight-year-old."

"So, wasn't your idea then?"

"Nope."

"Let it go. Let Evie spoil her. The child deserves it. Maybe Evelyn does too."

"Maybe."

"Anyway, thought I'd come out and offer my congratulations."

"Evelyn told you about the baby?"

"Yep. You're pretty quick off the mark."

"I don't fire blanks."

She laughed. "Spare me the details. I don't need to know."

"I'm a bit nervous about the whole fatherhood thing, though."

"You're already a dad to one cute little kid. You're a natural."

"Thanks for the encouragement."

"That's what big sisters are for." She pretended to punch him on the arm. "I better get back in there and help Evie."

"Thanks for the tea."

"I'll catch you later."

Over an hour later, Evelyn came to find him in the garage. He was sitting in the driver's seat, polishing the chrome on the dash of the De Soto. She opened the passenger door and slipped in beside him.

"What a day," she said, leaning back against the seat. "They've all gone home. It's safe to come out."

"What's Jackie doing?"

"She's in the bath. She's had a lovely day."

"That's good." He screwed the cap back on the bottle of polishing liquid.

"It will be early to bed tonight, though."

"How are you feeling?" He turned to look at her.

"Tired. But happy."

"Don't overdo it. Do you think you should be going up to Auckland next weekend?"

"There's no reason not to. Why don't you finish up here and come inside?"

"I'll be in shortly."

The rain had started again, and the ground squelched under his feet as he ran to the back door. Winter was depressing. Summer couldn't come soon enough.

Chapter 38

Evelyn was staying at the Embassy Royal Hotel in the middle of Auckland. It was a quick trip: up Friday and back on Sunday. Her manager, Tony, had booked her a gig that was too tempting to turn down. He had repeatedly told her if she didn't keep a profile out there, she would find it harder and harder to get jobs.

On Saturday morning, she had breakfast delivered to her room and lazed a little longer in bed than she should have. She read the paper and then rang Terry and checked that they were okay.

"We're heading over to Shannon to see the puppies today," he reminded her.

"Jackie will love that. Make sure she wears something warm."

"I will. You just look after yourself. And our baby."

"I will. Someone's at the door. I have to go. I'll ring you again tomorrow before I leave."

"Okay, love. Good luck tonight."

"Thanks. Love you." She hung up, pulled the robe around her and made her way to the door. Tony stood on the other side of the peephole. She quickly unlocked the door and opened it.

"Good morning, Evie," he greeted her cheerfully. He had a bunch of flowers in his hand and held them out to her.

"Thanks, Tony. What are you doing here?"

"Couldn't wait to see you again. It's been way too long since you were up here last. Thought I'd take you out for lunch."

"It's Saturday. Don't you have things to do with Jean? How is your lovely wife, anyway?"

"She was fine last time I saw her."

Evie put the flowers on the table and looked over at Tony. She had known him for ten years, and they had covered a lot of ground together during that time. It had been almost three months since she'd seen him last, and her life had been so busy lately. "What do you mean, last time you saw her? When *did* you see her last?"

"Well, I haven't seen her for four weeks."

"Four weeks? What's happened?"

"I left her," he replied, throwing his coat over the back of a chair and taking a seat on the sofa.

"You *left* her? Why?" Was the world going mad? She had no idea their relationship had been that bad.

"We decided we had nothing in common anymore."

"What about your children?"

"They're living with her. I see them when they're not busy with sport or their friends. It suits. We just grew apart. I was spending more time at work. We've got some great new talent coming through. It's an exciting time to be in the business."

"I don't know what to say."

"Then don't say anything. It happens all the time. It's a fact of life. How have you been?"

"I'm good. I'm expecting," she said, rubbing her stomach. She thought he looked surprised for an instant, but then he stood and walked over to hug her.

"Congratulations, Evie, honey. You deserve every happiness."

"Thanks."

"When's the baby due?"

"January twenty-eighth, approximately."

"The new husband's quick to have you barefoot and pregnant."

"What's that supposed to mean?"

"Nothing. I was hoping to have you up here all to myself. Working, of course," he added quickly. "There's plenty of money to be made at the moment, and you have such a great track record. Everyone loves you."

"Well, for your information, we plan to have a couple of kids of our own."

"That's right," he said, making himself comfortable again. "I forgot you had that kid you brought back from Vietnam."

"Her name is Jackie, and we adore her."

"Looks like you got out of Vietnam just in time too. Almost gave me a heart attack."

"I'll sing whenever I can. Terry's happy to look after Jackie on weekends, and we've got my mother and his mum. Just give me plenty of warning."

"Do you feel like going for a drive? Get some fresh air before lunch?"

"Sure. Give me a few minutes to change."

He stood and picked up his coat. "Great. I'll wait for you downstairs. Bring something warm. It's cold out this morning."

Chapter 39

Terry took Jackie to Shannon. He hadn't told her where they were going, just that they were going to look at something.

"We're here," he said, stopping the car outside a well-fenced house in a nondescript street.

"Can I come?"

"You sure can, kiddo."

She was dressed in a warm jacket and knitted hat, and the bottoms of her trousers were tucked into her gumboots, just like his. He closed the car door after her and took her small hand in his. He squeezed it, and she looked up at him and smiled, causing his heart to melt, just a little. He opened the gate, and pushed it closed behind them.

"Ah, you must be Terry Edwards." A rotund woman in gumboots and an oilskin coat greeted them as they rounded the corner of the house.

"I am, and this is Jackie. You must be Shona."

"I am indeed. Pleased to meet you, Jackie."

He could feel Jackie move closer to him, and he instinctively gave her hand another squeeze.

"I believe we have something here that you might like."

"Me?" Jackie looked up at Terry. He nodded at her.

"Yes. Right through this gate."

Over the gate, Terry could see a yard full of dogs: a couple of older Labradors and Springer Spaniels, and six young puppies also played in the enclosure. The woman opened the gate and held the excited dogs back while Terry and Jackie entered.

There was immediate chaos as the puppies all bounded over to where they stood, trying to jump up for pats and cuddles. Terry watched Jackie's face. Her eyes were as big as saucers, and then she laughed as one puppy tried to lick her face and another put his paws on her jacket.

"Do you think you might like to take one home, Jackie?"

"Can we?"

"Yes."

"Will it be okay with Evelyn?"

"Yes. But you can only choose one."

"Why don't you sit over there for a few minutes and play with them?" Shona suggested. "They love to play."

Jackie sat on the bench seat while the puppies crowded around her. Eventually, she picked the one she wanted. Terry paid the woman, and she gave Jackie a lead that clipped to the puppy's collar, so she could take him for walks.

"What are you going to call him?" Terry asked when they were all in the car.

"I don't know. I will think about names."

By dinner time, Jackie told him she had decided to call the puppy Biscuit. Terry laughed when she told him. She hadn't let the puppy out of her sight for five minutes.

"Where did you get that name from, kiddo?"

"It is my very favourite thing."

"Right." He didn't see the connection, but she obviously did, and it was her puppy.

That night, they stir-fried some vegetables and had them with noodles, which delighted Jackie. As they ate dinner, Jackie told him about the nuns and the work they'd had to do around the orphanage to help. It made him think about the hardships she must have endured. And once again, he found himself feeling guilty about having so much when Jack had died trying to achieve it. Perhaps, if things had been different? But there seemed to be far too many ifs.

"Do you want to watch a movie?"

"Yes, please. Can Biscuit watch too?"

"He sure can. Come on, kiddo, let's get this mess cleaned up and find a movie to watch."

She fell asleep on the sofa with her head resting on Terry's lap, and Biscuit curled up at her feet. As he smoothed the hair back from her face, for a split second he caught a likeness of his brother Simon, when he was young. He hadn't seen it before, but then he hadn't looked for it. It was soon forgotten as he gently carried her through to her bedroom, with Biscuit following behind.

If someone had told him ten years ago that he would be married and raising a young Vietnamese child as his own, he never would have believed them. How things changed. He tucked her in and went back to the television.

The following day, they took Biscuit for a walk across the paddock to visit her grandfather. Jackie wanted to show him her puppy. When they got back, Terry told her she had to put him in the bath and get all the mud off him while he put the fire on. She pleaded with Terry to allow her to have Biscuit sleep on her bed that night seeing as he was nice and clean, and he caved and let the dog stay, although he didn't know what Evelyn would say once she got home.

Later that night, after Jackie had gone to bed and he had done a quick check outside, he looked into Jackie's bedroom. Her bedside lamp was still on, and a book lay on the bed, partially covered by a sleeping puppy. He reached down and carefully slid the book out. Biscuit yawned, stretched, and went back to sleep. He stared at Jackie's peaceful face. He wasn't sure what it was, but there was something about this child that he couldn't help but love.

She was nothing like the scared child they had rescued from the orphanage at Long Hải. Her hair had been cut into a shoulder-length bob that shone where the light caught it. And pretty. Terry thought she was the prettiest kid he had ever seen. He was completely in love with the child. But maybe it was her connection to Vietnam that attracted him. Vietnam and all that had happened over there. He tucked her in, turned the lamp off and headed to bed.

Chapter 40

I'm coming, I'm coming. "Hello?" Terry got the phone on the fifth ring. He'd heard the ringing from the garage but had assumed Evelyn would answer it.

"It's Tony here. I was looking for Evie. Is she there?"

"She was, but it looks like she's not here now."

Silence.

"Can I give her a message?"

"Ask her if she could give me a ring as soon as possible."

"I will when I see her."

"Thanks."

The phone went dead. What was his problem? He didn't like Tony, although he'd only met him briefly in Auckland when he'd gone to a party with Evelyn and Jack back in the sixties. He had thought Tony was greasy then, and he didn't trust the man. He went back out to the garage.

The phone rang again that evening. They were watching television, and Evelyn got up to answer it. He heard her chatting to whoever it was, and five minutes later she hung up.

"That was Tony. He said he rang earlier and spoke to you."

"Oh, Christ, he did too. Sorry. Completely slipped my mind. What did he want? Another gig?"

"Yes. He wants me to go up to Auckland for a week this time."

"What did you tell him?"

She sat down next to him on the sofa. "I said okay."

"When?"

"Next month." She nestled into his shoulder.

"Are you feeling up to it? With the pregnancy and everything?"

"I'm fine. I've been taking it easy. I've had no problems so far. And I'll organise for one of our mums to help look after Jackie while I'm away."

For once, he would have liked it if she had put him first. He wasn't going to stop her; she loved to entertain, always had, for as long as he'd known her. And she was the country's darling. But he had no idea how Jack had coped with all the travel and attention and the loneliness. Not that he was alone; he had Jackie, and even Biscuit was good company these days.

"Do you want me to run you up to the airport in Palmerston North?"

"I'll let you know when Tony's sorted out dates."

Terry drove Evelyn to the airport on a Sunday morning at the end of July. Biscuit sat on the back seat, next to Jackie. The two had become inseparable. Where one was, the other was always close by.

"Now, are you sure you'll be okay?" Terry asked, placing a hand gently on Evelyn's growing baby bump.

"I will be perfectly fine. You fuss way too much," she teased, and then kissed him tenderly. "But I love you for it."

He picked up her case, and the three of them walked hand in hand to the terminal.

"Now, don't forget the meals I put in the freezer for you. And Jackie's music lesson. And–"

"Don't worry about anything," he interrupted. "We've made a list and, besides, I'm getting to be a pro at taking care of things at this end."

They waved Evelyn off and stood and watched the plane leave the ground before heading back home. This time, for a whole week.

On Wednesday, things were not going well for Terry. He had forgotten to organise Jackie's lunch the night before, they were running late, and she couldn't find the socks she wanted to wear. Then at work, Terry couldn't find what was wrong with a car a customer had brought in for repair. It was also the first day of his attempt to give up smoking.

He was later than usual to collect Jackie, and by the time he had prepared dinner for both of them that night, walked the dog and fed the bloody horse, he was buggered. All he wanted to do was sleep.

At ten-thirty, he did his usual perimeter check. He was craving a smoke. Oscar was standing in his shed, and Biscuit followed Terry around then rushed through the door ahead of him, pleased to be out of the cold. He noticed how clear the sky was, there would be a frost in the morning, but it should be a beautiful day. Everything was peaceful. *Stand-down, mate,* he said to himself, locking the door. As he kicked his shoes off, the phone rang. Who was ringing at this hour?

"Hello?"

"Terry?"

"Yes?"

"It's Tony here. I'm ringing you from Greenlane Hospital. It's Evie."

"What's happened? Is she okay?" Panic swept through him; it had to be serious to ring at this time of night.

"Calm down, mate. I think Evie is okay."

"You *think she's okay?*"

"She's upset and in shock, and the doctor gave her a sedative, so she's out to it at the moment. I thought I should ring and let you know."

"Know what!" Terry almost yelled down the phone line at him.

"It looks like Evie's had a miscarriage."

There was silence as Terry processed the words.

"I'm so sorry."

"She's lost the baby?" He couldn't think straight. "Is she all right?"

"I don't know the details. I followed the ambulance in, but they won't tell me much. You'd be best to ring the hospital directly or wait until she comes round in the morning and talk to her."

"I need to be there." He had to go; he didn't know how yet, but he had to go to her. He couldn't imagine what she must be going through.

"Ring in the morning first and get an update."

Stuff that. He wasn't going to sit here all night twiddling his thumbs while his wife lay in a hospital bed, eight hours away.

"Thanks for ringing, Tony." He hung up before Tony could answer. What would he do? He had to stop and think. Think. He picked up the phone and dialled. It was answered on the second ring.

"Hello?"

"Ray, it's Terry."

"Everything all right, lad?"

"No. I've just had a ring from Evelyn's manager." He gulped, trying to swallow the fear. "She's had a miscarriage. She's lost the baby. She's up in Auckland, and I've got to go up. I can't leave her on her own.

Could you come over and look after Jackie?"

"I'll come right over, lad. Get yourself ready. I'll be there in ten minutes."

If he drove through the night, he would be there at the hospital when she woke in the morning. He rang his boss and explained the situation and told him he would be away for two or three days. By the time Ray arrived, he had thrown a change of clothes in a bag and was ready to go.

"I've written Jackie a note to let her know where I've gone, and that I'll be back soon." He handed Ray the folded piece of paper. "I hope she's not too upset. I made up the spare bed for you. I'll ring you as soon as I know more."

"We'll be fine, don't worry about us. You just take care of that girl of yours. And drive carefully," he added. They shook hands, and Terry rushed out to the car.

The roads were quiet, and he made good time. There was no snow or ice through the Desert Road. He stopped in Taupo at a petrol station and again in Hamilton, and by the time he got to the hospital, it was almost seven in the morning.

A nurse directed him to the ward Evelyn was in, and after a few minutes of haggling, they let him in to see his wife. He walked up the corridor until he came to her room and tapped lightly on the door in case she was asleep. Evelyn was awake and when she turned her head towards the door, he could see she had been crying.

"Terry!"

"I'm here, love." It seemed to take forever to cross the room to her bed, and then he was holding her to him, wrapping her in his arms as she cried.

"I wanted this baby so much."

"It's okay," he whispered, not knowing what to say. "We can try again. We've got each other, and that's what counts."

"I'm sorry."

"I'm sorry too, but it's not your fault. I'm just so relieved you're okay." He wiped the tears from her cheeks and held her, trying to be strong for her.

"It was a girl," she said, once her tears had subsided enough to speak.

He didn't know what to say to comfort someone who had lost a child. As he sat on the side of her bed holding her, he realised he *too* had just lost a child. It had been Evelyn's second miscarriage, but for him, it was his first child. A daughter.

"Where's Jackie?" Evelyn finally asked.

"She's at home. Ray's looking after her. I left as soon as I heard."

"Thank you."

"How long will they keep you in for?"

"They'll probably let me go later today. Will you take me home?"

"If that's what you want, I'd be pleased to. I might need some sleep first though."

He climbed onto the bed and lay beside her, one arm around her as if to protect her from everything bad. When the nurse came through to check her blood pressure, she told them that Evelyn would be discharged before lunch.

"Just think of all the fun we're going to have trying to make a new baby," he whispered in her ear as he lay beside her.

"I don't think I can go through this again."

"There's no rush. We're young. There's still plenty of time to try again." And they were young, she was still only twenty-seven, and he was twenty-nine, but she'd already lost two babies; he didn't know if she would risk getting pregnant again and losing another.

But by August the following year, she was pregnant again, and her doctor ordered her to take it easy and rest as much as possible. He wanted to make sure she kept this baby. This time, neither of them wanted to talk about the pregnancy or the possibility Evelyn might carry to full term.

When she reached thirty-four weeks, they couldn't believe they still had the baby, and everything was going okay. The doctor ordered Evelyn into hospital for complete bed rest. She complained it would be too boring sitting in bed every day for two weeks, but Terry told her he and Jackie would visit every day after he finished work.

A week before the due date, Terry had just stopped work for some lunch when the boss came to tell him he had a phone call from the hospital.

"I don't want to take the call." He shook his head, and his boss put a hand on his shoulder.

"Come on, Terry. You've got to take the call. You need to know what's going on. She may have gone into labour."

"But what if it's something else?"

"Well, you won't know until you talk to them, will you?"

His stomach churned as he took several deep breaths, but what if Evelyn had delivered their baby this morning? He had to know. He picked up the receiver with shaking hands.

"Terry Edwards speaking."

"Mr Edwards, it's Nurse Caroline here from the delivery suite at the hospital."

He knew the nurse, had talked to her several times during visits when she was on duty. He liked her. She was gentle, with a calming voice.

"What is it? Is Evelyn all right?"

"The doctor has asked me to ring you to let you know Mrs Edwards was taken to theatre five minutes ago."

"Why did they take her to theatre?"

"Her blood pressure was a little high, and they couldn't find the baby's heartbeat, so the doctor is going to deliver the baby by caesarean."

The way she said it made it sound as though it was the most natural thing in the world.

"They couldn't find a heartbeat?" he repeated.

"The doctor wants to deliver the baby as quickly as possible, just in case it's stressed."

"But I don't understand, why has this happened at this stage?"

"I think you should come up to the hospital as soon as you can, Mr Edwards. Your wife will need you there with her when she comes out of theatre. And the doctor can explain things to you much better than I can."

"Okay. I'll come straight up."

It felt like it was happening all over again, except this time, they were so close. If they did lose this baby, he didn't know if he could be strong enough for Evelyn and everyone else too when it would be killing him inside.

When he arrived in the ward, she had just got back to her room, and the nurses advised him she was still groggy, but awake. He didn't know if he had a baby or not, but he had a sinking feeling they had just lost another child.

The doctor saw him walking towards his wife's room and stopped him to explain what had happened. One of the nurses had discovered Evelyn's blood pressure was higher than normal, and when she checked on the baby, she couldn't find a heartbeat. They made the decision to deliver the baby by caesarean as quickly as possible and they had rushed her straight into the operating theatre.

The baby had been stillborn. This time, it was a boy, and although he looked perfect physically, it appeared the baby's internal organs were malformed. The baby would not have been able to survive on his own without some major reconstructive surgery. The doctor explained he also suspected the baby had a cyanotic heart defect.

"What the hell is a cyanotic heart defect?"

"Basically, it's a structural defect of the heart."

"Was it something that could have been fixed by an operation?"

"If he had been alive at the time of birth, and he didn't have any of the other problems, we might have had a chance, but it would have been slim. His kidneys and liver had shut down, and we think his intestines would not have functioned either. We can do a post mortem if you require one."

Terry tried to swallow the lump in his throat but couldn't. The poor little kid. He hadn't stood a chance.

"Does Evelyn know?"

"Yes, she does. She has the baby with her now. She wanted a few moments to say goodbye. Would you like to join your wife?"

"Umm, I don't know." He turned and looked up the corridor and turned back again, running his fingers through his hair then catching both hands behind his head. He didn't know whether he could do this.

"I think she might like you there for a little support. Nurse." One of the nurses came rushing over. "Take Mr Edwards to his wife's room." She nodded and led Terry down to the room he had visited several times already. This time, he didn't want to go in.

The nurse opened the door, smiled reassuringly at Evelyn and nodded to Terry that it was okay.

Evelyn was propped up in bed, and he could see her face was red from crying. She was rocking a small bundle in her arms.

"At least this time I got to hold him," Evelyn said quietly as the nurse closed the door, leaving them on their own.

He didn't want to look down at the baby; it was hard enough looking at Evelyn.

She smiled up at him. "I think we should have a name for him. What do you think?" She was rocking the baby as if he were still alive.

"Yeah. Okay. I hadn't thought about it."

"What about…" She looked down at the baby's face. "What about Peter Terrence Edwards? I like that."

"That's a good choice."

"Here," she said. "Come and hold Peter. Just for a moment."

Terry stepped closer to the bed. He hesitated, swallowing hard. This was the hardest thing he'd ever had to do: take his own dead baby in his arms. He bent down and carefully took the bundle from Evelyn, surprised at how light he was. It was like the baby was sleeping, except he had no colour in his face as he lay wrapped in the pale green blanket Evelyn had brought into the hospital for him. Peter reminded him of Jackie when she was a baby: beautiful skin, perfect little eyelashes and tiny fingers.

He sat on the bed beside Evelyn, staring at his son's face. Everything about him was perfect. Terry felt tears well behind his eyes, he couldn't help it. He had been determined not to cry, but what they had been through needed more strength than even he could muster.

"Hello, little Peter," he whispered. "Know that your daddy and mummy love you so much." He ran a finger gently down the side of the baby's cheek, the skin was soft but cold, and he handed the bundle back to Evelyn. "I've got to use the bathroom," he said, standing up and walking towards the door. "I'll be back in a couple of minutes."

He hurried blindly down the corridor until he found a room that was empty. He rushed in, closing the door behind him. Leaning back against a wall, he slid to the floor. Tears streamed unchecked down his face. What the hell was wrong? Why did they keep losing babies? He sat there for a few minutes, crying openly, thinking about how much of a failure he was. And all he could see was Peter's innocent little face as he lay at peace in his arms. He put his head in his hands and wept.

After a few minutes, he wiped his eyes and his face, took several deep breaths and opened the door, looking for the bathroom. When he got back to Evelyn's room, the nurse had taken Peter away, and Evelyn told him a funeral director would be in touch to make arrangements.

He walked to her side and sat holding her, and they both cried for the child that had been so close, yet so far.

PART FOUR

1987

Chapter 41

"How's things going?" Terry's father asked as Terry sat down on a stack of tyres in his father's garage.

"I don't know."

"What do you mean, 'you don't know'?"

"I don't. These days, it feels like I'm just existing." Evelyn was devoting most of her time to her work: flying to Auckland, Christchurch or Hamilton, and once she had even gone with her manager to Melbourne for six days. Jackie was now nineteen and had shifted to Wellington at the beginning of the year to study at Victoria University.

Since they had lost Peter ten years ago, their relationship had slowly taken a nosedive. There was nothing specific Terry could put his finger on; the spark was just gone. They made love on the rare nights they were both at home and neither was tired, or when they had been drinking and were both feeling amorous. Evelyn had miscarried again eighteen months after having Peter, and although they didn't talk about it, Terry had the feeling that, like him, she didn't want to put herself through the anguish of losing any more babies. Their lovemaking had almost come to a standstill, and neither of them was prepared to talk about it–the subject sat in the corner of the room like the Grim Reaper.

"Have a beer." His father flipped the top off a bottle and handed it to him. "How's that wife of yours?"

"She's okay. Busy."

"How's work?"

"The same. The boss is thinking about retiring, and I was considering making him an offer on the place."

His father took a long drink from his bottle, and as he put it down, he studied his son.

"You know that business inside out, so it sounds like a good idea. And you? How are you?"

"I don't know." To be honest, he didn't know whether or not he wanted to talk to his father about it. "It's tough losing so many babies."

"I imagine it is. For both of you."

"My life has turned to shit lately, and I don't know what to do to fix it."

"How so?"

"Well, losing Peter for a start. He was a reality, you know, different from the others. With him, I got to hold him, touch him. And I've had more skin cancers cut out. That's twenty-seven all up now, mostly my arms, legs, and back–my body looks like a target on a bloody rifle range. Evelyn seems more interested in getting away to work than spending time with me, and when I do see her, she tells me I'm moody all the time. On top of that, I've been having trouble sleeping lately. And now the doctor says I have a stomach ulcer."

"It'll take time, son. Give it time."

"Jesus, how much time does it take?"

"As much as it needs."

"I don't know how to fix our marriage."

"Well, I'm hardly qualified to give out marriage advice, not with my track record, but sounds like you both need a weekend away. On your own. To sort out some of these things. Maybe you're both pushing yourselves too hard?"

"Maybe. There's a Victor Company reunion coming up in a month, at Queen's Birthday weekend, and the guys are getting together. It's been twenty years since we went over, and I've had a couple of calls from mates who want me to go, so I thought I might. Actually, Evelyn's been invited to sing at the do on the Saturday night."

"Sounds like the perfect opportunity to let ya hair down, have a bit of fun. And why don't you both go see the doctor? Ask him to run some tests."

"What kind of tests?"

"Shit, I don't know, son. They must be able to find out why Evie's losing babies all the time."

"I'm getting too old for young kids now."

"The hell you are. What are you now?"

"Forty-one this year."

"There you go. Still plenty of time to have kids."

Terry finished his beer and lit up a cigarette. He remembered old Smokey, who'd always intended to stop smoking, but could never quite manage it. He'd been thinking about his old mates a lot lately.

"You reckon it might be Evelyn? She lost Jack's baby too."

"Well, it could be her. It could've been Jack, or you. Let the doctors figure it out. That's what they've got all those qualifications for."

Terry nodded. His father didn't do much talking, but what he did say was always worth listening to. He seriously doubted he would be able to get Evelyn along to see a doctor though. She'd had enough of doctors and hospitals.

"Might talk to her tonight."

When he left his father's, he was feeling more positive than he had in several weeks. He and Evelyn needed to talk about trying for another baby, giving it one last shot.

As he drove home, he thought about it over and over and was pleased to see Evelyn's car in the drive. Pulling up behind it, he reached out to turn off the ignition. He would go and talk to her now, strike while the iron was hot. But when he went to open the car door, he felt dizzy, and as he put his arm out to support himself, he slumped forward.

He couldn't lift his arm, couldn't grip the steering wheel with his fingers. He tried to flex them: nothing. There was no feeling in them; they wouldn't move at all. What the hell was wrong with him now? Annoyed with himself, he tried to shift the gear stick with his good hand. Everything blurred beyond the dash. He tried to shake his head, but it seemed he had little control.

He couldn't move his left leg. He opened his mouth to call out but could only manage a incomprehensible mumble. He couldn't get out of the car. If he sat here for a minute, he'd come right. He'd be okay. He'd be okay.

He heard the back door open and tried to speak, but his voice was nothing but unintelligible noise.

"What's wrong?" Evelyn asked, ripping the door open.

Terry stared at her.

She bustled around him, helping him lean back into the car. She closed the driver's door and disappeared back inside, reappearing a few minutes later with a blanket and sliding into the passenger side.

"I've called an ambulance. It'll be here in about fifteen minutes."

Terry stared at her, and it was like he was looking at her for the first time. He felt as though he was waking up from a dream and needed to work out where he was.

"Ev–" He didn't need an ambulance. He would be right in a few minutes.

"It's okay," she reassured him, rubbing his arm. "It will be all right."

He closed his eyes. He had no idea what was going on. Maybe he was dying? Her voice sounded far away. Then someone else was talking. A man. He forced his eyes open. Ray came into focus. It was Ray.

"Terry, can you hear me?"

Terry attempted to make a thumbs up sign with his one cooperative hand.

"So you can understand what I'm saying?"

Another thumbs up.

"Good. That's a good sign," he said to Evelyn.

"Okay. Can you move your right arm? The arm closest to the door?"

"Yesss." Terry concentrated on pronouncing the word, surprised to hear it spill from his lips. It wasn't a riveting conversation, but at least words were coming out.

"Excellent. What about the arm closest to Evie?"

"Little."

While Ray spoke to Evelyn, Terry flexed his fingers on his left hand; the movement was coming back. He tried to lift his arm and got it to ninety degrees.

"Here's the ambulance. He'll be in good hands now, love."

"Don't need … ambulance."

And then someone helped him from the car, and he was standing up. They helped him walk to the ambulance, and he couldn't quite lift his foot when he walked. He was told to lie down; and they strapped something on his arm and put in an intravenous needle. And then Evelyn was there beside him; she was holding his hand, and he could feel it. Feel everything, and the fog in his head slowly disappeared as he took in his surroundings.

"I don't need—the hospital," he stated, sounding groggy. He felt like he had been in a deep sleep for the last five years and was just waking up. He didn't want all this fuss. All he wanted to do was have a good hot cuppa and crawl into bed to sleep.

"We're going to the hospital, so they can check you over," Evelyn stated.

It was comforting to know she was there with him. And then the ambulance moved, and he closed his eyes and tried to work out what the hell had just happened to him.

Hospital staff were waiting for the ambulance, and they rushed Terry into the emergency department. Evelyn followed him in, and for the next hour, they ran test after test. Later that night, the doctor spoke to them both and told them Terry had suffered a small stroke.

"A stroke? I thought only old people had those?"

"A stroke is more common in older age groups. It's very unusual for someone as young as you to have one. How's your arm? Can you lift it?"

"Yes." He demonstrated.

"And let me see you walking."

Terry stood up and walked around the side of the bed to where Evelyn was sitting and back again. He felt normal as though the events of the last four hours had been a dream. He flexed and curled his fingers. "All good again, doctor."

"Vision?"

"I can see that dark-haired nurse over there"–he nodded–"has a watch pinned to her pocket."

"I think you can take him home again, Mrs Edwards. He seems fine." He turned to Terry. "We'll give you a script for some blood thinners, just to err on the side of caution. Take one every day."

"We're a right pair," Evelyn said after the doctor had left. "If it's not me, it's you in a hospital bed. You gave me a heck of a fright."

"I parked the car, and then suddenly I couldn't move. I don't remember much else."

"Well, you're okay now, so I'll ring Ray and ask him to come get us."

As they sat in the waiting room, Terry wondered what else could go wrong with him. He was covered in scars from the skin cancers; his immune system was buggered, or so his doctor reckoned; he had scratches and cuts that weren't healing, and now he had suffered a stroke.

Apart from a few hangovers, he had never had a sick day in his life.

Until he'd got back from Vietnam.

Chapter 42

By Queen's Birthday weekend, all Terry could think about was catching up with his old mates from Victor Company. It had been twenty years since he had seen most of them, and up until now, he had been content to get on with his life and leave everything related to his time in Vietnam behind him. But now, the idea of spending a weekend catching up with his old Victor mates was stronger than ever.

They had been brothers once, and he deeply regretted losing touch. If he was honest with himself, he missed their camaraderie; it was different from his relationship with his mates back home. Smokey Harris and Murph had come to his wedding, and it was Murph who had rung, telling him to get his arse into gear and come to the reunion.

Terry was hoping it would be an opportunity for some time alone with Evelyn too. He remembered what his father had said and was determined to talk over their plans for the future; his desire to have one last try for a baby. He couldn't remember when they had last had a weekend away together, and he wanted this one to be special.

They drove up on the Friday, stopping at Taupo for lunch, and late in the afternoon, they checked into the hotel in Rotorua where the reunion was being held. Most of the registered attendees were staying there. It was a whole Victor Company reunion, almost two hundred men and their wives and girlfriends. The hotel was fully booked, and Terry suspected several other hotels in town were as well. They had a lovely room on the third floor, and from the picture window, they could see the lake.

After unpacking, he suggested they go for a walk to the lakefront and stop somewhere for coffee. Evelyn was happy to get some fresh air. Terry thought she had seemed a little anxious the whole trip and wondered if she was pregnant again and feeling off colour.

As they crossed the foyer, he heard someone call out, *"Romeo!"* He stopped. It was a long time since he had been called that. Turning, he saw Smokey and his old section commander, Craig Williams, walking towards him.

"Romeo!" Smokey put his hand out to pump Terry's and then embraced him in a bear hug. "Thought it was you. How the hell are you? You haven't changed a bit. And, of course, I knew you'd have that beautiful wife of yours with you."

"Smokey, you old bastard, how are you?"

"Good, mate, good."

Terry turned to Craig. "Boss, it's bloody good to see you."

"You're a sight for sore eyes, Edwards." He slapped Terry on the back and then shook his hand enthusiastically.

"This is my wife, Evelyn. Evelyn, do you remember Roger Harris? He came to our wedding."

Evelyn put her hand out, smiled, and shook Smokey's hand.

"And this is Craig Williams, our section commander." The two shook hands.

"Where's your missus, Smokey?"

"She cleared off about twelve years ago now. Had two more since. Don't think I'm good husband material. But hell, I've got you guys. That's all a man needs. His mates. Want to grab a beer with us?"

"We're going for a walk to get some fresh air. I'll take you up on that beer when we get back."

"Right. Look for me in the bar. I'll see you later." He tipped his cap to Evelyn.

Terry and Evelyn walked down Tutanekai Street until they came to Lakefront Drive. For a Friday afternoon in June, there were still lots of people walking, jogging, and sightseeing. He reached down and took Evelyn's hand as they walked. She looked up at him but didn't say anything, and he couldn't read the look on her face.

"It's nice you could come with me." He squeezed her hand. "I know it must bring back memories of Jack."

"I'll be fine. It was a long time ago."

They walked in silence.

"Let's sit here for a while," Terry suggested when they came to an empty park bench right on the lakefront. Evelyn sat down and pulled her coat collar up around her neck. She had a beanie on and blended in with everyone else out enjoying the afternoon. He put his arm around her shoulder and pulled her to him. He could have sworn she flinched, but he put it down to her feeling the cold.

Out on the lake, swans glided past. A seaplane was anchored several hundred metres offshore, and a family of Asian tourists gathered for photographs.

"We need to talk, Evelyn," he finally ventured.

"I know."

"About us. Our plans," he continued, trying to concentrate on the seaplane. "The boss is going to retire this year, and I want to make him an offer for the business. I wondered what you thought of me taking it on. And I think we need to talk about trying for another baby," he added. "One last try. Or perhaps we could even adopt?"

"I think it's a great idea–you buying the garage. You're a great mechanic, and you would have customers who know you already. It wouldn't be like you were starting a business from scratch."

"That's what I thought. I'll ask him next week for first right of refusal." He paused. "I think it's about time we looked at getting a place of our own somewhere too." He knew that the house had been a sore point ever since they married; he would dearly love to buy somewhere closer to town or maybe even out at Foxton Beach, closer to her parents. Somewhere that was their place, and not full of memories of Jack. The house had been the source of arguments for so long now.

"I know how you feel about the house," she said, watching the swans.

"I know you do. It's your place–or Jack's place–always has been. It's not mine. And these days, you're away a lot with your work. And that's okay," he added hastily. "But I've got to live with those memories too."

"So, this is about my work?"

"No." He turned to face her. "It's never been about your work. It's about us. About a last-ditch attempt at making a family."

"We've got a family."

"I know. And I love Jackie like she's my own daughter, but I'd love to have our own child too." He didn't want to argue with her about it, but he couldn't understand why she was being so defensive.

"And you think I wouldn't?" she snapped.

"Well, I just think it's something we don't talk about–and we should. We don't seem to talk about much these days. We're so busy with our jobs."

She shifted in her seat and looked down at her hands.

"I didn't want to tell you this here. This weekend. But perhaps I should."

"Tell me what? Are you pregnant again?" It was too much to hope for.

She turned to look him in the eye. He could see she had tears welling in them, and he wondered if she had already lost the baby and she hadn't told him.

"What is it, love?"

A tear spilled over and slid down her cheek, and she sniffed and dug in her coat pocket for a handkerchief.

"I *am* pregnant. With twins."

He couldn't speak. After everything they had been through, this time there were the lives of two babies at stake. He didn't know if he should jump up and down and laugh. Or wrap her up and take her back to the hotel and put her to bed.

"They're not yours."

The statement hit him like a blow from a Claymore. He felt like he'd been flung through the air and thrown to the ground and left winded and speechless. She was pregnant, but he wasn't the father? No. She wouldn't do that to him. Not after everything they had been through together. She wouldn't go and sleep with someone else.

He stood up and walked to the edge of the lake, then turned and walked back and sat down.

"I'm sorry, Terry. I was going to tell you after this weekend."

"You're sorry?" It was all he could think of to say. What she had told him had left him stunned. She had been sleeping with someone else, and now, all she could say was sorry? "I know we've been going through a rough patch the last couple of years, but Jesus, you don't just run off and sleep with someone else when the going gets tough." He felt like a stranger looking in from the outside. This was someone else's life, not his. Nothing made sense.

"I really am sorry. I didn't want to end things this way."

"End? What the hell are you talking about? We don't need to end things." Surely if it was an accident, a moment of weakness, they could fix things, work things out. "Hell, we all make mistakes." It was true, everybody did, but he had never slept with anyone else while he had been married to Evelyn. She was his wife; he was loyal, and he would have done anything for her.

"I'm moving to Auckland to live."

"Auckland?" It was like she was moving to the other side of the world. "What? Just like that? One minute you're driving around the country with me, and the next you're leaving me to go live in Auckland?"

"I've been thinking about it for a few months. It's best for the babies and my career."

"That's right. It's all about you. It always has been, hasn't it?"

"I'm sorry."

"Yeah, well sorry doesn't quite cut it anymore," he said bitterly, trying to control his anger. He thought she had been quiet in the car on the trip up, and he had wondered if she hadn't been feeling well. Now, he knew the truth. "Is that where your boyfriend lives?"

"It doesn't matter." She blew her nose and put the handkerchief back in her pocket.

"It matters to me." Everything was falling apart, and he had no control over any of it. "I don't know what to say."

"There's nothing to say." She stood up. "I think we should head back. I'll get the hotel to find me a room somewhere else for tonight and tomorrow."

"Are you still singing tomorrow night?"

"Yes."

She was destroying his whole life while everything around them continued as normal. A woman walked past them pushing a buggy with a baby in it, a young couple took photos of each other with the lake in the background, and two young girls threw bread to the swans. He took a deep breath and stood up.

He had come to Rotorua feeling hopeful and excited about spending the weekend away with his wife, to forget about everything they had been through and have some fun, and now he was going to go home without a wife. She was leaving him, and he still had so many questions he wanted to ask her, like how long she'd been having an affair behind his back. They walked back to the hotel in silence.

"How are you getting home on Monday?" he asked as she wheeled her bag across the hotel room to the door.

"I'll be fine. I'm going to head back on Sunday morning. I'll pack some things, and I'll be gone from the house by the time you get back on Monday."

"Are you going to live with–him?"

"Yes," she said simply.

"How will I get in touch with you?" He felt panicked that she was leaving, and he might not be able to see or talk to her again.

"I'll leave my address back at the house before I leave. And I'll let Jackie know where I am too. And my parents."

"You know I love you, don't you? No matter what you've done. I can't just turn that feeling off."

"I know," she said, half smiling at him. "And I love you too. I always will, but I need to move on. I can't handle all the miscarriages, the sickness, and the mood swings any longer. I want a normal life."

That confession was little consolation. With her job, her life could never be considered normal.

"So, I'll see you tomorrow night?"

She opened the door.

"I don't want to spoil your reunion any more than I have already. If you can stand to look at me, then I'll accompany you to the dinner. I'd like to think we'll still be friends. We've been through a lot together, and you've done so much for me. I'll never forget you for it. Anyway, I'm singing, so I have to be there. I don't want to let your friends down."

Fuck the reunion. She didn't want to spoil it for his mates, but she hadn't thought twice about screwing him over for some other guy. He didn't see any sense in that, but he didn't want to fight with her, it wouldn't achieve anything.

She walked down the hall to the elevator, footsteps soundless on the carpet, and he watched her step through the open doors, his eyes meeting hers as the doors closed. They had been married twelve years, lost three babies, and now it was over. Just like that. He sat on the bed and stared at the large bottle of champagne he'd had delivered to their room. Was he such an arsehole that she couldn't live with him any longer? Obviously, he was.

He gave Evelyn half an hour to leave the hotel, and then he caught the elevator down to the bar to find Smokey. He had some serious catching up to do.

Chapter 43

The following night, Terry was already down in the bar having a drink before the dinner, when Evelyn arrived.

"You look beautiful," he told her, unable to help himself. He had already had several drinks and was well on the way. He thought she looked stunning in her beautiful navy-blue dress. It was lacy on the top, almost see-through, and the skirt fell gracefully from her waist. Her hair was done up, and she glowed. Although he had asked her to accompany him this evening, it wouldn't be easy. Not for him. It was going to be a long night, but the alcohol would help.

He introduced Evelyn to the group he was drinking with and asked if she wanted a drink.

"Thanks, orange juice, please."

"Well, well, well," Dean Blackett said, grinning. "Evie Hallet wasn't it?"

"Took you a while, Blackie," Smokey said.

"Ignore him, you've got a good memory," Evelyn said, smiling.

"I went to one of your concerts at Nui Dat."

"You and almost everyone in this room," Murph replied. "How are you, Evie? Long time no see."

"I'm good, thanks. Busy with work as usual."

"I was sorry I missed Jack's funeral," Elvis Waata said. "I was over in Aussie visiting my sister and didn't hear about him until I got back. I had a lot of time for him. He was a good soldier. One of the best." There was a chorus of agreement.

"No disputing that, Elvis," Scott Taylor chimed in. Scott had been Jack's section commander in Two Section and had joined them at the bar when he saw them. "Ah, here's Red. Someone get that man a beer."

"Shit, we had a few laughs on Jack, didn't we, Horse?" Red said. "I remember the time you shot that snake. He thought you'd blown his ear clean off." He roared heartily.

"Anyway, how is our Terry?" Murph asked Evelyn. "He's looking well. You must be good for him."

She didn't answer.

The men talked for a while, trading memories and jokes, and when Evelyn excused herself to use the bathroom, the conversation shifted to her.

"You kept that a secret, Romeo," Elvis said. "Marrying Jack's missus."

"No secret, Elvis. It's a wonder you didn't see it in the papers."

"Any kids?" Blackie asked.

"One." He always felt like he'd been punched in the stomach when someone asked him that question. He wanted to say he had four, but people didn't understand what it was like to lose three babies, and he didn't need their sympathy. "How are your boys, Murph?"

"They're good. Both married, three little grandkids under five. Beautiful wee things. We tried again after I got back, but we lost it, and we didn't bother trying again after that."

"Yeah, I think that's why my missus cleared off," Smokey stated. "I told her I'd fired all the live rounds over in Nam, got nothing left but blanks now!" Everyone at the bar laughed.

"We have two kids," Horse said. "One's okay, trouble with asthma, and the other was born with Downs Syndrome. But she's a plucky kid. I admire her."

"Actually, we've lost three," Terry said. "Peter was stillborn." He never talked about the babies they'd lost. Not even to Evelyn. But here, amongst these men, it felt natural to share his problems. It seemed they were all experiencing the same things he was, and they understood what he was going through.

"Poor old Evie, she's had it rough."

"She lost one of Jack's too."

"What do they think causes it?" JJ Johnson asked, joining in the conversation. "Pat lost one, a girl, we decided to adopt after that. We've got three boys now. Two of them are doing well, but the third one's a bit of a rough bugger."

"Two outta three ain't bad, JJ," Blackie responded.

"There's a lot of shit going down about the chemicals they used over in Vietnam. That bloody Agent Orange, and all the tablets we took for fucking everything." Murph remembered the ladies in their presence and apologised profusely for his bad language.

"That's the stuff I sprayed all around our lines, wasn't it?" Terry asked.

"Sure was, and it was the stuff they sprayed on us from those C-123s. Completely harmless, they said."

"It's what's causing all these miscarriages and stillbirths," Murph stated. "I'm sure of it."

Evelyn arrived back at the table. She glanced around the group and then at Terry.

"Agent Orange is made up of two main chemicals: 2,4,5-T and 2,4-D." Murph continued. "They're not too bad on their own, but they're bloody dynamite when they're combined. They make a byproduct called dioxin. It's deadly."

"That's bloody lovely," Elvis said.

"You seem to know a lot, Murph," Terry commented.

"I've done a lot of research over the last ten years. I've had nothing but bloody health problems, mate."

"Story of my life."

"So have I," Elvis said.

"I've had that many skin cancers cut out, there's not much left of me. And I had a bloody stroke a few months back," Terry told them.

"Shit, Romeo, that must have been tough."

"I was scared shitless. I'll tell you that."

"Vietnam vets are dying at an alarming rate. Mainly from unusual types of cancers. But you know the worst thing about this toxic chemical?" There was silence around the table as everyone waited for Murph to continue. "The damage it causes is being passed down through us to our kids."

"Why hasn't anything been done?" Evelyn asked.

"Because of the implications."

"Who for? The company making the chemicals, or the government?" she asked.

"Both."

"Sue the bastards," Blackie chipped in.

"There are hundreds of millions of dollars involved, and no one will take the rap for dioxin poisoning. Not the company producing it, or the governments. You can imagine a company that sells thousands of gallons of the stuff isn't going to put its hand up any time soon," Murph said. "They've been selling it to farmers all over New Zealand for years."

"Agent Orange. It's like this huge fucking shadow over everyone who went to Nam," Terry stated.

"Yeah, you can run, but you can't hide from it. Ever," Smokey agreed. "And neither can our kids."

"There's no proof we were sprayed with that stuff though," Blackie said. "That's what they're saying.

"Change is in the wind," Murph stated.

"Bullshit. They will not own up to it. Not in my lifetime," JJ said.

"I think it's about acknowledging that we were exposed to dioxin, and I think if we could just get the government to listen to us, they'd have to do something about it."

"I don't think it's about us anymore, Murph. It's about acknowledging our kids have been affected by dioxin as a result of our exposure to Agent Orange," Craig Williams spoke up. "Our kids are the victims here. And who's going to look out for them when we're gone? How many generations will it continue to affect?"

"Actually, it looks like the health department's going to start a testing programme on us vets," Murph interrupted Williams. "Any of you lot heard about it?"

They all shook their heads.

"Apparently, they want to take blood and DNA samples and gather information about what level of exposure we had over there. Let me know if you're interested. The more of us involved, the better."

"What about if I don't have any kids?" Terry asked.

"You should still take part. We need all the push we can get to make it a success. Besides, you would have had more exposure than the rest of us, what with that leaky backpack you hauled around when we were in camp."

"I'll be into that. Let me know what I need to do. I didn't even think about it when I was spraying that shit everywhere and it was leaking down my back."

"None of us did. We had no reason to. I'll let my contact know. You'll get a letter in the mail, and you'll need to call in to your doctor's. Two-minute process."

They all agreed to put their names down.

The discussion continued as the remaining couples from One and Two Sections walked through to the dining room to sit down. After dinner, the band played and there was thunderous applause from their table as Evelyn took the stage.

"Tonight I sing for you all." A thunderous cheer went up. "But this is especially for the brave men of Victor One, The Originals."

She sang six numbers, promised everyone she would return, and walked back to her seat, stopping to talk to people along the way.

Terry couldn't face dancing with her, so she danced with some of the other men instead, and then rejoined the band on stage for her final set. She had the crowd eating out of her hand. She was a natural at what she did: polished and a true professional. For a moment, he remembered the dances all those years ago at the Astoria Ballroom in Palmerston North, when she got up on stage and sang, and he couldn't take his eyes off her. Hell, he still couldn't take his eyes off her.

Terry stood up. "Right, I'm going for another round, who's in?"

Murph stood up too. "I'll come with you, mate."

They walked to the bar in silence, and Terry ordered the drinks.

"So, are you really okay, mate?"

"Yeah, why?"

"You just seem, oh, I don't know. You're a bit quiet tonight."

"It's nothing." Terry gave the barman his room number.

"Doesn't look like nothing to me. Anyway, you're a lucky man with a wife as stunning as yours. She makes mine look a bit drab, as much as I love the old bird. Don't tell her I said that though." He tried to make light of it.

"She won't be for much longer," Terry replied, juggling four glasses.

"Won't be what?"

"Won't be my wife. It's all a sham."

"What is?"

"All this loving wife carry-on shit. She's leaving me. Tonight."

Murph let out a low whistle.

"Yeah, I had no idea. Came up here to have a bloody good weekend with her and my old mates, and she drops this on me."

"Sorry to hear that, mate."

"I reckon as soon as she's finished singing, she'll make some excuse and bugger off. Betcha a round."

"Things been a bit tough?"

"By the sounds of it, no tougher than what some of you lot have been through. Thing is, she's expecting twins."

"Aw mate, I'm sorry."

"Don't be. They're not mine."

"Jesus, that's a bit of a kick in the guts."

"Yeah, the boots are coming from all directions."

"Well, if it's any consolation, mate, you're amongst friends here. Don't ever forget it. Lifelong friends. We're only at the end of a phone."

"Yeah, thanks. You're not going to keep me warm at night, though."

Murph laughed. "Get a dog!"

"Thanks, you're a big help."

They carried the drinks back to the table. Evelyn was still singing, and the dance floor was peppered with couples enjoying the songs from the sixties. When her last song, "Green, Green Grass of Home," came to an end, she had sung for almost two hours and thoroughly entertained the whole room. When she'd finished her set, she thanked the crowd who clapped enthusiastically in response, and she walked back to the table. She didn't sit down.

"I'm going to call it a night." She smiled at those still seated at the table. "It's been lovely meeting you all."

Terry stood up.

"Good night, everyone." There were waves and goodbyes as Evelyn and Terry left the table.

"What will you tell Jackie?" Terry asked when they were on their own.

She sighed. "Simply that we've separated. She's old enough to understand."

Maybe she would. He didn't know. At least she was old enough to get a handle on things.

"When will I see you again?"

"Do you need to see me?" Evelyn asked.

"I don't know. I don't think it's even sunk in you're leaving."

"I guess we'll have to sort out what we're going to do with the house."

"I thought you loved that house?"

"I do. But if I'm living in Auckland, it makes more sense to sell it."

"It's Tony, isn't it?"

She refused to look him in the eye, and he knew he had guessed right. He couldn't help the bitterness. "It's your bloody manager. How long's it been going on?"

"I'm not answering that, Terry."

"I bloody knew it. How long has he been shagging you behind my back, eh? How long have you been making a fucking fool out of me?"

"I'll be in touch about the house," she replied, shrugging her arms into her coat.

"If it's no trouble."

She stopped and turned to face him, and he could see it was taking a toll on her too; she was close to tears. "I don't want to argue with you."

"That's some consolation," he replied, unable to hide the sarcasm.

"I never meant for this to happen. I know we've been through a lot together, but I can't do this any longer."

"Gee, thanks, and you think I have any option?" He couldn't suddenly wipe out his time in Vietnam, undo all the damage that had been done all those years ago. He couldn't help but feel bitter about her decision. Hell, he didn't even know where this had all come from. Had she been sleeping with her bloody manager for weeks? Months? It might have been going on for years for all he knew.

"I'll be in touch in a few weeks. We'll sit down and sort things out then." She pulled her coat tight around her and stepped out through the doors into a bitterly cold Rotorua night.

Terry wanted to make a grab for her, but he didn't know whether he wanted to try to shake some sense into her or pull her into him and hug her so tightly she couldn't leave. He stood with his hands in his pockets as he watched her climb into a taxi. She glanced in his direction as the car moved off, and he felt like his heart was being wrenched from his chest. It was the first time he could ever remember feeling like he wanted to hit something. Or someone.

When he finally turned to go back to the dining room, he spotted Murph sitting in one of the reception chairs. He stood up as Terry approached.

"You okay, mate?"

"Yeah, Murph, guess I have to be, aye."

"Come and finish your beer."

"Don't feel much like it, right now." He put an arm around Murph's shoulders. "Tell the guys I'll see them all in the morning for the service."

Mark Murphy slapped him on the back. "Sure thing."

He wasn't in a hurry to sit on his own in the room he had checked in to with Evelyn. It was hard to comprehend this had been coming for some time. Why hadn't he seen the signs? Why hadn't she said something? He would have been the first to admit that their marriage was flagging a little, but this weekend away was supposed to be the turning point. He was going to pamper her; try to rekindle what they'd had. They had raised a daughter together. Shit, they had made three children together.

It was twenty to eleven. Terry turned on the television and took off his shoes and jacket. He loosened his tie and pulled it off, then unbuttoned the top buttons of his shirt. He'd go to bed, but he probably wouldn't sleep, just lie there analysing everything, trying to understand why their relationship had got this bad; what he should have done. What *could* he have done? What had Vietnam done?

He reached for the unopened bottle in the ice bucket. A knock on his door interrupted him. Perhaps Evelyn had come back? He opened the door to find the boys milling around in the corridor, and he stood back as they filed in.

"The womenfolk have headed to bed, so we thought we'd have a few drinks with our mate," Blackie said as he walked carefully through the door, nursing two full jugs of beer.

The seven men were each carrying bottles, and Terry wondered if any of them would make it to the service and the march to the cenotaph in the morning.

"You know how hard it was to get these past the girl at reception?" Blackie asked.

"Right," Murph declared, raising a beer bottle. "I declare this party started!" And he promptly emptied a quarter of it then belched loudly.

"I second that," Smokey stated. He unscrewed the lid on a bottle of Johnnie Walker, took a swig, screwed up his face and then smiled. "To bloody good mates!" He passed the bottle to Terry.

"One Section!" Terry waved the bottle in the air. "It's beaut to be back together again."

There was a round of cheers.

"Anyone gotta a smoke?" Smokey asked, and there was a round of laughter.

"To absent mates," JJ called, and they all held their jugs and bottles in the air and thought about mates who had been killed in Vietnam or those who had died since they had returned.

"Remember that time Romeo got stung by a bloody scorpion?"

JJ roared. "Walked around for two days with his finger stuck in the air."

"You can laugh," Terry replied, laughing now himself. "I almost copped one from that Aussie bastard we had with us. He thought I was telling him to fuck off all the time."

"We told him you didn't like him!" Smokey added, pulling a packet of cigarettes from his shirt pocket.

Terry grinned. "I remember the shit you lot gave me when I got shot in the backside."

"Yeah, who could forget that one?" JJ said.

But now it was all in fun, and as he looked around the group, he realised just how important these men were to him.

"You're all bastards," Terry said, and then burst into laughter too. "The whole fucking lot of ya." He sure as hell had missed these guys.

Chapter 44

By the time Terry returned home, his animosity towards Evelyn was dissipating. It may have had something to do with the remains of two impressive hangovers in two days, and the men he had shared the weekend's activities with. He didn't hate Evelyn. How could he? He'd spent the last twelve years with her. And he couldn't blame her for wanting something he obviously couldn't give her: a child.

The loneliness was all-encompassing. The nights were the worst. Sometimes he went around to have dinner with his father, his sister, or Matt and Helen. Other nights he watched the television, or lay in bed, unable to sleep. He wondered what Evelyn was doing up in Auckland, and if she was happy. He spent hours thinking about their marriage and the relationship they'd had and what had gone wrong.

To keep himself busy, Terry searched the local paper for places to rent. He didn't want to hang around in Evelyn's house any longer than he had to. By the end of the week, he had found a comfortable looking house in Brown Terrace at Foxton Beach, and he made arrangements to go and have a look. He thought it looked great, and it had a decent sized garage. It was perfect.

It needed some new paint inside and out, and new carpet, all things he could work on. The only problem was, it wasn't for rent; it was for sale, and he told the real estate agent he was interested and would be in touch. Then he rushed home and worked out that if he was careful, he could afford to buy the house, and the garage from his boss, with a small mortgage from the bank.

Three days later, Terry made an offer on the house. His solicitor recommended he make an offer much lower than asking price and to his surprise, it was accepted. It felt like a huge weight had been lifted from his shoulders. The house wasn't flash, but it was solid, with a quarter-acre section and a double garage and carport. There was a decent fireplace in the lounge, and it had three small bedrooms, a kitchen, bathroom, and laundry. Although it was much smaller than the house on the farm, there was only him and Jackie's elderly dog, Biscuit, and they would both be very comfortable. It was also just a five-minute walk from the beach and the pub, which would be great during the summer months. He would give it a coat of paint and ask his mother about curtains. He had four weeks to wait until he could move in.

Two days after the offer on the house was accepted, he went to work and asked his boss for the first right of refusal when he finally decided to sell the garage. His boss was enthusiastic about Terry buying it and told him his wife wanted him to retire before Christmas.

The final thing Terry had to do was ring Jackie and tell her about the house. She was flatting with friends in Wellington now while she did her first year of a degree in architecture.

"Hello?" she said when she picked up the phone, and he heard her say thanks to the young man who had answered his call.

"Hey, kiddo." He loved calling her that.

"Terry!"

"How are you, love? How's it going?"

"Apart from the long hours of study and assignments, everything's good. How are you? I've been worried about you. Mum rang me last weekend. She told me she had moved out and was living in Auckland now. I tried to ring you, but there was no reply."

"I'm fine. It was a bit of a shock."

"I'm so sorry. I thought you guys would always be together."

"Me too." He paused. He didn't want to dwell on what had happened, and he certainly didn't want to burden her with how much Evelyn's actions had hurt him. "Anyway, I've got some news."

"What is it?" she asked. Her voice held almost no trace of her Vietnamese heritage now.

Terry smiled to himself as he relayed the details of the house he'd bought.

"So, there you have it. Biscuit and I will be shifting in four weeks."

"Would you like some help? I'll catch the bus up on the Thursday. I don't have any lectures on Fridays."

"If you want to, I would love to see you. I might need a bit of interior decorating advice while you're here."

She laughed. "You might too."

"And I have your Christmas present here for you, it's a bit early, but I figured you might need it."

"Sounds exciting. I'm definitely coming up now."

They chatted for a while; she wanted to know how Biscuit was and would she be able to come and stay with him over the summer holidays with her friends and he said any of her friends were more than welcome, any time. She promised to ring a couple of days before the shift and let him know what bus she'd be on.

The week of the shift, he hunted out Evelyn's phone number and plucked up the courage to call it. It wasn't that he didn't want to speak to her, he just didn't want to speak to the arsehole she was living with, the one who'd been sleeping with her and had eventually stolen her from him. Evelyn answered on the third ring.

"Evelyn, it's Terry. Have you got time to talk?"

"Terry–" She hesitated. "How are you?"

"I'm good. I'm ringing to see what you want to keep in the way of furniture in the house." He had to remember to keep things short and to the point. *Don't get personal.*

"Umm…"

Terry waited.

"I'm not fussed, Terry. Are you moving out?"

"Yes." *Don't get personal.*

"Oh. Take anything you need. I don't know what I'm going to do with the house yet, but I probably won't want anything. I guess I should come down."

"I'm moving out on the weekend." He hoped she wouldn't come down until he was well out of it.

"That was quick."

"I'll probably take some of the kitchen things, and the sofa, if that's okay? And Jackie is coming up to help out," he told her, ignoring her comment about how quickly he was moving out.

"It's fine. Take whatever you need. Give Jackie my love."

"I will. I have to go, Evelyn." He heard her mutter goodbye as he hung up. He wanted to ask how she was, and how the babies were doing and if Tony was looking after her. All the questions he no longer had a right to ask.

He picked Jackie up from the bus, and when they got back to the farm, he told her he had something he wanted to show her in the car shed. She helped him pull the big double door open, and inside was a shiny green Ford Escort.

"What?" she exclaimed, not understanding the car's significance.

"Here." He threw her the keys. "I've been working on it for a few weeks now, and she's good to go. You can take it back to Wellington with you or leave it up here, up to you."

"It's gorgeous!" she said, making a beeline for Terry and throwing her arms around him. "I love it!" She walked slowly around the car, taking in every detail. "How can I possibly thank you?"

"You're here. That's thanks enough."

When she got back to Terry, she threw her arms around him again. "I love my car, and I love you. Thank you."

She'd sat her driver's licence the year before, and he knew she couldn't afford to buy a car, but she was always the sober driver for her flatmates, driving their cars. Although Evelyn was paying Jackie's rent in Wellington, Jackie had been adamant she wanted to pay for her degree herself, and she had got herself a part-time job to help. Terry had slipped a few petrol vouchers into an envelope as a thank you for helping him shift and had hidden the envelope in the glovebox where she would find it later.

Matt arrived early on Friday morning and helped them get several heavy items onto the truck Terry had borrowed from a friend. Matt would call out to the beach and help him unload them after work. Between Jackie and Terry, they managed to get everything he needed onto the truck. And by the time Matt called in, there were only the heavy items left to unload. On Saturday, Jackie helped him unpack some of the kitchen things while he put the two single beds together. He hadn't wanted to take the double bed. It had probably been Jack's anyway, and he was leaving all that behind him. He would buy a new bed.

While Terry organised lighting the fire, Jackie went out in her new car to get fish and chips for dinner, and they sat on the floor of the empty sitting room, eating their dinner straight out of the newspaper.

When it was time for her to leave on Sunday afternoon, he was sorry to see her go. She had been wonderful company, and they had unpacked quite a few boxes while sixties songs played loudly on the radio, both of them singing along as they worked. She had made the place feel homely with her eye for styling. And as she hugged him goodbye, she promised she would come up again in a couple of weeks and maybe bring a friend with her, if that was okay. He laughed and said it was fine, and he would make sure there was plenty of food in the fridge.

She left him a list of things he needed to buy for the house, and he smiled as he read it in front of the fire that night. And when he turned the television off later and stepped outside for his walk, he thought about how strange life was at times.

At Labour Weekend, Jackie and three of her friends arrived to spend the holiday weekend. Terry was impressed when Jackie noticed he had finished painting the rooms, and she admired the new carpet and curtains his sister Judy had helped him pick. The house had been ready for visitors for the last month. He would paint the outside over Christmas when he wasn't working.

The girls spent the weekend walking on the beach, cooking wonderful meals, and playing Terry's old records, which they thought were brilliant. They even found an LP of Evie's that he had forgotten he had, and they asked if he would mind if they played it. He shook his head. Evie was part of New Zealand's history; he even heard one of her songs on the radio occasionally. He couldn't totally divorce himself from her, even if he had wanted to.

On the Saturday night, Jackie talked Terry into going to Hallet's Hotel for a drink with them, and although Evelyn's father made him feel welcome, he left them all to it after two beers.

Terry had promised himself he wouldn't ask about Evelyn, but when he found himself alone in the kitchen with Jackie the next day, he couldn't help it.

"How's Evelyn doing? Have you heard from her lately?"

"She's fine."

"That's good."

"Do you really want to know?"

"I want to know she's okay and happy. That's all that matters."

"I spoke to her two weeks ago, and the pregnancy was going fine so far." Jackie was well aware of how many babies her adoptive parents had lost.

"I'm pleased."

"How are you doing? Do you think you'll find someone else?"

"I don't know, kiddo. I've made an offer on the garage and should know in another week if it's mine. I reckon it'll keep me pretty busy. Might not have any time for chatting up women." He grinned at her, and she put her arm around his waist. Terry found her mature for her age, and he enjoyed the time they spent together. They had become close friends, and they talked about everything. She was a daughter any father would be proud of.

"I don't want you to be lonely," she said. "You're far too lovely to spend the rest of your life on your own. And you're still an attractive man."

Terry chuckled. She was such a tonic. "Thanks, kiddo. That's reassuring. But you can have all the friends or be the most successful person in the world and still be lonely."

"That's just sad and unnecessary," she said matter-of-factly as she put the last of the dishes into the cupboards.

"It is. But that's just how it is. And the hermit who keeps to himself may keep the best company and be the happiest."

"You're not turning into a hermit, are you?"

Terry grinned. "No chance."

"That's good."

He could feel her watching him as he wiped down the Formica bench.

"Can I ask you something?"

"Sure. What is it, kiddo?"

"Can I call you Dad?"

Terry stopped. "You don't have to."

"But I want to."

"Then I'd be honoured." He couldn't believe after all these years she felt the need to call him Dad. "You know I love you very much, no matter what you call me?"

"I do, and I know I have a birth dad, but in my heart, you are as much my father as he was, maybe even more, and I love you too. You've done so much for me."

"Go on. You're getting soppy now." He put his arms around her and held her tight. She was almost the same height as him now and growing into a beautiful woman. Her girlfriends were all attractive too, but Jackie was striking with her creamy complexion and straight dark hair. He couldn't have been prouder of how she had turned out and what she was doing. "Go and join your friends, kiddo."

Terry finished tidying the kitchen while Jackie went to find the girls. They were going to take Biscuit for a leisurely walk on the beach one last time before they headed back to Wellington. Before they left for their walk, they stopped to ask if Terry would like to join them, but he politely told them he had some work to do in the garage, and he'd see them when they got back.

The house was plunged into silence after they left for Wellington, and he was sorry to see them go. Even Biscuit seemed lost after all the attention. When he thought about the endless weekends he had spent looking after Jackie while Evelyn was away working, he guessed he should be used to being on his own.

He sank into the sofa with a coffee to watch the late news, but all he could think of was his conversation with Jackie. He would love to find someone to share his life with, and he was still a young man, but if it didn't happen, it didn't happen. At least he had his mates. And he had Jackie.

Chapter 45

The following month passed in a haze, and by the time December rolled around, the sale of the garage had gone through, and Terry was running the busiest garage in Foxton.

In the lead-up to the Christmas holidays, everyone wanted their cars, caravans and trailers ready for travel. It was hectic, but he had taken on the ownership with a strong sense of responsibility, and his customers rewarded him for his dedication.

He was working long days during the week and all day on Saturdays to ensure everything was done on time and his customers were happy. Although he needed another staff member, he couldn't afford to employ anyone yet.

To make matters worse, he had developed a burning pain below his ribcage. He didn't know what was causing it but wondered if it was the long hours he was putting in at work and not eating properly. Most nights, he was too exhausted to cook himself a proper meal so picked up something easy from the Four Square or burger bar.

In the third week of December, Jackie came to stay for a couple of nights, and he'd planned to finish work early so he could spend some time with her. But in the end, she'd had to come looking for him at the garage and tell him to leave the rest. She was driving to Auckland to spend Christmas with Evelyn before the babies arrived. She promised she would come and stay at the beach for a week in the new year, and she convinced Terry to close the garage for two weeks so he could take a break. He promised he would and agreed to teach her how to surf. She wasn't letting him get out of his promise.

At the end of January, he called into the Four Square for a few groceries on his way home and saw Evelyn on the cover of a women's magazine. Hesitantly, he lifted a copy. He flicked through the magazine to find the story: she had delivered two healthy boys, and there was a picture of her and her manager, Tony, holding a baby each. The headline: "Miracle Babies Arrive" blared at him. Miracle indeed. So now the whole country would know he hadn't been able to give his wife children. Great. He didn't read the story; he didn't need to, the photo said it all. She looked radiant. She finally had what he hadn't been able to give her for the twelve years of their marriage. He tossed the magazine back onto the pile.

Three days later, his stomach pain became so bad he had to pay a visit to his doctor. He had lost weight and even thrown up several times. The doctor ran blood tests to be on the safe side and four hours later rang to tell him he had a perforated gastric ulcer and needed to go straight to the hospital; they were waiting for him. They prepped him for theatre straight away; he didn't even have time to ring Jackie to let her know what was happening.

In November, Whiskey Company held their twenty-year reunion, and this time Terry didn't hesitate to register. It was in Auckland, and it promised to be just as good as the Victor Company one the year before. This time, Evelyn wasn't invited, and he felt more relaxed about going.

And just as there had been with his mates from Victor, there were plenty of laughs with his mates from Whiskey. Although each had been fighting their own private battles, as far as Terry was concerned, they hadn't changed a bit.

And like the previous reunion, the main topic of conversation was the progress on the investigation into the use of herbicides and insecticides in Vietnam. Everyone was talking about the anti-malarial tablets they had been given too; in particular, Dapsone, and about how the government was accumulating a large database of information on the veterans, its data indicating that the chemical dioxin was being passed down to the next generation.

"The government will never come to the table, and reports will never be conclusive in favour of us," Rusty Taylor stated.

"They will if we make enough noise," Terry said.

"How long have we been making noise for now?" Rusty challenged.

"Too long. But that's not the point."

"It is, from where I'm sitting," Rusty replied.

"The point is, even though we're dwindling in numbers, our voice still needs to be heard. In fact, probably louder than ever before."

"I agree," Lewis piped up. "We're bloody history now. It's our kids we need to speak up for."

The conversation continued until they each said their goodnights, and when it came time to leave at the end of the weekend, the men of Three Section agreed to meet every year. Too many of them were dying of cancers now, and it was important they kept in touch and supported each other.

Early March the following year, Terry heard from one of his customers that old Ray Coles had died. The news saddened him. During the years he had been on hunting trips with Jack, he had met Jack's old man many times, but it was during the years he'd been married to Evelyn that he'd had a lot more to do with him. He'd considered Ray a kind and caring grandfather to Jackie, and that was all that mattered.

The funeral was held on a drizzly Friday morning, and a large crowd gathered to pay their respects. Ray was an old identity in the district, and the majority of those present were friends of Ray or his sons Jack and Brian. Evelyn had come down from Auckland.

"Hey," Jackie said, walking up to Terry outside the church and putting her arm around him. She had driven up from Wellington for the funeral and was staying the weekend with him. "How are you, Dad?"

"Hey, yourself, kiddo." He put his arm around her waist and kissed her cheek. "Nice to see you. I'm good. I think you should go support Evelyn though. She's probably feeling it."

"I was talking to her earlier. She's pretty cut up. I think she feels she's lost the last link to Jack."

"Probably. Go. I'll catch up with you later."

She nodded and kissed him back, and then walked off to find Evelyn.

Terry stood at the back of the packed church. He saw Evelyn walk in behind her sister, Joyce, and Joyce's husband, Brian, and their children. Evelyn was carrying one toddler on her hip, and Tony walked beside her carrying the other.

At the end of the service, Terry watched the family members walk past him again. Amongst them, Evelyn, her eyes red. As if she sensed him watching her, she lifted her head, her eyes meeting his. For the longest second, he saw the Evelyn he knew when Jack died: beautiful, compassionate and grieving. His heart went out to her, and he stifled the urge to climb over the pews and hug her. Protect her. An instant later, she looked away, and the connection was lost.

Terry didn't want to hang around. He made his way through the groups of people standing around on the lawn outside the church, nodding his hello to those who recognised him. He had a trailer he was working on, and if he was lucky, he would be able to get it finished by the end of the day.

"Terry–"

He didn't need to turn around to know who the voice belonged to.

"Evelyn." She looked more composed now, and her eyes weren't so red-rimmed.

"I just wanted to say thank you for coming."

"No need. I liked the old boy. He was a bit rough, but he had a kind heart, and he was a bloody good grandfather to Jackie." He felt uncomfortable talking to her and shoved his hands in his pants pockets to keep from fidgeting.

"Yes, he was more than kind to me when Jack died. And happy for me when I married you, too."

Terry glanced around the crowd. He wondered where Tony was right now. "How's the family?" He wanted to say, *'the kids I couldn't give you,'* but he didn't. It was history now.

"The kids are good."

"I'm pleased." He rocked back and forth on his heels and studied the polish on his shoes.

"How are you doing? Health-wise."

"I guess I'm as fine as can be expected." He got the feeling she wanted to tell him something; that she was stalling for time or didn't know how to broach the subject.

He wanted to tell her that he missed her. But he no longer did. He was used to spending time on his own and had long ago, stopped missing her. He was a confirmed bachelor now.

"I wanted to–"

"Evie," a woman Terry didn't know, interrupted. "The hearse is about to leave."

"I've got to go. Sorry. It was nice to see you." Her smile looked strained as she turned and was led to a small gathering of the immediate family members.

Three months after the funeral, an envelope addressed to Terry with the stamp of an Auckland law firm on it arrived at the garage. It was a letter advising him Evelyn was seeking a divorce. He wondered if she finally intended to marry Tony.

He made himself a mug of tea and drank it while he thumbed through the wad of papers held together by a straining paperclip.

The lawyer advised the house at Himatangi had been sold, and he had been instructed to pay Terry fifty thousand dollars. *Fifty thousand.* He let out a low whistle and reread that section of the document, shocked to find it was his share of the value of the property.

He couldn't take it. He would have to ring Evelyn and tell her. It was her house. Jack had built it for them when he returned from Vietnam. Terry had no attachment to the property. He would ring her when he got home. Reading through to the end, he was relieved to find there were no more surprises.

He counted the rings, hoping that Evelyn wasn't working tonight and that it would be her that answered.

"Hello?"

"Evelyn. It's Terry."

"Terry. How are you?"

Terry didn't want to spend time making small talk.

"I got the divorce papers today."

"Oh." There was an uncomfortable silence before she spoke again. "If you can have your lawyer look at them and send them back signed, it shouldn't take long to finalise."

"Well." He hesitated. "The thing is, I can't accept the money."

"Why not?"

"It wasn't mine in the first place."

"That doesn't matter."

"It does to me."

"You looked after the house and maintained it for twelve years. If you hadn't done that, I wouldn't have been able to sell it for as much as I did."

"It doesn't matter. That was Jack's place."

"Don't be so stubborn."

"I'm not being stubborn. If you're so determined to give the money away, give it to Jackie. Or your kids." It was out before he realised what he'd said, and he instantly regretted it.

"I want to give it to you. Jackie just got half of Ray's farm. She doesn't need this too."

"I don't want to argue with you, Evelyn. I can't accept it."

"But what about keeping it, in case you need it for treatment or healthcare?"

"What healthcare?"

"I've heard how hard some veterans are doing." She hesitated. "They're struggling to pay the mounting costs of medical bills."

"Well, I can manage, thanks. I don't need your help."

"Just because we're no longer together, doesn't mean I don't care about what happens to you, Terry. And I'll never forget what you did for Jackie. I feel like I could never repay you for what you did back then. The least I can do is make sure you can afford the best medical treatment possible. If you ever need it."

"You don't owe me anything." He could hear a child crying in the background and wondered if she was at home alone with her children, or if *he* was there too. "I'll make the changes to the document and send it back."

"I wish you wouldn't."

"I better let you go, it sounds like you're needed."

"Terry, please reconsider–"

"My mind is already made up. Anyway, I have to go. I just wanted to let you know what I was going to do."

"I'd like for us to catch up sometime. I'm sorry I didn't have more time to talk to you at Ray's send-off."

"That would have been nice, but I'm not sure how your boyfriend would have viewed it."

"If I want to talk to you, I will."

"Well, it's probably not going to happen, anyway. I gotta go, goodnight, Evelyn." He heard her saying goodnight and hung up the phone. He hadn't had a drink since the reunion, but he sure felt like one now.

The lawyers sent letters back and forth until Terry eventually agreed to take the money and put it in a trust for Jackie, with the proviso he could access it if he needed money for medical reasons.

He hoped he never would.

PART FIVE
1998

Chapter 46

"You have to come down and stay with me for a couple of days, and this time I'm not taking no for an answer," Jackie argued over the phone.

"I've got a lot on at work at the moment, kiddo. What about if I came down in–"

"There are a couple of things I want to show you, and you need to come down this weekend."

"What are they? I'm coming down in three weeks to go to the parade, can't it wait until then?"

"I'd like to surprise you. Do you want me to drive up and get you?"

"Somehow, I think I'm not going to be able to get out of this, am I?"

"No." Jackie laughed. "You've got enough staff to run the garage for a couple of days while you take a well-earned break with your favourite daughter."

"Okay. Okay. You win. I'll drive down."

"When?" She wasn't about to let him wiggle out of it.

"How about I come down on Friday and stay until Monday?"

"I'll settle for three nights."

Terry hung up the phone and went back to watching *Fair Go* on the television. He hadn't been down to see Jackie for a while. It was high time he caught up with her, and he was pleased she still wanted to hang out with an old guy like him.

She was thirty now, and worked just as hard as Terry did. He was always telling her she devoted far too much time to her job, and not enough to finding herself a decent bloke. She had a nice home that she had bought with the money she'd inherited, and she owned an architectural design firm and had just employed four more staff members. She had told him several months ago that she was branching out into interior design too and exploring more sustainable ways to house people on low incomes, which she saw as an increasing concern in years to come. Her business was thriving, and he was happy for her.

The garage was also doing well. Terry had paid off his mortgage several years ago and had just taken on his fifth employee. He was even thinking about shifting into a bigger building and adding a sixth staff member. As a motor mechanic, he had long ago earned the respect of the district, and his customers were loyal.

He was looking forward to Parade '98 in three weeks. It was shaping up to be an emotional weekend and a long overdue 'Welcome Home' parade that the veterans should have had thirty years ago. All of the old gang would be there, and as far as he was concerned, it was all about catching up with his mates; but for some, the wounds ran deep, and this was a giant step towards healing them.

He rarely spoke of his time in Vietnam, except when he got together with his old mates, and he didn't even think about Evelyn much these days either, except when he saw her on a the cover of a women's magazine or heard her on the radio. Out of curiosity, he'd thrown the latest magazine in his trolley with his groceries, and when he got home, added it to the pile of papers and mail on the table to read later.

The hurt he'd felt when she had first told him she was leaving him had long gone. She had her life to live, and she was going places he couldn't have taken her. But he couldn't help the bitterness he felt when he saw pictures of her and the children smiling up at him from the pages of the magazines. It felt like she was rubbing it his face.

The credits rolled on *Fair Go*, and he got up to make himself a cuppa. While he waited for the jug, he caught sight of the magazine on the table. It was a couple of weeks out of date now, and he hadn't read it. Flicking through to the page featuring New Zealand's golden girl, a double-page spread confronted him: Evelyn with the two children beside her and another baby in her arms. She looked happy and radiant. There were several shots of her with the children, and he couldn't help but wonder if she would have left Jack for good if he hadn't been able to give her children either. He shook the thought from his mind. Evelyn was a lovely woman, and he was happy for her. He closed the magazine and tossed it in the bin.

On the Friday, he drove down to Jackie's. She owned an apartment in the middle of the city. Originally some sort of warehouse space, she had redesigned and renovated it, and it was now comfortable, stylish and homely. It was central to everything and close to her work. She had done all the interior design herself, and it reflected her style and personality. Terry was impressed with her talent and enormously proud of what she had achieved.

Jackie answered the door almost immediately and ushered him inside, hugging him tightly and kissing him on the cheek.

"So, what's this surprise you wanted to show me?" he asked, dropping his overnight bag on the floor.

"You just arrived, for goodness' sake. Let me make you some lunch first."

He laughed. "Do I detect an air of mystery?" He followed her to the kitchen and watched her gather ingredients and make sandwiches.

"You'll have to wait and see. How have you been lately?"

"Okay."

"Are you being honest with me?"

"All the normal problems. The rashes are back, blisters my doctor can't find a reason for, and I've had a couple more skin cancers cut out since I saw you last. The rate it's going, there won't be much left of me soon."

"I thought you looked a little thinner," she said, with a smile as she layered thick slices of rich red tomato on top of thickly cut fresh ham and lettuce. Jackie cut the sandwiches in half and placed them on a plate.

He loved that no matter how much she was part of the professional city vibe, she had kept her personal life simple and, in many ways, old-fashioned. She had an impressive collection of long-playing records that he loved to go through when he stayed over, it was clear they shared similar tastes in music. Sometimes he found one she didn't have and gave it to her to add to her collection.

"So, anyone on the radar yet?" he asked after he had finished eating. He worried that she was still single and hadn't found anyone yet. But she claimed she had far too many projects on the go for a relationship right now.

"I've been working on a major project the past few weeks and haven't even had time to catch up with my friends." She stood up and collected his plate and coffee mug. "Let's go for a drive. I want to show you something."

They took her little car: a newer model of the Ford Escort Terry had given her years ago. She knew the Wellington streets well. She had spent nearly half her life there now.

"Where on earth are you taking me, kiddo?" he finally asked, as they passed through Miramar and popped out on Marine Parade at

Seatoun.

"It's not far now." She was smiling as she drove, and he wondered what was so important to her. They followed the road around the coast to Scorching Bay Beach, and she pulled up right on the beachfront where they could see all the way across the harbour to Eastbourne.

"What do you think?" she asked, turning the car off and opening the door. "This is where we get out."

"It's very nice. But you didn't bring me all the way out here to show me a beach, did you?"

"Amongst other things," she replied.

Terry wondered why she was being so mysterious, but he followed her across the road and up a long driveway and through a tunnel of native trees until it opened out into a large plateau.

"So, what do you think of this?" She had her arms spread, and she spun around like a kid.

"It would be a great place to build a house." He stood with his hands in his pockets as he took in the size of the section and the views, and then he looked back at Jackie.

"I bought it two months ago!"

"This is yours?" he asked, surprised.

"Yes! I've been working on plans for a house, and the builders will start in a month."

"Have you had the site tested for stability?"

"Yes. There's no problem. It's an acre of land, it's private, and I have so many ideas."

"I'm seriously impressed. I can't wait to see the plans." He could tell she was wildly excited.

"Well." She stepped out towards the driveway. "The double garage will come to about here." She paced back towards where Terry was standing. "This will be your self-contained flat. Above me is the living room. Over there is my bedroom and a bathroom. Above that is the kitchen."

As Terry followed her around the site, she filled him in on where each room was situated and what views each would have. The whole project sounded wonderful, and he was proud of how determined she was.

"Well, I have to say, it's all pretty incredible. I can't wait to see it when it's finished."

"I hope you'll come down and stay more often. I don't like the idea of you living on your own. You deserve to have some fun while you're still young."

"Look who's talking." He grinned at her as they reached the car again. "Well, that truly was a surprise."

They walked the short distance to a dairy where he bought ice creams for them both, and they sat on the beach eating them, enjoying the last of the autumn sun.

"Are you ready for another surprise?"

"You haven't bought a second property, have you?"

She threw her head back, laughing. "No. Let me get this house built first. I'm taking you out to an exhibition opening this evening, and then I thought we might go for a meal somewhere, afterwards."

As she drove them back into town, Terry considered the prospect of making small talk with a crowd of people he didn't know, and decided it held little appeal. He took a deep breath. He'd do this for Jackie.

Later that evening, when she emerged from her room wearing a short black dress that, in his opinion, showed way too much leg, and strappy black heels, he thought she looked elegant and stunning and very young. And he felt old. He helped her into a woollen coat, and she pulled her long hair free of the collar.

"You scrub up well, Dad."

"Thank you. I was just thinking the same about you. I'm so proud of you, kiddo. You look beautiful."

She smiled and walked over to kiss him on the cheek.

"Next to you, I feel a little under-dressed though." He was pleased he had thought to throw in a tidy change of clothes. He wore dress jeans and a long-sleeved shirt under a smart jacket, but he hadn't brought a coat. It would have to do. He wondered if the exhibition was for one of her friends or someone she knew through her interior-design contacts.

As they walked up Taranaki Street, Jackie explained the gallery was two blocks away. She told him there had been a lot of talk about the exhibition, but she wouldn't tell him what it was. They crossed the road into Dixon Street and followed two couples down the street towards the gallery.

Terry felt his stomach roll and nerves kick in. At fifty-three, it embarrassed him that he got this anxious about meeting people and being in a crowd, but he was escorting his beautiful daughter to her friend's exhibition, and he could do this. Even if it was only for an hour.

As they approached, he could see the gallery was already busy. People were spilling out onto the footpath, talking and drinking, and a young man wearing an apron was circulating with a tray of wine glasses.

"This is it," Jackie said, taking his hand as they reached the large picture window on the front of the gallery.

The first thing Terry noticed was a large black and white photo. It hung in the window, and it stopped him dead. It was a photo of a soldier, his face covered in blood and grime, and he appeared to be crying as he reached out a hand out to someone who wasn't in the frame. It was taken close up and the face was shocking but mesmerising. He could tell straight away it had been taken in Vietnam during the war.

"Were these all taken in Vietnam?" he asked Jackie, trying to peer through the crowd, into the gallery.

"Yes, they were." She squeezed his hand. "Perhaps you could talk me through them."

"I thought we were coming to support one of your friends. Paintings or something. I wasn't expecting photos of Vietnam. Do you know the photographer?"

"No. But the exhibition has travelled the world, and now it has everyone in Wellington talking. I thought you might like to see it too."

He looked at her then, remembering that she had a Vietnamese birth mother. He nodded, peering closely at the image in the window. There was a stamp in one corner, but he couldn't read it clearly with the reflections.

"The exhibition is apparently only here until Parade '98."

Terry looked through the window. "I don't know if I can do this, kiddo." His heart was racing and he felt as if he were standing under a blast furnace.

"When I heard about this exhibition, it made me think more about the country I was born in. And my heritage. It's time I faced it." She turned to look him in the eyes. "Besides, I wasn't sure if I could face it alone."

"I don't know if I can face it either." He was being brutally honest with her. With himself. The exhibition was about to unleash a torrent of emotions. He was breaking into a sweat just looking at the image in the window.

"Perhaps we can do it for each other? We can do it together."

He took a deep breath and squeezed her hand. "Okay, lead the way, kiddo."

They manoeuvred their way inside. It was a large gallery; a commercial building renovated especially for the purpose. The walls were painted white, and, from what Terry could see, all the photographs were in black and white, and in the nearest corner someone had splattered what looked like a tin of red paint over the wall and onto the floor. It looked exactly like blood, and Terry thought it made a powerful statement on its own.

As they moved closer to the centre of the room, he noticed the words Associated Press and their logo on the far wall, and he instantly thought of Frankie and her cameras. But he knew the AP had used lots of photographers in Vietnam during the war years, and there were at least fifty photographs of different sizes here on these walls.

They were offered a glass of champagne; when Terry declined, they offered him a beer and he nodded. The waiter asked Terry if he was a veteran of the Vietnam War and when Terry told him he was, the waiter welcomed him home. Terry nodded his thanks, and as he stood there amongst the images and the people, he felt overwhelmed by his emotions. The memories these young men in the images brought to life had been buried and forgotten for a long time.

They moved towards another framed photo, this time, two young soldiers were the focus. He told Jackie he thought they were Marines and couldn't have been much more than eighteen or nineteen. One was bent double with his head in his hands, both bandaged legs, ended at the knees, his face was almost completely hidden by bandages. The other Marine had his arm around his mate's shoulders, a mixture of shock and terror on his face.

Memories of the firefights flooded back as he stood in front of the images. He remembered his first contact, how terrified he'd been, especially when he realised that if he didn't kill, he'd be killed. He'd had to grow up mighty quickly, as they all had over there. It dawned on him that he had never talked about the horrific side of the war. When he got together with his mates at reunions, they always talked about the laughs they'd had. Never the bad times. This exhibition brought all the bad memories back.

He looked around the room. Most of the people gathered were young enough not to have been around during the war. Or too young to remember. Beside him, a couple was discussing the American involvement in South Vietnam, and on the other side, two young women were talking about film speed and exposure.

Terry moved on to the next image. He inched closer to the photograph, peering at the stamp in the corner.

"I'd like to know who took these." There, on an angle, was the photographer's embossed stamp with Associated Press on the top and F. Proctor in relief on the bottom. He stepped back in shock. *Frankie?* This was one of Frankie's photos? He wanted to reach out to it as if to renew a friendship, reconnect with the woman who took it. He knew there had to be at least one of her photos amongst those here.

They inched through bodies to the next photo. It had Frankie's name on the bottom too. Another brutal image of suffering. And the next one had her name on it as well. And suddenly he knew he was seeing a collection of her photos; they were all taken by her, and he felt an urgent need to see them all.

As he manoeuvred his way to each framed image, some large, some small, he forgot all about Jackie; all he wanted was to see the images, and then he stopped short in front of a photo someone had taken of Frankie. She was lying on the ground, blood on her face, her eyes closed; a young soldier crouched beside her, holding her hand, while another held an IV bag. And Terry wondered if she had been killed while out on an assignment. He could feel the tears well and spill down his face, and he took a handkerchief from his pocket and quickly wiped them away. Shit, he didn't even know if she was alive or dead, if she had made it out of Vietnam after the fall of Saigon, or if she had got caught up in the fighting in the last days of the war.

He felt a hand on his arm.

"You okay?"

He sniffed, wiped his nose and grinned foolishly at Jackie as he shoved his handkerchief back in his pocket. "Yeah, kiddo. The memories are pretty rough though."

"Do you know any of the people in the photos?"

"There were thousands of people over there. I think many of these are Marines."

"This one is interesting. Isn't that a woman on the ground?"

"It is. She was a combat photographer—the photographer who took these photos." The soldier leaned over her, panic etched onto his blood-splattered face. Frankie looked like she was dying. His heart sank, and he took a deep breath, trying to calm himself.

"There were a lot of female journalists and photographers over there," he finally said, not knowing if he was ready to tell his daughter about his relationship with Frankie. He hadn't told anyone, not even his mates. He had been surprised no one at the reunions remembered her; they seemed to have forgotten about his kiss with the woman on the tarmac the day they left.

"They were pioneers and bloody good at their jobs," he continued. "There were a lot killed too." Being good at your job over there, often came at a high price.

They moved to the next photo. They all told stories of the loss of youth, innocence and life: legs with no bodies, boots with feet still in them, bandages and blood. They were hard hitting, and he knew why the exhibition had attracted a lot of attention. Frankie had done an admirable job of telling the stories she'd said she wanted to. He felt his heart swell with pride for what she had achieved.

At each photo, Jackie asked questions, and it helped him to talk about some of the things he had seen.

It took them almost an hour to get to the last photo, and it shocked Terry when he saw it right at the back of the gallery, hanging on its own. It wasn't of young men dying, or even of death. It wasn't of men being carried to dustoff choppers, or men crying or comforting each other in the midst of death. Instead, it was a simple portrait taken to expose one side of the face and hide the other. It was of a woman wearing fatigues, the collar of her shirt turned up on one side and over on the other. Sweat matted the hair around her face and blood was splattered across her jaw and neck; one lone tear sat on her grimy, dust-covered cheek. He was staring straight into Frankie's eyes.

Her image sucked all the air from him, and he took gulps, trying to force air into his lungs.

"Dad?"

"Give me a minute," he managed, as he fought to control his breathing and his shock at seeing the portrait.

He couldn't help the huge surge of emotion as all the old feelings swept through him. All the love, the admiration. His feelings for Frankie had been much stronger and more real than anything he had felt for Evelyn. What he'd had with Evelyn had felt more like a duty. It was easy to look back now and think that, but as he stood rooted to the spot, staring at the portrait, he knew there was never any doubt. He'd married Evelyn because he'd confused love with a sense of duty and guilt; pure and simple.

Terry dug in his pocket for his handkerchief again, wiped his eyes and blew his nose. In black and white, the photo didn't show her trademark copper hair, and the eyes–the eyes were dead. Lifeless. As if she were an empty shell. It brought tears to his own eyes, and he dabbed at them again. As if he were the only person in the room, he reached out to the portrait, as if to touch Frankie herself. As though she were there standing in front of him. As if by touching her he might make her smile, might wipe away the tear on her cheek, might crinkle the corners of her eyes just a little while the freckles bounced around on her skin. As though to restore life to her eyes.

"This is the photographer, isn't it?" Jackie asked. "She's beautiful."

He snatched his hand back, remembering where he was.

"She was beautiful, all right. And she had the prettiest copper hair."

"Did you know her?"

"Yes," he said, barely louder than a whisper. He couldn't tear his eyes from the portrait, and he didn't want to. He wanted to be transported back to the sixties and the times he had spent with her. As he smiled at all those gorgeous freckles he'd loved to trace, he wondered if they would sell this photo, or maybe a copy of it.

"I used to call her Copper."

"You were the only one who ever did," a voice beside him answered.

The world stopped. In slow motion, he turned. He'd know that voice anywhere, but it couldn't be–

"Frankie?"

Chapter 47

Frankie stared at Terry in amazement. The Vietnam War had brought Terry to her again, and she couldn't believe her eyes. Here he was, standing in front of her, large as life. The telltale threading of grey through his hair made him look even more handsome than she remembered, but his eyes were full of sadness, pain, and now shock. If she hadn't been in shock herself, she would have laughed at the look on his face. He was staring at her as though he'd seen a ghost.

"You're alive," Terry whispered.

"You better believe it," she replied, smiling, trying to keep the conversation light so she wouldn't cry. "Although, sometimes it doesn't feel like it." She smiled at him. Then she took a deep breath, leaned in and kissed him on the cheek; enjoying, for the briefest second, the feel of his skin.

Life had taught her many lessons, and she had long ago made a pact with herself to be more spontaneous, act on impulse more often. This was the impulsive moment she had been waiting for.

"I thought—I mean," Terry stumbled. "I saw the photo with you on the ground, and I thought you had died over there."

"It's me. Large as life. But, I think a part of me did die over there." She took a sip of her beer. "So. What do you think?" She glanced around the gallery at the collection. She knew every photo, every detail, every soldier, and every minute of drama that she had captured on film. She had travelled with the exhibition for the past ten years, meeting some incredible people and hearing some wonderful stories of bravery, love and dedication along the way.

"I think they're brutal in their honesty," the striking young woman hanging on to Terry's arm, stated. "And extremely sad. They make me want to cry."

"Human devastation is certainly something to be sad about. I hope you never have to experience anything like that," Frankie replied, wondering what the connection was between them. She remembered the day she had seen Terry at Tan Son Nhut Airport just before the fall of Saigon. He had been with a woman and a young child. Was this woman that same child? Or maybe she was his wife? She knew a number of veterans who had gone back to Vietnam and found a wife.

Frankie smiled at the woman and offered her hand.

"Sorry for being so rude. I'm Frankie Proctor. Combat photographer back in the day. You must be Terry's … wife?"

The woman looked at Terry and burst into laughter. She still had her arm through his, and she slipped it out to shake hands with Frankie.

"It's an honour to meet you, Frankie. I love your work and your dedication to a cause, but I'm Terry's daughter, Jackie Coles, JT to my friends. I'm not his wife."

"Sorry. Your father hasn't aged over the years as badly as I have."

"You haven't changed a bit in my eyes," Terry stated.

"So, your eyesight is going too, eh?" Frankie asked.

They all laughed.

"The photo of you back there, were you badly injured?" Terry asked, changing the subject.

"I was on assignment with the Marines, and we came under heavy shelling. I got caught helping out a wounded soldier, wrong place at the wrong time. A mortar blast lifted me up and threw me through the air. I got a concussion, shrapnel wounds, a couple of cracked ribs, and sprained my wrist. The NVA kept up the shelling for almost two days before it eased enough to get me out. I ended up in the hospital at Da Nang." She waited for Terry to remember. It had happened at the end of sixty-eight when they had planned to meet at the Continental. She saw a flicker of remembrance in his eyes. She didn't want to say anything, in case his wife was also here in the gallery somewhere.

He nodded. "I remember."

Frankie also remembered making it to the airport as he was leaving the country with Whiskey Company. She wondered if he was thinking of those times too.

The two of them stood for a moment in awkward silence. Each with their own memories.

"I'm going to refresh my drink," Jackie said, lifting her empty glass. "Can I get anyone anything?"

"No, thank you." Frankie watched the young woman move away and stop to talk to a couple in the middle of the room.

"She's a lovely woman. You must be very proud of her."

"I am. She's already achieved a lot in her short lifetime."

"I can't believe you're standing here after all these years." Her heart skipped and fluttered, and she felt like a teenager.

"Neither can I. Jackie persuaded me to come down and stay with her for a couple of nights. I had no idea she was bringing me to see this exhibition."

They were silent again. There was so much to say, so many questions, Frankie didn't know where to start.

"I'm pleased she did."

Several people interrupted them to congratulate her on the exhibition, and she spoke with each one, thanking them.

"Can I get you another?" Terry nodded to her empty glass.

"No, thank you. One's enough these days." And then she had to ask; she couldn't help herself. "Is your wife here with you tonight?" She had always wondered if the woman he was with at the airport all those years ago had been his wife. He had obviously fathered a Vietnamese girl. Or maybe adopted her, but the woman looked a lot like Terry. Frankie had so many questions, and she didn't know if she had the right to ask any of them.

"No. Actually, I'm divorced. Have been for a couple of years now."

"I'm sorry to hear that."

"Don't be. Our relationship was probably buggered from the start. I just didn't know it. What about you?"

"Never married. Never quite found the right man."

"I find that hard to believe."

"Maybe the bar was set too high? I don't know. I was engaged once, but it only lasted eight months, and then he got sick of the real me."

"Who is the real you?"

He had asked a hard question. She'd thought about it a lot after Josh had broken their engagement and accused her of being bipolar and moody. But she wasn't bipolar, and it was Vietnam that caused her mood swings. Even now, although she managed things, she still got cranky from time to time. She had cut back on alcohol and cigarettes and had stopped chasing ideals instead of reality. And when she finally came to terms with who she had become, what the war in Vietnam had turned her into, she accepted life would probably be better managed if she lived on her own.

"That's a hard one to answer. Sometimes I forget who the real me is." She studied him. "I blame the war."

"Don't you get lonely?"

"Sometimes. If I stop and think about it. As long as I'm busy, it's not a problem. And I have my friends."

"Did you not want kids? Shit, sorry. This is turning into twenty questions."

Frankie grinned. She had so many questions of her own she wanted to ask.

"It's okay, I've got twenty for you too. I decided against having kids. I heard about all the problems the vets had been having with miscarriages, stillborn babies, and deformities. I decided I wouldn't even try. Mind you," she added, "for that you do need a man at some point in the equation. What about you?"

"I don't need a man."

She laughed. Couldn't help it. He was the same Terry she had met and fallen in love with all those years ago. He carried a few battle scars. But underneath it all, he was still that same man. Just older. More experienced.

"That's not what I meant," she managed when she'd finished laughing. "I meant children. Do you have any other children, apart from Jackie?"

And for a second, she caught a glimpse of pain in his eyes, and then it was gone.

"We had three attempts. Lost all of them at one stage or another."

"Jesus, *three?* I'm so sorry. It must have been a tough time for you and your wife."

"Yeah." He glanced around the room, and then his eyes settled back on her. "How long do you have to stay here for? When can I smuggle you out?"

"Oh, I'd say"–she glanced at her wristwatch–"in about fifteen minutes. The gallery owner can take it from then."

"Jackie and I are going to grab some dinner. Would you like to join us?"

"I'd love to. If I'm not intruding?"

"You wouldn't be. I'll leave you to your guests, and I'll go find the kiddo and let her know."

She smiled her acknowledgement and watched his back as he moved through the guests. Who would have thought? A sleeping giant had been awakened. All those feelings, buried under thirty years of life, were bubbling to the surface. She hadn't even asked him if he had a girlfriend or anyone special in his life. But it didn't matter. She would take what she could get. If there was one thing the war years had taught her, it was to live for the moment. And in this moment, tonight, a miracle had happened, and Terry Edwards had walked back into her life.

Chapter 48

Terry and Frankie sat in a small Italian pizzeria a block from the gallery. When he had asked Jackie if she minded Frankie joining them, she'd said she had met some friends she hadn't seen since university days, and she would go out with them for dinner and a few drinks and leave Terry to catch up with Frankie. He had his key to the apartment and could let himself in when he got back if she wasn't home.

"I still can't believe you're sitting here," he said, finishing the last slice of pizza and wiping his fingers on the serviette.

"I'm pleased I am. That was bloody good pizza." She pushed her plate away and lifted her head to look at him. "Terry, I owe you an apology."

"For what? You've done nothing except share dinner with me."

"For not answering your letters, all those years ago." She lowered her gaze and absently picked at crumbs on the chequered tablecloth.

"I was pretty cut up about it. I couldn't understand why, or what I'd done."

"You didn't do anything."

"I thought you'd found someone else over there. Some quick-talking journalist who knew all the moves."

"I thought you'd go home and meet someone else too, and I didn't know when I'd be back—it seemed selfish to make you wait. It wasn't fair on you."

"You were worth waiting for," he said quietly.

"Did you know I saw you in Saigon in seventy-five?"

"You saw me…?"

"Yes, boarding a plane at Tan Son Nhut."

"In seventy-five?" It took him a minute to figure out what she was talking about. "I didn't see you."

"I know. It looked like you were in a hurry."

The waitress interrupted, asking if they wanted desserts or coffees, and he ordered a coffee for himself and tea for her and waited for the girl to leave.

"I was," he continued. "I was with Evie Hallet. It's a bit of a long story. I'm not sure if you want to hear it."

"*The* Evie Hallet?" She was impressed.

"Yes."

"If you feel like telling me, I'm happy to listen."

He told her about his infatuation with Evelyn before he went to Vietnam, and how she had been engaged to his best mate, Jack Coles, and had eventually married him."

"Coles? Isn't that Jackie's last name?"

"It is. You see, Jack had an affair with a Vietnamese woman. She had a child and claimed it was Jack's. Before Jack left in sixty-eight, we were out on an op, and he stalked and shot a couple of snipers who ambushed us. One of them was Jackie's mother. Turned out she was a high-ranking Viet Cong officer and a sniper. Jack then got sent home, leaving a four-month-old baby over there somewhere. Anyway," he continued. "Evelyn fell pregnant, but after they lost the baby, things got rough for Jack and ... cutting a long story short, he took his own life. He had been suffering from depression, couldn't sleep, couldn't hold down a job or even commit to his rugby anymore. His death devastated Evelyn and affected everyone who knew him."

"That sounds horrible. I'm so sorry."

The waitress delivered their drinks, and he nodded his thanks.

"So, a couple of years after Jack died, Evelyn decided she had to go back to Vũng Tàu and try to find the child–Jack's daughter–and bring her back. I couldn't let her go on her own."

"And you found the girl?"

"It was nothing short of a miracle. Believe me."

"And that child is the woman I met tonight?"

"Yeah."

"And I'm guessing Evelyn was the woman you married?"

"Good guess. But when she left me, I realised I'd married her out of a sense of duty." He grinned across the table. "You know, macho male protecting his woman. I think there was an element of survivor's guilt thrown in the mix somewhere too." He remembered his coffee, which was now lukewarm.

"It wasn't love. Not when I compare that relationship to what we had." He was being brutally honest. He was too old to play games or worry about consequences. "She was away a lot, working, and I was always left to look after Jackie. I think that's why the kiddo and I are so close."

"I'm sorry you had to go through all that. Makes my life seem boring in comparison. So, what are you doing now?"

"I bought a garage in Foxton a few years back. And a cottage out at the beach. That's my lot. Are you living here in Wellington, or just passing through?" he asked, moving the topic of conversation back to her.

"Living here. For the time being at least. I've spent a long time travelling, and I've been thinking it's about time I settled down and made some sort of home for myself. I found a little place in Island Bay to rent for a few months."

"Sounds nice."

"It is. I do a lot of walking, and I write a column for a paper. Some days I sit watching the sea roll in and out and it takes all my effort to find the motivation to get out of the damned chair."

"You know, I think you're even more beautiful than you were back then."

She laughed, and he felt embarrassed for speaking his mind. But in his eyes, she was the same girl he had met all those years ago, and he couldn't believe they were sitting here talking about things like it was an everyday occurrence.

"I guess I should be getting home before I turn into a pumpkin," she said, smiling at him. "What are you doing tomorrow?"

"I haven't thought that far ahead yet. I don't think Jackie has anything planned."

"Would you like to come and have lunch with me? At my place. Will Jackie mind if I kidnap you for a few hours?"

"I'd love to. Thank you. I'm sure she won't mind."

She rummaged around in her bag for a pen and scribbled her address and phone number on one side of a serviette then slid it across the table to him.

He agreed to come at one o'clock, and as they stood on the footpath waiting for her taxi to arrive, he took the liberty of kissing her lightly on the cheek and was relieved when she didn't flinch. As the taxi pulled up outside the pizzeria, she put her arms around him and gave him a hug.

"Thank you for coming to my exhibition tonight. I'll see you tomorrow."

He nodded and closed the car door for her. She waved, then the car pulled out, and she was gone.

Frankie Proctor. Was it too late? Was it worth hoping? Dare he hope for a second chance?

He walked back to Jackie's apartment with a spring in his step that he hadn't had in a long, long time.

Chapter 49

The following day, he arrived at the address Frankie had given him. He pushed the gate open and walked up to her front door with a large bunch of flowers he had picked up on the way. When she opened the door, she was wearing faded jeans and a baggy sweatshirt with an American flag on it. She'd pinned her hair up untidily, and she wore no make-up. He thought she looked absolutely wonderful.

She ushered him in, and as she prepared lunch, he admired the view from the huge picture windows that overlooked the bay and the harbour beyond.

"I can fully understand why you don't want to tear yourself from this view."

"I've thought about taking up painting as a hobby, but I wouldn't know one end of a paintbrush from the other. Would you like a beer?" She opened a Diet Coke for herself and then handed him a beer.

They ate lunch watching the inter-island ferries enter and exit Wellington Harbour and gulls swoop down to balance skilfully on her front fence. He told her he thought the house suited her perfectly, and she shared the fact the house had come fully furnished. She had brought a few cases with her, everything else she owned was still in storage for the time being.

He got up to use the bathroom, and as he walked back to the kitchen, he passed what appeared to be her bedroom, and something in there caught his eye. He hesitated, and then, knowing it was wrong, stepped into the room. There was a picture window on one wall that looked out at a planting of large tree ferns, and apart from Frankie's large bed, there was a bedside table, a set of drawers and a coat stand. He knew he was invading her privacy, but he couldn't help himself; he was being pulled in to the room by the memories they shared. What had caught his attention was the collection of Buddhas that sat on her drawers. Seven of them, all different sizes.

And when he turned to leave, there it was.

On the table beside her bed, a small marble Buddha; it looked to be the one he had given her thirty years ago. The same one he'd had tattooed on his chest above his heart after he got back to New Zealand. He had wanted something to remember her by. No one had ever known how much that tattoo had meant to him. Not even Evelyn.

How come she still had it? He picked it up and held it in his hand, feeling the cool marble under his fingers, cherishing the memories. As he put it down, he noticed a framed photo. He picked that up too, stunned to find it was the one of him taken on the beach at Vũng Tàu with that bloody fish in his hand. He smiled then turned when he heard a noise in the doorway.

He hastily put the frame back.

"I'm so sorry. I shouldn't have intruded. It was wrong of me."

"No need to apologise."

"You kept this picture? Why?"

"I think you already know the answer," she replied.

He reached down and picked up the little smiling Buddha again and ran his thumb over the rounded curves, his mind miles away.

"It's always, only, been you."

"No wonder your fiancé left," he said, trying to make light of the situation. He had no idea how to react or what to say, and he was embarrassed she had caught him looking at her things. He had only truly loved one woman passionately in his lifetime. And she was standing here in front of him, telling him she still loved him.

Hell, he was fifty-three, and she was even older. Who would want an old guy like him? But they were two people who had met under extreme circumstances and lost each other in them too, with no guarantees they would see each other again. And thirty years later, here they were, like some giant hand of fate had been guiding them through everything they had experienced, to this weekend.

"I told him you were my brother, and that you were killed in Vietnam. I told him you were my hero, and that I loved you very much and missed you every day."

He looked at her, shocked, trying to imagine how the poor man would have felt with Terry watching on all the time. Then he realised she was joking, and he laughed with her. The clock had just been rewound thirty years, only now, they finally had their chance to be together.

There was nothing left to do but kiss her. He took her face in his hands, his thumbs caressing the freckles, now faded with time. He was done with waiting. Life was too short, too full of sickness and unwelcome surprises. It was time he acted on instinct, grabbed whatever good things came his way, and Copper was definitely a good thing.

Her lips tasted even better than he remembered as she responded willingly to his touch, to his passion. And he let his need for her consume him. Memories, passion, and a love much too strong for either of them to restrain. Whatever it was that each of them felt, it was more powerful than either of them realised.

Parts of his body reacted in ways they hadn't in a long time. All the feelings he had locked away years ago were released. When he finally stepped back, he didn't know what to say, except how he felt. He studied her face, remembering it when she was only twenty-three and he was twenty-one.

"I love you, Copper. And this time, I'm not going to let you go." Slowly, he lifted the sweatshirt up and over her head, discovering she wore nothing underneath, and his heart melted at how beautiful she still looked. And then he noticed she had a little smiling Buddha tattooed on the inside of her wrist and he laughed, aware that she had no idea what he was laughing at and probably thought he was crazy.

Suddenly, they were frantically undoing zips and buttons, tearing off their clothes, desperate to make love and rediscover each other's bodies. And he knew what she was thinking when she took his shirt off and discovered the matching Buddha on his chest. She ran her fingers over it, and he found her touch just as erotic as he had all those years ago. Every part of his body responded.

As Frankie lay asleep in his arms two hours later, he thought his heart might burst with happiness. They had come full circle, and he couldn't believe how lucky he was to have found her again.

"Hey," he whispered and kissed her forehead through the tangle of faded copper hair.

"Mmmm."

"Are you awake?"

"No." She nestled closer into his side, an arm across his stomach.

And then he asked the question he should have asked her thirty years ago before he got on that damn freedom bird home.

"Will you marry me?"

Chapter 50

When Terry got out of the shower, the bed was empty. He pulled on his jeans and wandered out to the kitchen, still drying his hair on a towel. The house was warm even though it was windy and cold outside.

"What in God's name are you making?" he asked, leaning over her shoulder and kissing her neck. "You're not going to drink that are you?"

"It's chamomile tea with a little Valerian root added if you really must know. Want some?" she teased.

"It would probably kill me." He chuckled.

"Chamomile helps keep me calm, helps me sleep and"–she turned to look at him "it has antibacterial, anti-inflammatory and liver-protecting properties. Plus, it helps with anxiety and headaches."

"You won't need it once we're married." He threw the towel over the nearest chair and put his hands either side of her on the kitchen counter, trapping her.

"Why not?"

"You'll have me. It'll be my job to make you nice and relaxed, to get you off to sleep. Give you something nice to dream about. Every. Single. Night." He leaned into her and kissed her again, and he felt her hands slide over the skin on his back.

"Is that so?" she challenged.

He could easily have made love to her again, right there and then.

"I need proof," she said. "Perhaps you should stay over tonight. Would your daughter mind?"

"What say I ring her and let her know?" She nodded her agreement. When Jackie answered her phone, she sounded surprised.

"Dad? Where are you?"

"Hey, kiddo. I'm still at Frankie's place. Would you mind if I stayed with her tonight?"

"Dad!" She laughed down the phone.

He felt like their roles had been reversed.

"I want you to be happy and have some fun. You've been on your own far too long. You're owed big time."

"Thanks, kiddo."

"I love you, Dad."

"Right back at you, kiddo. I'll see you in the morning. Oh, and I've got some exciting news for you. I'll tell you tomorrow."

"Well, why don't you and Frankie come for breakfast at my place in the morning? I'll go into work later."

"Hang on…" He turned to Frankie. "Can you come and have breakfast at the kiddo's place with me in the morning?" Frankie nodded. "We'll see you about eight."

When the wind died down, they went for a walk around the bay. He held her hand as they walked, and in the middle of the footpath he stopped and kissed her while passing cars tooted at them, but he didn't care. They stopped at a café for coffee and finally walked back to her house as the light started to fade. He couldn't get enough of her. The woman he loved, whose long copper hair billowed about in the wind.

They sat on the sofa, eating toasted sandwiches, watching the small fishing boats come into moor and the lights of the other houses in the bay flicker in the dark.

"Where are we going to live? I didn't even think about that," he remarked, thinking out loud.

"I don't care. Maybe at your place?"

"I can sell the garage and the house at the beach, and we could buy something closer to Wellington if you want." He was prepared to do anything for her, even if it meant it was time to move on from the garage and Foxton.

"Could I come and stay with you at the beach for a while? I don't want you to have to sell your business."

"Let's decide later," he suggested, collecting her plate and taking it to the kitchen.

"What say I come up tomorrow? I've got a couple of things to do when I leave Jackie's, and then I'll drive up later in the afternoon."

"The sooner the better," he replied, grinning at her. It would be a whirlwind engagement, but neither of them cared. They were both done waiting.

"We have to set a date."

"Is tomorrow too short notice?"

"A little, unless I can get married in my baggy sweatshirt?"

"Knowing you wear nothing underneath it, except a tattoo, I'd be happy with that." He grinned at her, and she shook her head in mock disgust.

"I think I should make a bit of an effort. This will be my one and only wedding."

He was happy to wait as long as necessary, to allow her time to find the perfect outfit.

They spent all evening talking about the last days in Saigon before it fell to the North. He couldn't believe the horrors she had seen and the stories she told, and he was saddened to hear about Louis.

Then finally, late in the night, he took her by the hand and led her into her room, and they made love again, this time more slowly, enjoying each other. Savouring what they had found and what they would have for the rest of their lives together.

Just after two, Terry got up to use the bathroom and remembered he hadn't checked outside as he always did. It was the first time in years he had forgotten. After pulling on his jeans and his jumper, he walked to the door and stood on the doorstep while lighting a cigarette. He loved the sound of the waves on the beach and the smell of the sea air. He pulled the door to and followed the path alongside the house and down to the front gate. The air was still now, but although the wind had died down, it was icy cold outside. Normal for the middle of May. He stood watching the lights blinking across the bay as he finished his cigarette.

Frankie propped herself up on an elbow and stared at the hands on her bedside clock. It was almost three. Terry's side of the bed was empty. What was he doing? The house was silent.

She rolled over, threw the covers off and got up, shrugging her arms into her robe as she walked out into the kitchen, glancing into the bathroom and toilet as she passed the open doors.

"Terry?" Nothing. She walked across the room to the front door; it wasn't properly closed. He had to be outside. She pulled the robe tighter, slipped her feet into her Ugg boots and followed the path.

As she got closer to the gate, she could make out the shape of someone lying on the path. Her stomach dropped. *NO!* Panic gripped as her heart pounded. Her mind was scrambled. She ran to where he was lying.

"*Terry?*" He felt so cold. "Terry! What's wrong?" *Oh, God.* How long had he been there? She stood and ran as fast as she could to the phone and, with fingers shaking, dialled emergency services. She grabbed blankets off the sofa and ran back outside.

"Terry!" He couldn't do this to her, not now, it was too unfair.

He hadn't moved, and when she put her face to his mouth, she could hear him breathing, but it was shallow, and she didn't know what to do to help him. She rolled him into the recovery position, propped a folded blanket under his head and carefully covered him with the others. He was cold to the touch, so she lay beside him and put her arm around him, willing him to keep breathing as she tried to help warm him until the ambulance arrived.

Nothing she had experienced in Vietnam had prepared her for this, and as she prayed over and over that he would be okay, the tears began to flow.

"Stay with me," she begged. "There's an ambulance on its way. Just hang on." As she stroked the side of his face, she sniffed and willed herself to be strong for him. And he surprised her by opening his eyes and staring at her. "Don't you dare leave me now, you hear me, Terry Edwards. *Don't you dare.* You fight this." There was no recognition in his eyes, and he moved his mouth a fraction, but didn't speak. She didn't know whether he had heard or understood.

Frankie wrapped her arms around him. She had to stay strong even though all she wanted to do was cry. She had no idea what was wrong, except he looked like he was dying.

Flashing lights stopped outside the gate and she heard the ambulance doors open and footsteps running towards where they lay.

When the ambulance officers reached them, one gently helped her to her feet and wrapped her in a blanket as the other worked frantically on Terry. They were asking so many questions, and she didn't know how to answer any of them. They inserted a cannula in his arm and prepared to feed in some drugs. One of them asked her if she wanted to come in the ambulance with Terry, and she nodded.

"While we're getting him ready, put some warm clothes on, get anything you need and lock your house. Okay?"

She nodded.

"We'll be ready to leave inside three minutes."

Frankie fled. She pulled on her jeans and threw on the sweatshirt and grabbed her jacket, then grabbed her bag and keys.

The ambulance officers had Terry on the stretcher and were wheeling him into the back of the ambulance. She hurriedly collected the blankets and ran up to the house, throwing them onto the doorstep. They could stay there until she got back.

She held his hand as they sped through the suburbs towards the hospital. Terry looked like he was sleeping as the ambulance officer worked quickly to attach small round pads to his chest.

"Everything points to a cardiac arrest," the officer said, checking the monitor. "Has he had a heart attack before?"

"I don't know."

"Problems with his blood pressure?"

"I, I … I don't know."

"Is he diabetic?"

"I don't think so."

"It's okay, love. Do you know if he's taken anything, drugs of any sort?"

"No!"

The questions kept coming, and she couldn't answer any of them, and she wanted to shout at them to work harder, not to let him die, but she knew they were working as hard as they could, and all she could do was sit and watch.

All she knew was that she loved him, and she wanted to spend the rest of her life with him, and finally she blurted out that he was a Vietnam veteran, as if it would somehow answer all their questions.

"Okay, don't worry. I think we might have got to him in time."

"You *think?*" She was almost hysterical. "What if you didn't? What if he dies?"

"Time is critical with a cardiac arrest, but the signs are positive. The team is waiting at the ED for us, Mrs Edwards. He's in the best hands."

Frankie was numb. She sat with one hand clamped over her mouth, the other holding Terry's hand. What if he didn't make it, if they never got the chance to spend the rest of their lives together? She thought about all the death and loss she had seen in Vietnam, but this was different; it was Terry whose life was on the line. She couldn't lose him now, not when they had just found each other again. After all this time.

She was strong, and she'd be strong for Terry. She squeezed his hand as if transferring her strength to him.

Don't you dare leave me, Terry Edwards, don't you dare.

Chapter 51

In a whirl of activity, Terry was rushed away on arrival at the hospital. Doctors shouted instructions while nurses ran to keep up. A nurse eventually told her they were running tests to confirm he'd had a heart attack and to see what damage had been done. They would come and talk to her as soon as they knew anything.

Frankie found a chair and collapsed, exhausted and terrified, to wait for news. Oh God, she had completely forgotten about Jackie. She had to let his daughter know. She asked the woman on the reception if she could use the phone and flicked through the phone directory searching the Wellington names. She found a J.T. Coles listed and with shaking hands, rang the number. It was almost quarter to four, but this couldn't wait. What if Terry never regained consciousness?

"Hello?" a groggy voice answered.

"Is this Jackie Coles?"

"Yes?"

"Jackie, it's Frankie."

"Frankie, what's wrong?"

"It's Terry, he's … he's in the hospital."

"Is he okay? What happened?"

"They think he's had a heart attack. They're running tests now." Frankie explained, her voice wavering.

"I'm coming down right now. I'll be fifteen minutes. Where are you?"

"In the emergency department."

"Okay. Stay there. I'm on my way."

Frankie put the phone down and walked back to her chair. She closed her eyes and offered a silent prayer to whoever might hear her. He had to be all right. He just had to.

True to her word, Jackie arrived fifteen minutes later. They let her into the emergency department, and when Frankie saw her, she ran to her. The two women held each other while Frankie cried.

"I'm sorry. I didn't mean to cry all over you."

"I understand. Is there any news?"

"Nothing yet," Frankie replied, blowing her nose and trying to regain some composure. "Do you think we should have heard something by now?"

"They'll let us know as soon as they have something to tell us."

After they'd spent twenty minutes worrying and pacing, a doctor walked across the ED towards them. Frankie took Jackie's hand in hers and held it tightly. She was terrified by what the doctor might tell them, and she felt Jackie squeeze her hand in return and put her arm around her. She was so thankful Jackie had come.

"Mr Edwards has been extremely lucky," the doctor began, looking at Frankie. "From the tests we understand he's suffered a heart attack. Thanks to you, the ambulance staff got to him in time to save his life. The response time is critical in these cases, and fortunately, the ambulance staff ran an ECG and were able to determine Mr Edwards had suffered a heart attack and administer the appropriate medication immediately." He looked from one woman to the other. "Response time determines the quality of survival, how the patient recovers, and whether there is likely to be any lasting damage to either the heart muscle or the brain. In this case, you saved your husband's life."

"Can we see him?" Jackie asked.

The doctor looked at Frankie, who explained Jackie was his daughter.

"He is still in recovery, and we have a couple more tests to run, but he's stable and comfortable. He will be taken to a ward in about thirty minutes and you can see him then. I'll get a nurse to let you know when you can see him."

"Will he be okay?" Frankie asked.

"We've done an angiogram, to see if we can find any blockages, and have just finished running an echocardiogram. That checks all parts of the heart are pumping normally. At this stage it appears there is very little, if any, damage to the heart. We didn't find any obvious blood clots or blockages, which is good news, but a little puzzling at the same time. He's undergoing an electrocardiograph at the moment, which records the electrical activity of the heart. We have also taken bloods, to confirm he did actually have a heart attack. He isn't overweight, and he's in reasonably good shape, so he should recover well. Although, it's still too early to predict the outcome."

It all sounded so clinical. Frankie didn't like the thought he was going through it all alone, but for now, there was nothing she could do but wait.

"Come on, Frankie," Jackie said. "Let's go and sit down. He's in good hands, and we can't do anything to help right now. They'll let us know when he's up in the ward."

Frankie followed Jackie back to their seats. She felt numb.

"What happened to him tonight?" Jackie asked.

"I woke up and he wasn't in bed, so I went to look for him. I looked everywhere, but he was nowhere in the house, and I figured he must have gone outside for a cigarette." The words tumbled out, and Frankie had no idea if she was making any sense. "I found him on the ground by the front gate. I didn't know how long he'd been there. He was so cold." She wiped at the tears that had begun to spill down her cheeks again and dug in her bag for a tissue.

Jackie smiled, putting her arm around Frankie. "He goes outside at night before bed. He's done it since I was a kid. I think it's from his time in Vietnam. It's like he's doing a perimeter check, making sure everything is secure for the night."

"They asked me lots of questions in the ambulance, and I couldn't answer any of them. I felt completely helpless. I didn't know anything."

"The doctor said you saved his life. Thank you for acting so quickly. You must realise how special is to me."

Frankie nodded. "I'm so sorry."

"For as long as I can remember, Terry's had one medical problem after another. Sometimes it can be scary. Sometimes, I can understand why Evelyn left. I hope you know what you're getting yourself into."

"I know enough veterans to know what's ahead."

Jackie remembered her earlier conversation. "On the phone, he said on the phone he had something to tell me? He sounded pretty excited."

Frankie turned to look at this beautiful woman beside her. Her perfectly tailored clothes, her long jet-black hair pulled up into a loose ponytail. She was the daughter of Terry's best friend, who had died a lifetime ago, and a mysterious Vietnamese woman, yet Terry loved her like she was his own daughter and always would. She knew he wouldn't mind if Frankie told her.

"He asked me to marry him." The tears began to spill again.

Jackie's eyes lit up, and a huge grin spread across her face.

"Congratulations!" She wrapped her arms around Frankie and hugged her, then pulled back. "You did say yes, didn't you?"

"I did." Frankie started to laugh, and cry, and needed to blow her nose, all at the same time. "I love him so much."

"He must love you too, that's a big step for him."

"Perhaps I should fill you in while we're sitting here. You probably don't know much about me, except that I went to some strange places and took depressing photographs."

"He's never even mentioned you before."

"Do you remember the tattoo he has on his chest?"

"Yes."

Frankie pulled up the sleeve of her sweatshirt to reveal her tattoo.

"They're *matching?*"

"I met your father in nineteen sixty-seven. On a plane from Singapore to Saigon. I was twenty-two and heading to whichever press bureau would employ me as a photographer. I had huge ideas about changing the way the world saw what was happening in Vietnam. Terry was nineteen and heading over with Victor Company for a six-month tour of duty. We met up again when I was walking along a street in Saigon some weeks later, and he walked into me and sloshed my drink all down my front. I still don't know whether or not that was on purpose." She smiled.

"Our relationship grew from there. Sometimes things happen in extreme situations like war, and you can't tell if what you have is real or just a need for two young people to prove that they are alive. We wrote to each other for almost a year after he came home, and then I stopped answering his letters. I thought it was totally unfair to make him wait for me when I didn't know when I'd be back home, or even if I'd survive the war. I wanted to give him the chance to move on with his life."

"I never knew."

"I saw him again in Saigon just before the city fell to the communists in seventy-five. He was with a blonde woman and a young Vietnamese girl with dark hair, and they were rushing to board a plane. I hadn't known he was in Saigon, but when I found out later, I knew my decision had been right. I assumed the woman was his wife and the child his daughter."

"I remember that day too," Jackie said.

"I never stopped loving him, and there's not been a single day pass where I haven't missed him."

"Did he never come looking for you after the war ended?"

"No. I told him not to. I intended to travel. Asia, Europe and the States. I never married. Never found anyone who measured up. Now I keep thinking, what if he doesn't make it and…"

"He'll be fine. He's strong."

"Mrs Edwards?" a nurse interrupted them.

"Yes?"

"Mr Edwards has just been taken through to the cardiac ward. You can go on up and see him if you like. Third floor."

They hurried to the elevator and stood in silence as it climbed. They were met at the nurses' station and told that Terry was in room twelve. He was very tired, and they should keep their visit brief. He needed to sleep.

Frankie nodded. The ward was quiet, and they made little noise as they walked past doors until they reached number six. Frankie stopped outside and took a deep breath. She turned and looked at Jackie. They had both had a huge fright tonight and knew it was far from over. But Terry was alive, and that was the only thing that mattered.

Frankie pushed open the door and stepped inside. Terry lay still. His eyes were closed, and he looked peaceful. She noticed he was starting to get the colour back in his face too. She looked at all the monitors he was connected to; he had wires everywhere. All she wanted to do was hug him and tell him she loved him.

As if he sensed they were there, he opened his eyes, looking first at Frankie and then to the other side of the bed, at his daughter.

"Sorry." His voice was a hoarse whisper, but to Frankie, it was as if he had yelled the word, and she had never been happier to hear his voice.

She leaned down and kissed his cheek.

"I love you so much, Terry Edwards." She took his hand in hers and squeezed it. "You're not getting out of marrying me that easily."

<h1 style="text-align:center">Chapter 52</h1>

Two weeks later, on Queen's Birthday weekend, people from all over the country gathered in Wellington in unprecedented numbers to watch the proud men and women who had served in Vietnam march with their families in Parade '98. Terry had been determined to walk alongside his mates, and with Frankie on one side and Jackie on the other, he did.

He had been discharged from the hospital three days after his attack, and the doctors reported they couldn't find anything wrong with his heart. They told him it may have happened as a result of being exposed to dioxin, and that the stroke he had suffered years ago was also most likely a result of his exposure to the chemical, as were all his skin cancers and the lost babies. But they were unable to positively prove it.

At fifty-three, he was still a young man, but the experience had driven home the need to enjoy the day, prepare for tomorrow, and ensure the next generation never forgot the consequences of war. It also meant it was time he faced something that had bothered him for years.

After the parade, the three of them went back to Jackie's apartment. Terry needed to rest before the cabaret later that evening. Although Frankie had agreed to go with him, she was limiting him to a couple of hours' maximum. They still had the service to attend on the Sunday, and they were making sure Terry didn't overdo things.

He was sitting on the sofa drinking green tea that Jackie had made for him, watching the two most important women in his life talk about the wedding. It made him happy to see they got on well together. They all agreed the wedding was to be a quiet affair, just family and their closest friends. Jackie had told them they could married at her new home at Scorching Bay. She offered to organise everything as her gift to them, and they had gratefully accepted her offer. It was one less thing for Terry to have to think about.

"I need to talk to you, kiddo," he said to Jackie, when they closed the book they were working from.

Frankie stood up and grabbed her coat.

"Well, I'm popping out for about an hour. I need to collect some things from my place." She walked over to Terry and kissed him goodbye then grabbed her bag. Jackie had asked her to stay with them for the weekend of the parade, and Frankie had been delighted to accept.

"What did you want to talk about?" Jackie asked after Frankie left.

"There's something I need to tell you. I should have told you years ago, but I've been too bloody gutless. I thought I'd lose you."

"Are you sure you want to tell me now?"

"It's time I did. And since my heart attack, I need you to know … just in case something happens, and I don't make it next time."

"Nothing's going to happen. You're far too tough."

"I can never be too sure, kiddo. I reckon I've been on borrowed time since the day I came home from the war. If I were to die and I'd never told you this, well…" He took a breath. "I think you need to return to Vietnam."

"Why? Everything I need and want is right here. My life is here."

"Because you have family back there too." There, he'd said it. He waited a minute for his words to sink in.

"I have family in Vietnam?"

"I'm so sorry I didn't tell you sooner."

"But why didn't Evelyn tell me? I always thought I was orphaned because I had no family, except Dad's."

"Evelyn wouldn't have known. In fact, I don't think Jack knew either." He felt ashamed at himself for withholding the truth from her all this time. Now it worried him that she might never know any of her mother's family.

"No one has ever told me about my mother."

"When Jack found your mother, Mai Linh, she was badly injured and hiding in a village with an elderly woman who she claimed was your great-grandmother. They told us she died while Mai Linh was in the hospital. Your mother refused to speak to anyone, so they sent Jack to see her, and she spoke to him, in good English too. I think she felt indebted to him for saving her life. Jack met her again months later at a bar in Vũng Tàu." He stopped and looked at Jackie, unsure whether to continue.

"Go on."

"She was working the men, and she remembered Jack and singled him out. They formed a relationship. He would go and see her every time he was on leave. Eventually you came along."

"She was a bar girl?"

"No, she wasn't. Your mother was a Viet Cong officer, and she had been using Jack to get information on the Kiwi and Australian movements, poor bugger." Terry stopped and looked down at his shoes, but it was too late to stop now.

"We were out on an operation and got pinned down by two snipers. It was a common occurrence. We seemed to get ambushed a lot. Anyway, they had us pinned down and Jack, being a brilliant marksman, shot both of them. One was your mother. Your father was hit in the shoulder, and they choppered him to hospital. He was beside himself with worry. He didn't know where you were. You were four months old, and you could have been anywhere."

"Poor Jack, he must have been so upset."

"He asked me to visit him in the hospital in Vũng Tàu, and he wanted me to look for you–in case you were still in town."

"And did you find me?"

"Yes. I went to the house where your mother had lived. I found a young woman with a baby, and I looked for the birthmark on your arm, to make sure it was you." He nodded towards her arm. "She claimed she was your mother's sister, and she couldn't, or didn't want to, look after you. She wanted me to take you, but I couldn't. I had to go back to camp, and Jack was in hospital and being shipped home in a matter of hours. I thought the best thing for everyone would be to give her all the money I had on me and not say anything to Jack. I was trying to protect Jack and Evelyn, and in the end, I did nothing but cause you seven years of hardship in an orphanage." He dug his handkerchief from his pocket and wiped his eyes.

"But you didn't give me to the nuns. My own family did."

"The years after Jack got home, all he thought about was you. And when Evelyn finally found out he had a daughter, she left him. Then, after Jack died, Evelyn made it her mission to go back to Saigon to try to find you."

"Frankie said she saw us in Saigon in seventy-five."

"I couldn't believe we managed to find you. It was more than a miracle. You were such a beautiful child. It wasn't hard to love you." He smiled at her. "But I've felt so guilty ever since, that I turned my back on you and walked away when you were so little. So helpless. I owe you so much."

"I think it's me who owes you," Jackie said quietly. "You raised me and loved me like I was your child. That's not something an uncaring man does. You were always there when I was growing up. You taught me compassion and to be strong, and to fight when the situation calls for it. Your strength and love inspire me." She took his hands in hers. "I could never repay you for the love you have given me." Jackie wrapped her arms around Terry and hugged him as they both cried. When their tears subsided, they both blew their noses and laughed.

"So, promise me someday you'll go back to Vietnam and find the rest of your family. You don't have to live there, or even like them, but you need to know if they're still alive. See the country you were born in." Terry felt a huge weight lift from his shoulders.

"I will. I promise."

They heard a key in the lock downstairs, and a moment later Frankie appeared in the lounge.

"Is everything okay?" she asked nervously.

Terry looked at his daughter. "*Is* everything okay?"

"Everything is fine. I love you, always have and always will. And I think I'm going to love your new wife too," she said, breaking out into a large smile.

Terry put his arm around his daughter and squeezed her.

"I have something special for you, Jackie," Frankie said, digging in her bag. "This has been with me since nineteen sixty-eight. It has been my most prized possession." She handed it to Jackie. "I'd like you to have it. I no longer need it. I have the real thing now."

Jackie looked at the photo. She hadn't seen it before. It looked like it had been taken on a beach; it was a photo of Terry and Frankie. Frankie was laughing and holding Terry's hand, and Terry was holding a fish in his other hand, his head thrown back in laughter.

"It was the start of a love that has spanned thirty years."

A tear slipped free and slid down Jackie's cheek.

"Thank you," she said, finally. "I will take great care of it."

"And there's one more thing." She reached into her bag and then handed Jackie a small marble Buddha with a huge smile and long earlobes.

Jackie looked at the Buddha and then at Terry.

"This looks familiar."

"Your father gave me this to help get me through the hard times and times when I was lonely. It made me smile. Every time. I don't need it anymore, his work with me is done."

And at that moment in time, despite the Nam shadow that hung over them all, life couldn't have been any richer or filled with more love. Everything in their world was perfect.

Ministerial Statement to Parliament – Crown apology to Viet Nam veterans

Helen Clark
28 MAY, 2008

The Crown formally acknowledges the dedicated service of the New Zealand Regular Force personnel deployed during the Viet Nam War, and those many servicemen and women who supported them in their mission.

Further the Crown records that those armed forces personnel loyally served at the direction of the New Zealand Government of the day, having left their home shores against a background of unprecedented division and controversy over whether or not New Zealand should participate in the war.

The Crown extends to New Zealand Viet Nam Veterans and their families an apology for the manner in which their loyal service in the name of New Zealand was not recognised as it should have been, when it should have been, and for inadequate support extended to them and their families after their return home from the conflict.

The Viet Nam War was a defining event in New Zealand's recent history, and one during which significant divisions and tensions emerged within our own society. Old allegiances and alliances were tested, and New Zealanders began to question the role their country was playing in global affairs.

On all sides, strong views were held with conviction. My own party, the New Zealand Labour Party opposed New Zealand involvement in the war, and acted immediately to withdraw the troops on election to office in 1972.

Many others also spoke out, often coming under attack from the government and other establishment voices of the time for doing so.

Viet Nam itself suffered huge damage from the war–to its people, its cities and ports, and its countryside. The consequences there have been long term and intergenerational. Today we count Viet Nam as an Asia Pacific partner, and welcome its leaders to our shores.

Today's focus, however, is on those who served, regardless of what our personal views on the decision to send them were. It is time for reconciliation.

The Crown is placing on record its respect for the service of the nearly 3,400 New Zealanders who served in Viet Nam during the war between June 1964 and December 1972. We honour the 37 personnel who died on active duty, the 187 who were wounded, some very seriously, and all those who have suffered long-term effects. The service of those who fell and all who served in that conflict should now be honoured, alongside that of other brave service personnel deployed to other conflicts in the service of our country.

For too long, successive governments ignored concerns being raised by Viet Nam veterans. It was the emergence of Agent Orange as a serious health and veterans' issue in the United States which began to change the way in which issues surrounding Viet Nam veterans came to be perceived and then treated in New Zealand.

In 2003 the Health Select Committee undertook its own inquiry into the concerns raised by veterans. It investigated whether New Zealand defence personnel had been exposed to Agent Orange. It also assessed the health risks to defence personnel and their families, and the health services available to them. The Committee concluded that New Zealand personnel who had served in Viet Nam had indeed been exposed to Agent Orange, and that this exposure had had adverse health effects not only for the personnel themselves, but also for their children.

A Joint Working Group on the Concerns of Viet Nam veterans was established in July 2005, under the chairmanship of the former State Services Commissioner, Michael Wintringham. The Royal New Zealand Returned and Services Association, and the Ex-Viet Nam Services Association participated in the group.

In their report of April 2006, the Joint Working Group proposed that the Crown apologise formally to veterans and their families for the history of pain and suffering experienced by many of them. That recommendation was accepted as part of a wider package of measures proposed under the themes of "Acknowledging the Past", "Putting Things Right", and "Improving Services to Viet Nam Veterans". A range of steps under each of these headings was agreed.

Today the Crown has offered a formal apology to the New Zealand Veterans of the Viet Nam War and their families. The Crown places on record recognition of the service of those personnel; and acknowledges the many consequences of that service, including the physical and mental health effects. The failure of successive governments and their agencies to acknowledge the exposure of veterans to dioxin contaminated herbicides and other chemicals is itself acknowledged, as is the way in which that failure exacerbated the suffering of veterans and families.

The recommendation of the Joint Working Group report that the earlier Reeves and McLeod reports, should no longer form the basis for policies towards Viet Nam veterans and their families is accepted by the Crown.

Finally, there is the commitment to put things right, where government action is the appropriate means of achieving that resolution. The commitments the Crown has made to the treatment of Viet Nam veterans who were affected by toxic environments in Viet Nam and to their families are set out in the Memorandum of Understanding of 6 December 2006, and the Crown will adhere to them.

In concluding, the Crown thanks the members of the Joint Working Group who provided a way forward for dealing with these troubling issues of New Zealand's relatively recent past. This has led to the opportunity for the Crown to put on record its thanks for, and its apology to, those brave service personnel who became the veterans of the Viet Nam War, and to pay tribute to those who never came home. We will remember them.

Helen Clark
Prime Minister

A word of thanks from the author

Huge thanks to all those who have, in someway, helped me get this novel to completion. I've been researching and writing about the Vietnam War for far too many years now. It's an exhausting business—but you, the reader, via reviews, emails and messages, make it all worthwhile.

I'd like to thank two special Kiwi veterans: Brian and Stewart. Brian, your friendship and enthusiasm for my writing has been appreciated more than you will probably ever realise. You're a talented storyteller, and as such have certainly kept me smiling. I treasure that first meeting we had over a coffee and the legendary bayonet! And my dear friend Stewart, your encouragement and friendship over the last fourteen years has been a gift. I admire you for your drive and determination in all you do. I feel privileged to know you both as friends.

My deepest thanks to New Zealand's Prime Minister of the time, Helen Clark, ONZ SSI, for her kind permission to reprint her Ministerial Statement to Parliament of 28 May, 2008, in the pages of this book.

Meredith, Liz, Jesse, Lise and Susan, and the team at Graphic Press, together you have helped me create another book I'm damned proud of! I have to mention my fabulous street team, you are the best supporters ever, thanks so much for your enthusiasm!

And as always, my love and thanks to Dennis, you keep me sane in this mad world of storytelling.

Finally, if you enjoyed reading this book, please consider leaving a review on goodreads.com to let other readers know what you thought. If you'd like to know more about what I'm working on next, feel free to subscribe to my newsletter, you can find the sign-up over on my website, www.carolebrungar.com or pop in and visit me on Facebook at facebook.com/carolebrungarauthor

The Nam Legacy

The Nam Legacy is an epic love story set during the 60's and 70's. When the Rolling Stones and Jefferson Airplane drove parents crazy, teenagers found sexual freedom and peace slogans covered placards. When the Vietnam War abducted the nation's young men and sent them to fight in New Zealand's most controversial campaign.

After eighteen months in Vietnam, New Zealand soldier Jack Coles thought killing others to stay alive would be the hardest thing he would ever have to live with. He was wrong.

Although the nightmare of what he saw and did haunt him constantly, what tortures him the most is what he has left behind.

'Not everyone who lost his life in Vietnam died there, not everyone who came home from Vietnam ever left there.'

The Nam Legacy is Jack's story.

"To those people who love a good read, this book is a MUST READ."
"The Nam Legacy is evocative, disturbing and beautifully written."

"It is a powerful, gritty story with authentic characters."
"I congratulate you on your work and this book will hold a special place in my library."

Foxton Beach, NEW ZEALAND, 1964

Chapter 1

Jack considered himself in the rear-vision mirror of the Hillman. He looked the same as he had the other twenty times he'd checked. Stop pissing around, he reprimanded himself. That's what his old man would've told him. Though if his old man knew he was here, he'd be telling him he was wasting his time. No girl in her right mind would want to go out with a lazy bugger like his son. Jack hated milking bloody cows and if he had a choice, he'd look for a carpentry apprenticeship, but according to his father, real men worked the land.

He skimmed a hand nervously over the front of his shirt. He was tired of all the sneaking around with Evelyn. Their coincidental meetings at the Bella Vista at the end of Darwick Street where any one of a dozen people could have told Evelyn's father they had seen her out with one of the Coles boys. And trying to rendezvous at the beach for half an hour on a preplanned day at a certain time was bloody near impossible.

There was only one way to find out if he could take Evelyn on a date, and that was to ask her old man and he had been awake most of the night going over what he was going to say. Now he wouldn't even be able to string a decent sentence together he was so nervous.

With another quick glance in the mirror he climbed out of the car, took a deep breath, walked up to the door of Hallet's Hotel and pushed the white painted door open. Shouts from the smoky interior momentarily interrupted his focus. At nineteen he was too young to drink in the pub and had never been inside Hallet's, though his father drank here on occasion.

To his right was a door with the words Private Bar over it in gold lettering, and a small notice which declared it was also the entrance to the restaurant. On the far side of the room sat a pool table. A selection of pool cues were racked beside a dart board. Men stood at tables drinking, while others crowded around a radio. To one side, leaning partially against the bar, sat Bob Hallet. Jack had heard about him from his mates. He had a reputation every drinking man in the district knew about. You only picked a fight with the publican of Hallet's if you didn't know about his left hook.

Shit, he had to be mad coming in here and asking to take his sixteen-year-old daughter out. What father in his right mind would say yes?

Bob Hallet shifted his weight on the bar stool, flicked the hanging column of ash from his cigarette into the ashtray and appeared to study the pages of a Track Digest. From the radio a commentator relayed the line-up of horses. As they approached the home straight, the noise in the public bar intensified by several decibels.

"Come on, you beauty!" Bob Hallet bellowed.

Most of the men in the bar were yelling at the radio, punching holes in the air. Jack couldn't even hear the commentator now.

A middle aged woman swept through the bar collecting glasses and Jack wondered if that was Evelyn's mother. He watched her for a moment as she went from table to table placing the empties on a tray.

"Double Delight is out by a nose!" the commentator relayed in a frenzied high-pitch.

"Run, you little bugger!"

"Bob."

"Shhhh, woman!"

"Double Delight takes it by a head, closely followed by Sydney Sider and Night Song."

"You beauty!" Bob Hallet bellowed, slapping his racing guide back onto the counter and turning to pick up Ida mid-step and swing her around.

Jack thought how different they were from his parents. He could see where Evelyn got her enthusiasm from.

"Put me down, Bob Hallet. For goodness sakes, you'll put people off their beer." She blushed as her husband set her down and planted a kiss on her forehead. She readjusted her hair and smoothed her skirt.

"She was payin' a tenner to win and I had ten bloody quid ridin' on her." Beaming he folded the well-thumbed Track Digest and filed it in his back pocket.

"Very good. Don't forget to check the bottles."

"Onto it," he confirmed, rounding the bar with a light step and noticing Jack. "Yes, lad. What can I do for you?"

"Name's Jack Coles." Jack hesitated, swallowing hard. At least he'd remembered his own name. It was a good start. "I'd like permission to take your daughter to the dance at the Town Hall Saturday fortnight."

A silence fell on the room as the men in the bar stopped what they were doing and turned to look at the unfolding situation before them.

"Is that right?" Bob answered, arms folded across his chest as he eyed Jack.

"Yes, sir."

"Ida!"

Evelyn's mother came bustling through from the small reception area, wiping her hands on the heavy-duty apron she wore tied around her generous waist. She stood looking from one to the other.

"This here's Jack Coles. He wants to take our girl to the dance next Saturday fortnight. What do you think?"

Evelyn's mother looked from Jack, to her husband and then shook her head in disbelief.

"How old are you, lad?" Ida asked.

"Nineteen." He tried to swallow, but his tongue was stuck to the back of his throat.

"Are you from around here, Jack?" Ida continued.

"Up at Himatangi. The old man has a dairy farm."

"You're not Ray Coles's son are you?" Bob inquired.

"That's right."

"I was sorry to hear about your mother."

Jack shifted his weight and thrust his hands in his trouser pockets to stop them shaking. His mother had been thrown off her horse after a rabbit had spooked it. Although she had broken both legs, she was recovering well, until two weeks later when she suffered a heart attack and died before anyone could get her to a hospital. Evelyn was the only one who knew just how much he missed her.

"And how long have you known our girl?" Bob asked.

"Six months."

"Well, she kept that quiet. Nineteen, you say?"

"Yes, sir."

"Ida, do you have any objection to them going to the dance?"

Everyone craned to hear Ida's answer over the noise of the radio.

"I don't think so," she finally replied, eye-balling Jack, despite the fact he was almost two feet taller than her. "But, there'll be no funny business, you understand?"

Jack let out a breath. "Yes ma'am. If nothing else, Mum taught me to be a gentleman." Shit, they said yes!

Ida smiled. "I'll go get her, you'll want to say hello while you're here." She disappeared from the bar.

"So," Bob continued, picking up bottles from a crate and placing them one by one in the nearest refrigerated cabinet. "You're working on the farm now?"

"Yes, sir. Milking, some fencing, bit of cropping, whatever needs doing."

"And how's your brother? I haven't seen him in here for some time."

"He joined the Army. He's down at Burnham Camp right now."

"The Army?"

"Yes, sir. Reckons farming isn't for him. The old man blames the engineers that came over from Linton Army Camp and blew up the old swimming pool. That's all Brian could talk about for weeks after."

"I remember that. Does he realise he'll probably get sent to Vietnam?"

"The old man reckons we won't send troops because the British won't get involved."

"Well, lad, we've already got engineers over there rebuilding roads and bridges. We'll have to see what those Yanks get up to."

"Brian would probably be the first to put his hand up to go."

"Holyoake's doing a great job of stalling, but, it's only a matter of time and America will be putting pressure on the Prime Minister to send troops. Mark my words." Bob lit a cigarette. "So I hear talk Jack Coles is the best winger to ever come out of Foxton."

"Not sure about that."

"Who are you playing for next season?"

"Manawatu. Unless I get a better offer."

"Your father must be proud of you."

"He doesn't say a lot, except it takes me away from the farm too much, you know, with practice and games."

"You wanted me, Dad?" a dark-haired girl, interrupted them. She glanced briefly at Jack, ignored him, and looked to her father to speak.

"Jack here wants to take you to the dance in town."

Jack's mouth fell open. He'd clean forgotten Evelyn had a sister. He could feel perspiration bead on his forehead.

The young woman looked at Jack and burst into laughter. "He doesn't want to take me. He wants to go with Evelyn."

Jack felt a flush of nervous relief wash over him and at the same moment realised what a bloody mess he was making of things. "I think you've misunderstood me, sir," Jack interrupted, instantly regretting the accusation. The room shrunk as the conversations in the public bar stopped once again and everyone hung on Bob's reaction.

Bob glared at Jack. "How's that, then?"

Jack cleared his throat. "Umm, well sir, I wanted to take Evelyn to the dance." He shifted from one foot to the other, feeling like a fish under a heat lamp. Perhaps he should just leave now.

"Ida!" Bob bellowed again and turned his attention back to the lad in front of him. "Well now, Jack, that's a whole different matter. You know how old Evelyn is?"

"Yes, sir."

"Sixteen," Ida exclaimed, catching the end of the conversation. "She's sixteen."

The contents of Jack's stomach rolled and settled. He ran a hand across the back of his neck.

"I'm not sure I'm too keen on the idea," Ida said.

Bob filled a jug with beer for one of the Oldfield brothers, slid it across the bar and swept the coins from the dark polished wood into the palm of his hand. "I think he's a good lad and I think he'll look after our girl."

Cheers broke out from the listening drinkers, followed by loud clapping.

"Thank you," Jack felt only slightly relieved. "I'll take good care of her and I'll have her back . . ."

"Wait," Ida interrupted.

Jack swallowed hard. Of course there had to be conditions. And he was going to agree to any condition in order to take her out on a date.

The room went quiet again as one by one everyone lined up along the bar. Jack suspected they were more interested in hearing what was going on than the sudden need for a refill.

"You can both go, as long as you take Joyce along with you as chaperone."

"Aw, do I have to go, Mum?" Joyce pleaded.

"Go and fetch Evelyn please." Ida directed, ignoring her eldest daughters protest. Joyce turned and stalked off.

Jack watched Evelyn enter the bar. He could see the delight hidden behind her eyes.

"Evelyn, Jack wants to take you to the dance in two weeks," her mother informed her.

Evelyn was speechless.

Jack watched her look from her mother to her father, across to him and then at everyone who was propped against the bar listening waiting for her response.

"Well, sweetpea, do you want to go?" her father asked.

"Can I?"

"You can," Ida stated authoritatively. "Providing you take Joyce with you."

"Thanks, Mum!" She threw her arms around her mother and then reached around the bulk of her father to give him a squeeze as well.

Relief flooded through Jack like a tidal wave. Right now he could happily have reached across the bar and kissed Bob Hallet himself.

Available in bookstores throughout New Zealand, online at all good e-book retailers and the author's website, www.carolebrungar.com

a tide too high

Life of an international rock musician is fast and furious. Work hard and play harder. But when Mac collapses on stage in front of a packed Auckland stadium, she has no choice but to make some serious life changes.

She disappears from media scrutiny to spend time recuperating at a private beach in the winterless far north of New Zealand.

London-based Alec wants what his twin brother has, a home, a wife and children. But just because he's one of the world's most successful and respected businessmen doesn't mean he's good at personal relationships. With a divorce pending, maybe he's just not marriage material.

Then he meets a burnt-out rock star who's in hiding and she manages to shift the whole axis of his universe.

A novel about two people from different worlds who find a soulmate in each other and stand to lose everything in the process.

"I couldn't put it down. It took me on a journey of laughter, sadness and excitement."
"Had me hooked from the first page. Awesome from cover to cover."
"Loved it! Lots of twists & turns."
"I loved the fast-paced story-telling style and the grittiness of the characters."

Chapter One

"Shit, you look gorgeous with a hangover."

McKenna Morgan dropped on to the sofa beside the band's drummer. They had been up all night on an alcoholic bender and neither had got more than three hours sleep. She smiled back at Jimi through long lashes. "Shame I couldn't say the same for you."

The band had arrived in New Zealand on the last leg of their six-week Australia New Zealand tour. The bender was a way of washing the jet-lag away, but for Mac it dulled the anxiety about seeing her mother again.

Jimi winked at her, wrapping the tattooed snake on his right arm around her shoulders so the forked tongue caressed her chin. "What are you running on, babe?"

"Piss off, Jimi. Right now I think I'm running on bourbon. Nothing else." She was dressed simply in jeans and a black dress jacket over a white sleeveless singlet. Her long hair was casually pulled back from her face in a classic ponytail and dark shadows crept from her eyes. At five foot ten she was the equal of most of the guys in the band, but when she shrugged out of her jacket she looked like she hadn't eaten for a month. Anyone who didn't know her would have guessed she was doing hard drugs. But those who did know her knew she constantly pushed herself to the limit when it came to her work, and even harder when she was having fun. Her lifestyle required a little adjusting.

Jimi leaned in, ignoring her reply and his regenerating stubble, to kiss her playfully on the cheek and squeeze her shoulder.

She caught a hint of stale aftershave and weed. "You're all bullshit, Jimi McMaster. You'll crash and burn before I do." She loved teasing him. She considered it a sport. Surveying the room she noticed Brian and Magpie were sleeping on sofas and Ray, the band's bass guitarist, was going over a riff on an acoustic guitar.

"Anyone been out for coffee yet?" Although the recording studio had a well-stocked fridge, it lacked a coffee machine and good coffee.

"Yeah, Stretch's gone for it," Ray answered, not looking up from his strings. Jimi dug out a pack of cigarettes, offered Mac one and lit both.

Breakfast this morning had consisted of strong black coffee–she was eager to get to the studio, she'd eat later when she was hungry. Her mobile sang from the depths of her satchel.

"Jules, where are you?" *Late*, she mouthed at the others.

"Sorry, love, you guys make a start. I've got great news, I'll fill you in when I get there." When her manager sounded this excited it usually meant he'd scored them a top gig.

"Okay, see you when you turn up." She dropped the phone back in her satchel. Jules had been with them for the last six years. She had managed the band herself until they had got too big for her to organise gigs and negotiate dollars.

The recording studio was full of people–most she didn't know, but they'd been employed because they were the best. *Polar Blaze* was renowned in the music industry for having the best road crew, and that included their management and production teams. They were surfing a huge wave of popularity partially due to the team they had working for them. They were recording tracks for another album, and then they had a two-week break planned before they headed back home to the States to prepare for a four-month tour of Europe. The recording studio in Auckland was one of the best and they were lucky to have been able to buy time in it.

Mac loved the concerts. Nothing compared to performing live, even sex, although she hadn't had much of that for quite some time. She smiled, remembering the first time the band had played to a crowd of eight-thousand. She had been a nervous wreck. As she sang, the fans whistled and danced, and the vibes that bounced around the packed rugby stadium gave her one hell of a high. And by the end of the concert, with her clothes stuck to her body with sweat, she realised just how much she loved what she was doing.

She poured her heart into her performances and the crowds loved her. Her work schedule didn't allow for relationships, too much time touring and not enough in one place. And she could do without the guilt trips the morning after when she woke and wondered what the hell she was doing in bed with a total stranger.

She stubbed out the cigarette and swallowed a mouthful of the aromatic brown liquid that Stretch had placed in front of her. "Right guys, let's get this record rolling."

"Sweet," Jimi answered.

They worked through until early evening, recording two new songs. Mac wanted to lay down the rhythm tracks for another but the guys were bitching at each other. They were tired, hungry and complaining that she was going to kill them from over-work. After spending all day in the studio none of them wanted to spend the night there too. They all had things they wanted to do.

She felt they'd made a good start on the new album, but she was always unhappy about the progress. The recording process always seemed to take forever. Jules had arrived with news of a guest appearance on national television and he'd heard rumours they were going to be asked to do a music video for a film, but it was too early to confirm anything. He had disappeared as abruptly as he had arrived.

Mac unlocked the door to her hotel suite. The quiet interior screamed loneliness. Years of touring had taught her they all needed their personal space, but she was thankful that most of the time they all congregated in her suite to watch movies or work on new lyrics, or sometimes just to jam with each other and chill. Sometimes it was good to be able to let your hair down and have a few drinks without the prying eyes of the media.

Music was her first love and she suspected it always would be. Her family was musical. Her father had played trumpet and piano in a band, her mother sang at functions for many years and her sister Gabby had a voice that was about to take her on a scholarship to one of the best operatic schools in Europe. But her parents were older now and Gabby was gone.

She dropped her swipe card and satchel on the polished table next to a large basket of fruit and walked around the breakfast bar to the phone. She needed to ring her parents, she'd been putting it off since she arrived. With a sense of dread, she dialled their number and waited as it rang. They would be expecting her to visit them and she might as well get it over with. Her stomach churned. It had been almost two years since she had seen them last and she still let her mother affect her. Mac counted five rings then recognised her father's voice.

"Hello?"

"Dad, it's McKenna, how are you?"

"McKenna! Your mother and I saw you'd arrived."

She could hear the smile in his voice. She doubted she'd hear it in her mother's.

"Your picture was in the paper this morning."

She hadn't seen the paper, but she remembered seeing photographers at the airport the day before. There were cameras and cellphones everywhere they went.

"Thought I'd come out and see you and Mum tomorrow, if that's okay."

"I'll check with your mother." A muffled silence followed. With the phone to her ear she crossed to the bench, switched the jug on, checked the water level as an afterthought and took a mug from the cupboard. Her father was discussing the situation with her mother–it was pretty much routine. She could hear her mother's monotone voice in the background. Why did he have to ask her? Why couldn't he have just said, *come any time you want to?* But that was their relationship.

"We'll be having dinner at five-thirty if you'd like to come and have something to eat with us." He hesitated and then continued. "Will you be bringing any of the others with you?"

"No, I'll be on my own. Five-thirty is fine, I'll see you then."

They said their goodbyes and she made coffee, lit a cigarette and walked across the room to stare at the cityscape spread beneath her. Her mother never failed to make her feel anything but inadequate, even though she was now the driving force behind one of New Zealand's most successful exports. Her father was different and she missed him the most.

She never forgot their birthdays and when she played in New Zealand she made the effort to visit them. Slowly, over the years, they had become almost strangers to each other. In her mother's eyes she was the daughter who could never replace the daughter they'd lost, no matter how successful she became. The more they distanced themselves from her the more she avoided travelling to Auckland to see them.

Below her the city glittered in the darkness, a sign that it was alive and full of people doing things. Although she was tired as hell, she didn't feel like an early night. She didn't do early nights. She picked up the phone again. This time it was answered instantly.

"Good evening, Miss Morgan. How may I help?"

"Hi, can you put me through to Jimi McMaster's room please?"

"Certainly, ma'am, one moment." Recorded music.

"Yeah?"

"What are you up to?"

"Shit, Morgan, don't you ever take a break?"

"You know me, Jimi. You guys in or out?"

"Out. I'm heading down with Magpie and Stretch to check out that new nightclub we've been hearing some serious shit about. Don't suppose you wanna come?"

She laughed. It took a whole two seconds to think about it. "Count me in."

"Sweet. We'll drop past about nine."

"Perfect." That would give her more than an hour, plenty of time to shower and change.

When she opened the door at ten minutes to nine she was greeted with low wolf whistles. Magpie helped her into her coat and together with a couple of minders they caught a taxi downtown to the nightclub. For Mac some good music and a nice slow one-on-one relationship with Mr *Daniels* would take her mind off visiting her parents the following day. Or at least seeing her mother.

The nightclub was packed when they arrived. Mac could feel the vibes radiating from the building before she even entered it. The bouncer, recognising them, let the six of them in, and another stocky bouncer arrived from nowhere and ushered them to a table in a dimly lit corner of the room. He offered his services should there be any unwanted attention from the patrons. They thanked him, but they had it covered. From their table they could see the band and watch the punters dancing. They could also keep a low profile if they wanted to. But tonight Mac didn't feel like it.

Removing her jacket, she slid along the polished leather bench seat. She was wearing a figure-hugging black number that was attracting attention from both men who wondered if they stood a chance, and women who wondered how she did it. Her dress was far shorter than Jimi had seen her wear and was completely backless. It draped way below her hips, so that you could tell she wore nothing under it. Sheer black lace on the halter-neck top exposed a glimpse of firm breasts while bare arms revealed the pale skin of her shoulder blades. A wreath of red roses was tattooed around one wrist and black heels lifted her to Jimi's height. She wore thick black eyeliner and her long lashes curled upwards to expose gold flecks in brown eyes. She looked much younger than her twenty-nine years with her hair loosely curled and cascading wildly against the pale skin. She also looked ill, borderline anorexic from the late nights and unhealthy living, but no-one had the courage to tell her.

Jimi wondered how the fabric of her dress held together. He was getting a fuckin' hard-on just sitting next to her and shifted uncomfortably in his seat.

She stubbed out her cigarette, swallowed the last of the Jack Daniels and beckoned to the barman. She wore almost no jewellery except for a trickle of tiny diamonds that hung from her ears and two leather bracelets around one slender wrist.

"C'mon." She grabbed Jimi's hand, pulling him up out of his seat and through clumps of swaying bodies on the dance floor. "I've got a reputation to keep."

"Happy to oblige," Jimi yelled above the music. He wrapped an arm around her tiny waist, pulling her against him. Their bodies pressed together with the rhythm of the music, her arms swaying high above her head. Jesus, she was hot tonight, something about her that made him as horny as hell.

As the evening progressed she danced less with Jimi and more with others. Everyone knew who she was and the minders were discretely vetting her dancing partners. After consuming more than her fair share of alcohol, they wanted to make sure she was safe and didn't leave with anyone.

When Jimi got up to get a round in, he couldn't help notice every guy in the room was watching her. Shit. He knew how they felt. He'd had a hard-on all bloody night. Jesus, life was a bitch.

Available online at all good e-book retailers and the author's website, www.carolebrungar.com